For Barry… who led me to the mountains.

*"Travelling—it leaves you speechless,
then turns you into a storyteller."*
Ibn Batulla, 13th century Moroccan scholar

CONTENTS

Map of Dharapani and Ratmate XI
Upper Mustang XII
Prologue XIII

Silver Star Mountain
January 2014
Chapter 1 Stepping Out of My Comfort Zone 1
Chapter 2 Second Thoughts 14

Hong Kong
April 18, 2014
Chapter 3 Keep Paddling 27

Kathmandu, Nepal
April 20, 2014
Chapter 4 Birthplace of the Buddha 44

Ratmate Village, Gorkha, Nepal
April 25, 2014
Chapter 5 Teacher, Teacher! 57
Chapter 6 On (and Off) the Grid 73
Chapter 7 Pheri Bhetaula Ratmate 87
Chapter 8 Namaste Aprik 101

CONTENTS

Pokhara, Nepal
May 12, 2014
Chapter 9 Lonely in Lakeside 114

Upper Mustang
May 15, 2014
Chapter 10 Gateway to the Forbidden Kingdom 124
Chapter 11 Mero Sathi, My Friend 134
Chapter 12 Reaching New Heights 146
Chapter 13 The Greatest Library of Lo 159
Chapter 14 Return to Lo-Manthang 174
Chapter 15 Medieval Monarch 187
Chapter 16 Age-old Rituals, Contemporary Connections 197
Chapter 17 Retail Therapy at 3,840 Meters 211
Chapter 18 Kindred Spirits 225
Chapter 19 Restoring the Heart of an Ancient Culture 238
Chapter 20 Will this Trek Ever End? 247
Chapter 21 The Long Stairway to Heaven 258
Chapter 22 Homeward 269

Silver Star
June 2019
Chapter 23 Nepal One Day at a Time 275

Reading Guide 285
Acknowledgements 287
Resources 290
About The Author 293

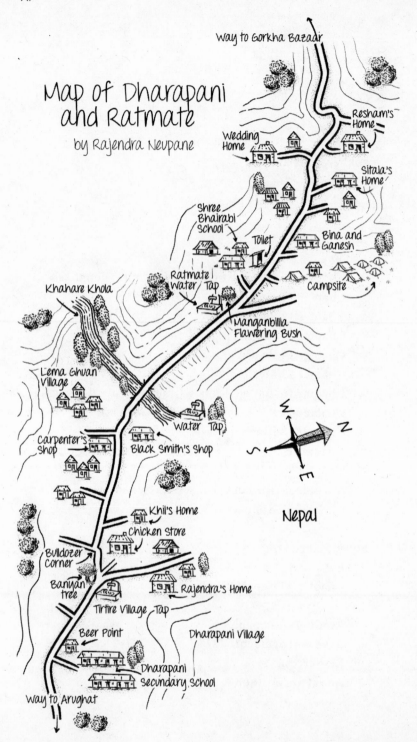

Map of Dharapani and Ratmate
by Rajendra Neupane

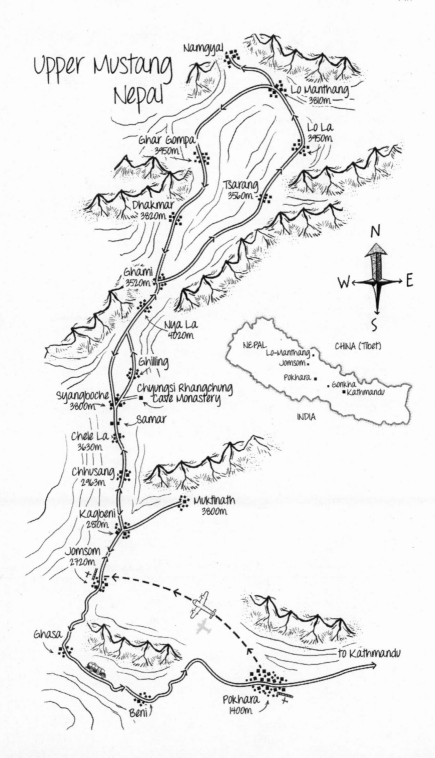

PROLOGUE

Upper Mustang; June 2, 2014

"So what's up for today?" I asked my guide, Raj, requesting his usual blow-by-blow of the day's trek. We'd been teaching, trekking, and conducting interviews together in remote areas of Nepal for more than two months. Over steaming cups of coffee cooled with fresh goat milk we sat side by side in the drafty Syangboche Village guesthouse kitchen planning the day ahead. I was tired. He seemed upbeat, ready for adventure. When I had whined about fatigue after an especially long and arduous trekking day he had threatened to hire a Jeep. Instead he rewarded me with a half-day's respite, an afternoon to curl up and read after a short morning hike. Now he was upping the ante, suggesting an alternate route.

"Do you want to try the trail through the canyon to visit the Chyungsi Rhangchung Cave Monastery?" he asked. "Monks from Ghilling Village discovered it about thirty years ago."

I've never been much of a risk taker. "Is it longer and harder than the normal route back to Samar?"

"A bit longer, I think. I've never gone that way." He hesitated.

"There is one extremely steep part."

"Is the trail really narrow?" The image of a friend from home flashed across my consciousness. A friend whose one step near the edge of a narrow, rugged trail in Portugal had resulted in a horrific accident.

Our heads almost touched as we leaned over the map in the smoky kitchen. Raj traced the route described to him by the man of the house. It was time to step out of my comfort zone, to take a risk. What better place than on a desolate plateau high in the remote Himalaya? Unlikely to return to the area and eager to research stories worthy of publication in newspapers and magazines, I agreed to the alternate path.

"*Hazure, hazure.* You convinced me," I said, using one of my newly acquired Nepali words, roughly translated as "okay." I smiled bravely, masking my trepidation of yet another high pass to climb, a rarely travelled, unmarked route to find, and a hidden cave monastery to search for. Excited but apprehensive, I shouldered my pack and followed Raj out of the guesthouse.

CHAPTER 1
STEPPING OUT OF
MY COMFORT ZONE

SilverStar Mountain Resort; January 2014

My journey of thousands of footsteps on Himalayan trails started with a single step, an escape from a January snowstorm into a yoga studio.

I kicked the snow off my boots. Puddles had already formed from snow melting off the boots belonging to women who had arrived before me.

Like others, I had walked through the plump snowflakes falling through the sunset skies of a peaceful winter afternoon at SilverStar Mountain Resort, in the Okanagan Valley of the British Columbia interior. Gentle snowflakes drifted down to kiss my eyelashes, reminding me why I loved living here. Bundled against the cold, some of the others came from hotels, but most, like me, had sauntered through deep snow from nearby mountain homes. The laughter of children enjoying family ski vacations briefly interrupted the silence. Through the frosted window I could see groups strolling along, swapping stories of the ski day. A classic late 1800s Currier and Ives tableau of a pick-up hockey game and figure skaters on Brewer's Pond complemented the scene. The slap of frozen wooden sticks against hard rubber pucks punctuated each move by youngsters lost in their dreams of the NHL.

Strings of white lights framing the commercial buildings of the village glittered amid the flurries. Tall Douglas firs flaunted capes of teal and purple icicle lights, each tree topped with an ice-blue star. At the far end of the village, bright lights illuminated a section of hill for night skiing.

Easing into the warmth of indoors, I hung my down coat on a hook in the entryway and slipped around the corner into the toasty L-shaped room. On the left was a wall of mirrors, an aid to checking *asanas*, poses. Candles placed around the perimeter of the room twinkled against the deepening pink of the early evening alpenglow.

On the floor at the end of the room our resident yogini, Gillian, sat cross-legged on the floor. Her open notebook signaled this wouldn't be the usual stretch-and-strength class. We were here to be guided through a series of activities designed to help us release fears, thoughts, and habits no longer serving us. We had come to realize our true selves.

Twenty soul-searching women wandered into the space and unfurled their yoga mats. Aged twenty to seventy, some were tall and slim, some small, some not so slim. I was at the top end of the age range. Most were athletic women, toned from downhill and cross-country skiing and woodsy snowshoe walks with their dogs. A few wore trendy lululemon coordinates, but most, like me, preferred the comfort of leggings and an oversized T-shirt.

The small studio was crowded. Apparently I wasn't the only one with baggage to dispose of, looking for a fresh start in 2014. Some sat down. Some stretched, showing off their flexibility. Others collapsed on their backs with a sigh, glad the holidays were over and company had departed. No one knew what to expect. I positioned my mat in an alcove so I was close to Gillian in a safe, quiet corner.

"Namaste," Gillian said, her palms pressed together close to her heart. "The divine light in me acknowledges the divine light in you." The chatting stopped. "Congratulations to all of you for setting aside this time from your busy lives on this special evening, time just for yourselves to explore your personal limitations, to discover and commit to your true intentions."

Locals loved Gillian's classes. She generously shared her own fears, joys and stories.

"I've never offered this class before," she said. "It's new for all of us, so we'll work through the steps together." My breathing quickened. I was excited but apprehensive. Gillian looked around the room, lips curved in a gentle smile, making eye contact with each of us. "Some of you look nervous. I'm nervous, too. Some of this inner work can be frightening. We'll just forge ahead together and see what unfolds."

That made me edgy. Would I be asked to share private thoughts?

Sadness had overwhelmed me lately. I'd missed too many days of cross-country ski training. My leaden legs had refused to drag me out the door. What was the point? I trained best when I had a goal. Why work out when there was no chance of a trekking trip in the increasingly distant future? Even reading the shortest paragraph in *HELLO Canada Magazine* required more concentration than I could muster. And forget getting any writing done. Deadlines loomed. I had feature articles due for *Okanagan Woman* and *Okanagan Life* magazines and a snappy travel piece in the works for *The San Francisco Chronicle*. Uninspired and fighting depression, I procrastinated.

My usual self-disciplined focus on healthy diet and daily exercise had crumbled. Lately I'd been compounding the issue with my melancholic, self-destructive overconsumption of chocolate chip cookies, mugs of coffee, fistfuls of lavishly salted cashews and jumbo glasses of red wine. No wonder I wasn't sleeping well. I'd even stooped to daytime binge-watching South Asian movies. In an effort to conjure up the evasive Nepali Hindu culture of my daydreams, I'd lie on the couch in a slump of mid-day self-pity, a stack of cookies and my fourth latte of the day close at hand. Even watching *Slum Dog Millionaire* and *The Best Exotic Marigold Hotel*—movies I had loved since my first trip to Nepal in 2011 with my husband and trekking partner, Barry—couldn't haul me up out of the doldrums. Unable to shake my negative attitude, I longed for things to return to normal. After thirty happily married years spent enjoying each other and rewarding careers as teachers and administrators in Vancouver, we were now in our seventh year of retirement in a location we loved. How many months would it be until Barry and I were riding the chairlift together again, chatting, squabbling happily over whose turn it was to choose the next ski run?

Lately the house was quiet. We didn't seem to laugh together any more. My once vibrant sister, now in the late stage of Alzheimer's, had been placed in a care home. My best friend had recently beaten, narrowly, a bout of cancer. And just as we were beginning to plan our second trip to Nepal, Barry had ruptured his Achilles tendon. I needed some help to climb out of my despair. I hoped this workshop would be it.

"We'll begin on our backs," said Gillian. When we had settled, she led us through the usual stretches and breathing exercises. That felt good, familiar. My breathing deepened.

More stretching, some dancing, bouts of giggles and throaty laughter followed. Gillian's abandon was inspiring. She waved her slim thirty-something arms joyfully above her head to the music, looking like a woodland fairy in *Midsummer Night's Dream*. At first my dance movements were stilted and tentative, but soon the music swept me away. My inhibitions melted into the sunset. We wove and wiggled for several songs, then collapsed on our mats, warmed by the activity.

That's when it got serious.

"Make a thorough list of all the obstacles and fears in your

STEPPING OUT OF MY COMFORT ZONE   5

life that prevent you from realizing your true self, the self you wish to be," said Gillian.

We sat quietly, notebooks on our laps, consumed by thoughts. Sounds of earnest scribbling and pages turning punctuated the silence.

My list was extensive: my fear of Barry being hurt and angry that I wanted to go back to Nepal, even if it meant going without him. Did I have the nerve to travel alone? Was I physically fit enough for another high altitude trek? Was I being selfish leaving Barry behind? Should I wait until he could go with me? What would friends and family think? Why did I care? It was our business. We knew we had a solid marriage.

Then, Gillian invited us to ceremoniously rip up our paper, symbolically ridding ourselves of the millstones dragging us to murky depths.

The toughest part for me came next. "Now describe who you wish to be in your life from now on." Doubts bubbled to the surface, fighting to be acknowledged. Despite having published 200 magazine and newspaper articles I still wondered if I had enough talent to fulfill my dream of becoming a travel writer. Did I really have a unique voice? Was I smart enough? Would anyone want to read my scribblings?

Then we wrote down our commitment to our intention, and the steps we planned to take to make it happen.

"Now," said Gillian, "it's time to own your intentions." This final step, sharing them with the group, was optional. I longed to go first to get my turn over with, but shyness prevailed. My heart raced. I waited and listened. I had been attending yoga classes off and on for the past ten years, but this was the first class where we were asked to share internal thoughts. The brave ones went first. Each woman stood and took her turn, some more tentatively than others. One intended to be stronger, another more independent, a third vowed to find more joy in her life.

We applauded each effort. Their goals were so general. Mine was incredibly specific. Had I misunderstood the instructions?

Finally, I gathered courage. Surrounded by warmth and support I wiped my eyes with my sleeve and declared my vision, several times over, more confidently each time. "I will be a strong, independent, confident solo traveler and travel writer." It was a simple declaration. Saying it out loud to be witnessed by others was huge.

At the end of the ninety-minute session we sank to our mats. In regular yoga classes, ten minutes of Vipassana or mindfulness meditation offered a perfect rest or, for some, a quick nap after a strenuous class. This night was no different.

The silent interlude cemented my intentions. My muscles melted into the mat like the folds of a wrung-out blanket. After a period of stillness Gillian started some music. No *Zen Garden* or *Yoga Zone* selections for Gillian. This non-traditional yogini preferred to end her classes on a whimsical note. First the mellow music of ukulele strings, then the warm tones of Israel Kamakawiwo'ole singing "Somewhere Over the Rainbow" filled the room. My heart swelled with joy. Tears trickled down my cheeks to stain my pink yoga mat with dots of happiness, exhaustion, and resolve.

Each of us rolled up to a cross-legged sitting position. "Namaste," said Gillian. We returned the greeting in unison, rolled up our mats, and hunted for our coats and boots. Gillian stood at the doorway. Her strong gaze held mine. The warmth in her brown eyes sent a message of love. Despite the almost forty-year difference in our ages, we had an undeniable connection.

"That's exactly what I needed right now," I said. "Tonight will get me going with a definite plan for solo travel."

She clasped my hand in a firm squeeze. "Messages come when we are most ready to hear them. Do your homework, follow the steps you outlined in your plan. You'll be okay. You are already, just as you are." Her compassionate arms pulled me toward her, drawing me close for goodnight hug.

Snowflakes snagged my damp eyelashes as I wandered up the hill to our house. Which each step I reviewed my intention to travel to Nepal, to spend time volunteering at a village school followed by a full month in Upper Mustang, and to write stories, or even a book, about the trip. There was still one huge obstacle to overcome. Before I could deal with all of my personal fears and goals, I had to convince Barry that going alone was a safe and acceptable proposition.

——— • ———

My homework was to set a proposed travel itinerary and send it to the trekking agency we had previously travelled with for a price estimate. Then I would have a concrete plan to discuss with Barry. It felt vaguely disloyal to send the itinerary without discussing it with him first. I didn't like it. We hadn't lasted for more than thirty years together by keeping secrets. But, captivated by possibilities, I forged ahead.

Magical places danced through my brain, conjuring thoughts of adventure and exotic cultures. I longed to return to the frenetic streets of Thamel, the assault to the senses that is Kathmandu. I dreamed of teaching children in Ratmate Village, the home of our first Nepali guide. I imagined myself back in Lo-Manthang, the medieval capital of Upper Mustang, interviewing locals. Possible travel schedules veered perilously close to the dreaded monsoon season, the torrential rains that engulf Nepal from mid-June to mid-September causing mud and rockslides, and leaving roads impassable. I needed enough time for volunteer teaching as well as trekking to Lo-Manthang to attend the three-day Buddhist festival, then time to stay to discover the ambiance of the walled city after the majority of other trekkers had left. The categories of possible interview candidates— hoteliers, artists, shopkeepers, lamas, teachers, local citizens and fellow trekkers— jumbled like an incomplete puzzle in my weary consciousness.

A week later Prem Khatry, owner of Ace the Himalaya, returned the itinerary for me to review, discuss with Barry, and make a decision. It was simultaneously scary, exhilarating, and challenging. This trip would signify my next steps in journaling, writing, independence and strength. My bookshelf was crowded with travel writing guidebooks; this might be my one chance in life to try out my talents while travelling on my own. Was I brave enough? Would I be resentful of Barry if I didn't go? How would it affect our relationship?

It was time to discuss my plan with him.

At 4:00 a.m., after fitful, sleepless hours of mourning the health issues faced by loved ones and recurring interruptions to our active lifestyle, I still lay wide-awake. Unable to sleep I went downstairs. Following my usual morning ritual I booted my computer and muddled through preparation of my morning latte. Steaming cup in hand, wrapped in my sapphire yak-wool blanket, I sat in my office watching the electric-blue Steller's Jay frolic around the bird feeder outside my window. From the windowsill I picked up my statue of the elephant-headed Hindu god Ganesh, said to be the remover of all obstacles, and waited for the sunrise.

If I found it this difficult to tell Barry what I wanted to do, would I have the nerve to travel alone? Winter conversations at the dining room table had swirled around the subject of a return trip to Nepal. I longed to fill in the blanks left by our abrupt departure two years earlier. Periodically the thought of going alone crossed my mind, but fear kept burying the idea.

Three hours later I heard his uneven footsteps on the stairs. He still walked with a slight limp from the Achilles injury. It had happened so unexpectedly and so quickly. The prospect of six months more of recovery, and even longer before he was eligible for travel insurance, hung over us like a sinister cloud.

"Come sit with me for a minute," I said. "I need to talk to you."
My crying jag started before I could begin. I put words
together between sobs. "I really want to go back to Nepal to
volunteer in the school in Ratmate and trek to Upper Mustang.
I can't wait another year. I'm afraid I'll be the next one with a
health problem." It wasn't Barry himself I feared. He was unfailingly supportive and understanding. I was afraid of how my
leaving without him and more than two months apart would
affect our relationship.

A long silence followed. Painfully long. I could almost see
his brain working to formulate a response. Neither of us moved.
"It's not the way we usually do things," he said, his voice shaky.
He was right. We enjoyed the same outdoor activities and exploration of new cultures. We wanted to travel to the same places,
so we went together.

I didn't cry often. Barry once told me I was emotionally the
strongest of my siblings. I didn't cry when my parents died or my
best teaching pal passed away far too early from breast cancer.
It wasn't necessarily a good thing, keeping things bottled up
inside, but I dealt with grief and tragedy privately, then sucked
it up, took care of myself and others, and moved on. Like my
father, I'm stoic and self-contained. I don't dwell on the past.

So when I sat crunched up and sobbing on the living room
couch, Barry knew it was time to pay attention. We both stared
straight ahead, as if studying the flames in the fireplace, not
touching, unable to look at each other. I hugged a cushion. His
back was rigid. Outside the wall of living room windows balsam
firs towered tall above the ski trail, the weight of last night's
snowfall heavy on their drooping branches. Above the mantle
the painting of the Everest trekking route, a spot I remembered
well from our first trip to Nepal, was a blur. But I knew the scene
by heart. It showed all I had been missing: the snowy summits
of the Himalaya against a pink and mauve sky; prayer flags

fluttering above a white, bulb-shaped sacred Buddhist *chorten*; shaggy gray yaks laden with bundles of supplies lumbering along the dusty trails, a red-shirted Nepali porter following behind, his tiny frame dwarfed by his overloaded basket.

My sobbing continued. I felt uncontrolled and unattractive, my eyes swollen and, no doubt, rimmed with red.

I stumbled to the kitchen for a tissue. "It's your fault I want to go," I called back. "You're the one who made me to be this way. You're the one who transformed me from a cottage girl to a wilderness travel junkie."

I blew my nose, grabbed a fresh tissue and blew again, purposely hesitating, considering what I wanted to say. I wandered back and stood by the fireplace. "You know when we first met at Capilano College I wasn't at all interested in you. I thought you were really smart and knew a lot about the outdoors, but those faded rugby shirts, baggy track pants, and your red hair and glasses just weren't a turn on for me. Then my friend Annie persuaded me to look harder." He always laughed when I told this story when someone asked us how we met. Now he stared at me, eyes a watery blue. I carried on. Over the years so many things had been left unsaid; it seemed important to me to remind him of things we both knew.

"But, you know, ever since our first day rock climbing together thirty-seven years ago, I've always felt second in command. I've been following you around the mountains winter and summer long enough. It's time for me to prove I can do something adventurous on my own." He nodded slowly. For years he had been an unfailingly supportive partner and coach, waiting patiently for me when I trailed behind, always greeting me with words of encouragement. "As a teacher and principal I felt like a leader, but when we went skiing or paddling or climbing together I never felt confident or independent. No matter how hard I tried I was never fast enough or strong enough to keep up with you." He lowered his head in another knowing nod.

I sat down beside him again, faced him and took his hand. Like many long-married couples we went about our lives in long practiced harmony, rarely delving directly into the deep, complex issues of our relationship. Now, it seemed crucial to address an episode that had terrified us both.

"You're my personal mountain guide, my mentor and my best friend. When you had to be air evacuated from Namche Bazaar on our trip in 2011, I was scared—more scared than I've ever been in my life. I thought I might lose you. Waiting outside the surgery in Norvic Hospital at midnight in Kathmandu for you to have an angiogram and then a stent put in one of your arteries was terrifying. You've made an amazing recovery, but who knows what might happen next to either of us. It's time for me to try going solo. I really want to visit Raj's home village and volunteer at the school. And with a longer time in Upper Mustang I can interview locals about the effects of tourism. Our single day in Lo-Manthang on our last trip was too short to really understand how things are changing. The story could make a great article or even a book. No one else is writing about it.

"We've always agreed we should do the more physically demanding trips, the high altitude, strenuous adventures first, while we still can," I went on. We had thought the cut-off point for joining the cruising set was still at least twenty years away when we would both be in our late eighties; these days, I wasn't so sure.

"We've been messing around with plans for the past year," I continued. "We never seem to get it together. Now, we can't go at all because of your Achilles."

Silence was his only reaction to my thoughtless comment. My obsession with the idea of a return trip to Nepal had deepened as Barry's waned.

Compared to obstacles others face in their lives, Barry and I have had a pretty easy time. Since retirement in 2006 we have spent summers at our cottage on an island in a pristine Ontario lake, and winters at our home at SilverStar. We have comfortable pensions. We get along. I dust and he vacuums. I cook and he does the dishes. I'm our social secretary. He takes care of finances. We discuss major life decisions and large expenditures. We're lucky and I am grateful. Barry was fit again—that is, until he ruptured his Achilles.

When it happened, all I could think was, "Oh no. That's it for Nepal or any other trip. Stuck at home for another year." My thoughts vacillated between how selfish I was being and wondering if I would still be able to trek in another year. Was I going to be the next one with a health problem? We had been T-boned twice since the year 2000 by another car hitting the passenger side door, where I was sitting. Years of physiotherapy and exercises had never completely solved the problem. How long would it be before I needed a hip replacement?

We never went to bed on a fight; each day ended with a kiss and a cuddle. But now each night I kissed Barry then crawled into my sleeping bag in the guestroom, too fearful of kicking his injured foot to sleep in the same bed. We weren't used to sleeping apart. I could feel the distance between us expanding. How could I find the elusive balance between being supportive and sacrificing my own wants and needs?

Neither of us seemed able to make things better between us.

And, every time I forgot to turn off the electric kettle I was certain that I would soon succumb to Alzheimer's. I was haunted by the memory of my older sister, Donna, once a vibrant yoga instructor, wasting away in a care home. My brother was still healthy at seventy-two, and although our parents were gone we had longevity in our family; my paternal grandfather William Shales lived well until the age of 103. Still, I knew good genes were no guarantee. I might soon to be the last one standing of our tightly knit nuclear family.

I was troubled by the image of my once-fit and active husband confined to a armchair in our living room, gazing out the window at skiers schussing the trail behind our house. For an expert skier an armchair with one foot enclosed in a cast, waiting an entire year for a ruptured Achilles to heal was torture.

There was no guarantee I wouldn't be next.

I sat blubbering beside my supportive, caring husband. One foot raised on a pillow on the coffee table, he listened attentively. Then he reached over and took my hand. I was afraid to breathe. The wait seemed an eternity. "It sounds like this is really important to you," he said, compassionate as always. "I think you should go."

CHAPTER 2
SECOND THOUGHTS

E very night I lay awake. Frightening scenarios of getting lost, plummeting off steep trails or being squished against rocks by overloaded yaks haunted my dreams. I stared at the moonlit shadows on the bedroom blinds. Hemlock branches swirled like sadhus, the mystical white-faced ascetics who line the smoky cremation sites of the Pashupatinath temple on the shore of the Kathmandu's Bagmati River. Their vacant expressions intrigued yet also frightened me. I was unsure if their wild eyes exuded serenity, or madness brought on by a fanatical search for holiness.

Overheated, I threw the covers off. Five minutes later I was shivering in the grip of my latest imagined fear. What if I never found a female trekking partner? Was I brave enough to go alone?

I remembered a conversation I had with my friend Patti that morning as we had wandered along the snowshoe trails of SilverStar. "I'm getting freaked out about this trip," I said. "I'm determined to go, but still not sure about going alone."

"What's your biggest fear?" she asked, her voice coming from behind me on the trail.

Patti's gift was seeing the positive in every situation so I hit her with one of the worst. "I'm scared I'll get sick and have no one to take care of me," I said.

"Did you get sick on other trips to Asia?"

"No, I'm careful about water and food. It's more altitude that scares me. In Upper Mustang I'll be between 3,000 and 4,000 meters for a whole month. I've been as high as 5,630 meters on Drolma La, the high pass on the Mount Kailash trek in Tibet, but that was only for a few hours."

She stopped to refasten the binding on her snowshoe. "There's never any guarantee. Depends on how much you really want to go. I thought you said you'd been fine with elevation on your other trips."

"I have. But it can be different every time. On the Annapurna Circuit, I got a horrible headache in Manang Village at 3,500 meters. We stayed an extra day so I could acclimatize and I took Diamox."

"What's that?"

"Basically a water pill, a diuretic, so you don't get the headaches, nausea or shortness of breath caused by fluid buildup. It worked for me. I took it for three days and got over Thorang La, the high pass on the route, easily. That was at 4,500 meters. After that I didn't need it for the next two months, even at higher elevations."

We continued in silence on a steep uphill. When the trail leveled off in a meadow, we stopped. "OK. So what else are you worried about?" she said.

"I guess I'm mostly scared of getting into the Kathmandu airport late at night and not being able to find Raj or somebody from the trekking company. It's so dark and there are mobs waiting outside."

Patti and I are the same height, an inch or two above the five-foot mark. She's a kickass downhill skier despite a half knee replacement. We hiked at the same pace, both loved going to bed early and rising early. My perfect trekking partner stood right beside me.

"Ever thought of hiking in Nepal?"

"I have," she said. "But there's things higher on my bucket list. Didn't I tell you I'm training to walk the Camino de Santiago? I'm going with two women friends next September."

No surprise she was booked already. Patti's sunny personality and ability to call everyone in our mountain community by name made her a popular choice of partner for any activity.

A few days later I had a similar discussion with my friend Therese, one of the most well-travelled women I knew. Born in Switzerland, she thrived on challenging trekking trails. She and her husband Bruce had visited Nepal several times. She's fun, my age, a take-no-prisoners backcountry skier, and not afraid of lumpy beds and squat toilets.

"So, Therese, have you ever travelled alone?" I asked over dinner at her home.

"Sure, lots of times," she said. "In Nepal last year I hiked for seven days with a female guide while Bruce stayed in our rented flat in Pokhara. Her name is Hira. I can give you her email. You might want to trek with her sometime."

"Maybe, but I've already booked Raj. The school where I'm volunteering is in his village. So what are your next travel plans? Would you consider coming to Nepal with me? Two weeks volunteer teaching in Gorkha, then a month's trek in Upper Mustang to study the effects of tourism and the new road, and then a week in Lhasa, Tibet."

"That would be fun," she said between bites of her signature Swiss dish, *raclette*, crafted with cheese and fingerling potatoes. "But Bruce and I have plans to go back to Nepal in the fall. Our itinerary is set."

I was disappointed but in some ways relieved neither Patti nor Therese was available. Travel could make or break a relationship. I didn't want to risk losing either of them because of my own idiosyncrasies or annoying habits, or theirs.

My shortlist of likely candidates exhausted, I had asked around for other suggestions. Several SilverStar women showed interest in travelling to Nepal, but like most first-time Himalayan trekkers, it was the Annapurna or Everest Circuit that attracted them. Five weeks prior to my mid-April departure date, Barry suggested another SilverStar acquaintance named Roseanne. A naturalist and snowshoe guide, Roseanne seemed energetic and positive. Fifteen years younger than me she stood a head taller and was fit and muscular. The idea of her coming with me seemed worthy of investigation. "I'll email her the itinerary," I said.

The next day, Roseanne and I settled on opposite sides of a scarred wooden table at Out of Bounds, one of the SilverStar Resort hangouts.

"Your trip sounds exciting," she said after I'd summed up. I began to feel hopeful. "I've wanted to go to Nepal for a long time." I leaned forward in anticipation. "But your itinerary doesn't really match what I want to do."

I slumped back in my seat, defeated.

I was okay with that. I didn't know her well. With that she stood up, tugged a rainbow wool toque over her long chestnut mane, and left. With her my last chance of finding a trekking partner walked out the door.

It wasn't long before I realized my search for a sister-in-trekking had ended the way I had subconsciously intended. I would be heading out solo. Physically I was doing okay. Due to an active lifestyle of summer swimming and stand-up paddleboard workouts, fall hiking and winter downhill and cross-country skiing and snowshoeing, I had a good fitness base. Living most of the year at an altitude of 1,600 meters gave me some advantage. A ninety-minute cross country outing on my skate skis—the narrower, stiffer racing ski cousin to touring skis—was doable every second day but daily sessions of up to three hours in length and some stretch and strength training were what I needed.

So many tasks remained: writing projects with looming dead-lines, income tax forms, packing, and lesson plans and charts for two weeks of teaching English at Bhairabi School. During my career I had taught most elementary school grades, but as a principal for the last twenty years of my career and retired for nine, I had now been out of the classroom for thirty years. As a beginning teacher I taught French as a second language and used action songs to teach vocabulary. Now my vocal chords were sadly out of shape. I printed song charts and drew flashcards of animals, family members, parts of the body and clothing items. I wanted to do a good job. Raj was taking me to his home to meet friends and family. I didn't want to let him down.

Emotionally, I ran the gamut of fear, apprehension, excite-ment, joy, and delight. I had a wonderful secret: I was going back to Nepal, by myself. I relished the thought of travelling on my own; no one else to worry about, time to reflect, write and decide things just for me.

Technology would be one of my biggest challenges. I'd never even used an ATM; Barry always got the cash. I often sat staring into nothingness, mentally reviewing the imagined terrors of my decision. I still had so many fears that may seem petty to some, but to me they were terrifying.

The usual routes from Vancouver to Kathmandu are via Hong Kong or Bangkok. I chose Hong Kong. I had been that way before. The airport was huge. I pictured myself lost, forever riding the subway beneath the length of the airport, searching for my duffel bags. What would happen when I reached Kathmandu? I replayed the scene from our last arrival at Tribhuvan International Airport. I visualized myself encountering the familiar seething mob of taxi drivers, thirsty for tourist dollars, nylon shirts and shiny synthetic pants stuck to their bodies in the humid midnight air. In one mass they pressed against the security barrier. "Taxi, madam. Let me take your bag," they called out. "AC, madam.

Cool and comfortable. Come with me."

I searched the melee for Raj's comforting smile. What if he didn't turn up? The recurring scene was exacerbated when a stern email warning arrived from the trekking company: "Do not go with anyone except the Ace the Himalaya guide or staff member. If you are not met by a guide displaying an Ace the Himalaya sign, do not leave the airport. Stay where you are and call one of these numbers." The numbers were no use to me. Intimidated by technology I had chosen not to bring a cell phone. Why were they sending this email now? Had single women been abducted and carried off into the warren of dark, smoky alleyways of Kathmandu? My head spun with frightening scenarios scented by polluted air, fragrant incense, and the pungent sweat of illegal taxi drivers.

If I made it to Kathmandu unscathed, what would stop me from ending up in a crumpled heap on the edge of a narrow street in Thamel, the city's bustling tourist area, after some bold thief had spotted me as a single female tourist and stolen my pack? The image played before me: I sat crouched in despair, face in hands, sobbing, the sludge from the soaking-wet pavement seeping up the legs of my trekking pants. Incense mingled with motorbike exhaust from the morning commute choked me. My passport, camera, bank and Visa cards and emergency phone lists were long gone.

And what if I did navigate my way through this fantasy of horrors and make it to the trekking routes? Nightmares of altitude sickness, headaches, and vomiting on some remote high altitude trail plagued me.

Refusing to give my fears decision-making power over my life, I listed them. My statue of Ganesh, remover of obstacles, watched from the windowsill.

First on the list: Hong Kong International Airport.

"Barry," I called into the living room, "do you remember how many stops there are on the Hong Kong airport subway to get to the baggage carousels?"

A pause. "One," he yelled back. "Follow the crowd."

Should have asked him a few days ago. I'd be better rested.

Second was the midnight congestion outside the Kathmandu airport. I tucked the emergency phone numbers into my passport wallet. I would ask for help. "I'm not stepping outside the airport until I spot Raj."

"Sounds like a plan," said Barry, now peering into the open fridge.

The third, the threat of altitude sickness, was harder. I could pack my inhaler, down the two liters of water per day suggested by doctors and make sure our daily itinerary limited us to gaining altitude slowly – that was easy – but there was no guarantee how my body would react to altitude higher than 3,500 meters.

I vowed to keep training and pack Diamox.

As for being lost, I decided to pack my own maps and trust Raj wouldn't abandon me or purposely fall off a cliff.

Then I remembered currency issues. Mathematics has never been my strong point, so money exchange, possible corruption and theft were authentic issues. I bought a tiny calculator and created a miniscule chart of exchange rates.

My most consuming fear was being sick and alone, holed up in some hostel, dehydrated by diarrhea and vomiting, flattened and shivering. I stashed sufficient chlorine pills to ensure there were enough to purify two liters of drinking water a day.

But what truly sent shivers down my spine was leeches—the blood-sucking tyrants rampant on some trekking trails, vampire-worms ready to sneak into your socks and up your ankles to who knows where. At the school in Gorkha in the lush green hills northwest of Kathmandu I'd be in a subtropical area, heaven for leeches.

I once read Broughton Coburn's terrifying yet strangely hilari-

ous travel story about leeches in the 1997 edition of *Travelers'*
Tales Nepal: True stories of Life on the Road. It tells how Coburn
made the ill-fated choice of combating the heat of trekking by
leaning over a stream and splashing water over his face. Soon
after, he kept experiencing regular, inexplicable nosebleeds. They
continued for weeks until an embarrassing encounter in a teashop
made him realize something was wrong. The waiter kept staring
at his nose and finally refused to serve him, retreating in horror.

At home in front of the mirror Coburn saw a tiny speck of
something dark brown protruding from his nostril. He examined
the area with a magnifying mirror. Finally after several visits to
the doctor a leech was discovered living happily on Coburn's
blood in the warm cavity inside his right nostril. Eventually the
doctor was able to extract the twenty-five centimeter wormlike
creature.

I scratched my nose every time I thought about it. There would
be absolutely no face-splashing from rivers, lakes or streams,
not even if I was fainting from the heat.

I continued skate skiing, wearing a backpack, for two to
three hours at a time several times a week. Two weeks before
boarding the plane for Hong Kong my knees puffed up like
balloons. Medicinal rub and Advil, followed by a bit of après ski
wine, helped. Barry suggested rest, ice, liniment, and a compress
bandage. If it happened on the trail rest would be out of the
question and ice unattainable. I'd make do with liniment and wine.

With one day to go I still hadn't packed. My throat was hoarse
from singing. Barry surprised me with an altimeter watch small
enough to fit my slender wrist. Why had I ever doubted his
support? Unruly piles of fleece, merino wool, down and cotton
jumbled amid rows of Ziploc bags bursting with bottles of Advil,
packets of water purification tablets, and Imodium. Extra water
tablets went with my toothbrush; it amazed me how many tourists
bought bottled water then brushed their teeth with village tap

water and were surprised when they got sick. Enough blister pads for several pairs of feet, and masses of clothing blanketed our guestroom bed.

I slouched against the bookcase. Over the years I had replaced books on educational strategies with travel literature showcasing my passion for the outdoors and fascination with all things Himalayan. The collection began with *Lost Horizon*. The 1930s novel by James Hilton, required reading in Grade 10, had introduced me to the mystery of Tibet through the story of a fictional utopian lamasery in Shangri-La hovering high on a cliff, almost obscured in delicately veiled mountains.

Leaning against Hilton's tome was the well-worn scrapbook from my Ontario Grade 13 year at Neuchatel Junior College. The charming Swiss town of Neuchatel initiated my love affair with mountains and wine. Hundreds of mini Buddhas smiled down from Bob Thurman's *Essential Tibetan Buddhism*. Barry and I often discussed the teachings and felt empathy for the plight of Tibetan refugees in India as well as those left inside China in the Tibet Autonomous Region. We were attracted by the Dalai Lama's message of compassion towards self and others. Whenever I said something bitchy Barry would invariably respond, "Is that what the Dalai Lama would say?" in an effort to tease me toward becoming a better version of myself.

Mountaineering, Freedom of the Hills, the outdoor bible first published in 1960 by The Mountaineers of Seattle, Washington, signaled the beginning of my more practical approach to the mountains. Thirty years before, I had enrolled in the Wilderness Leadership program at Capilano College in Vancouver. My quest landed me the skills necessary to travel to remote areas, and a mountain-guide husband.

My daypack would contain items needed every day. A headlamp, toilet paper, and hand sanitizer went in the top pocket. These were indispensable for navigation and comfort in dark squat toilets. I'd been caught out before and it wasn't pretty.

In a Ziploc bag I encased my journal, lightweight lined pages with slots inside the covers. My latest Valentine card from Barry showed a couple walking hand in hand along a forest trail. *Dearest Patti, My love and spirit will forever be with you on every trail. Love, Barry.* I tucked it inside the front cover. In the back, a few pages of journal writing advice filled the slot. I threw in a few Ziploc bags for collecting travel brochures, business cards, and recipes. The final item was a tiny aluminum-cased lemon-scented travel candle.

I filled two single-liter water bottles and loaded them into the side pockets. My shoulders complained instantly when I hefted my day pack for a test run. I'd have to get used to the weight.

Barry appeared in the doorway. "Here are eight numbered camera memory cards, and a bag of charger plug adapters for Hong Kong, Nepal and Tibet, labeled as to country." I gave him a hug. His perfectionism made things easy for me.

The red duffel with most of my gear was almost at capacity I slipped in a few extra Mars bars and a second roll of double-thick, ultra soft toilet paper. In Nepal toilet paper was thin and oddly stretchy. I'd make my private stash last as long as it could. I had barely enough room for the last crucial item, my talisman, Roger, a pint-sized golden retriever who always traveled with me. Enchanted with Dell comics as a preschooler, I had insisted on naming our puppy after my cowboy hero, Roy Rogers. My siblings agreed and shortened his moniker to Roger. This toy version, from the gift shop at the Kingston General Hospital, had comforted my dad during the last week of his life in September, 2010. He had almost made it to his ninety-fourth birthday.

The real Roger was with my family through my childhood and teen years. I had kept the stuffed version of Roger close every day since my father's passing. His matted fur reeked of the inside of my backpack. His brown plastic eyes reminded me of the security of our tight-knit family. My dad: advisor, math coach, personal tennis and swimming instructor and biggest fan. I respected and adored him.

Deep in my daypack, I stashed copies of my personal documents then went downstairs to email them to myself.

In the second duffel I packed felt pens and hand-printed conversation and song charts. Nepali maps and phrasebooks overlapped English songbooks and sheaves of reward stickers. I wasn't confident in my athletic ability but I did feel self-assured as a primary teacher. These items would, I thought, ensure success with village kids. My naïve North American assumptions were soon to be shaken.

I added school supplies, lesson materials, and four-dozen toothbrushes donated by my dentist. I lugged the second duffel upstairs and plunked it on the bathroom scales. I hauled in the red duffel from the guest bedroom. Magically, each weighed slightly less than the allotted fifty pounds. My pack tipped the scales at twenty-two.

———— * ————

That night I rotated through sleepless positions, consumed by my personal baggage—my fragile sense of self. My body held the scars, the stories, of my life. Aging muscle fibers clung faintly to past years of figure skating; the swim, bike, run maneuvers of triathlon competitions; and the freedom of cross country skate training and racing. My legs and feet held reminiscences of excursions over the mountain trails of North America, England, Tibet and Nepal. Had they stored the wisdom and strength to do it again?

The soft tissue surrounding my right hip harbored the residual resentment of two car accidents. My left shoulder nagged at the memory of three dislocations. And my back, a victim of congenital scoliosis, caused me to tug constantly on the straps of my daypack, adjusting and readjusting to the curvature of my spine.

Digging deeper I sorted through my inner inventory.

While my adult sense of self had been honed during a success-ful thirty-seven- year career as a teacher, educational consultant, elementary school principal and occasional competitive athlete, there remained inside a shy, chunky girl with strawberry blond frizzy curls, and an all-encompassing lack of confidence.

My petite blue-eyed mother, a dedicated 1950s housewife, despite considerable competence as a mother, chef, swimmer, tennis player, choir singer, and nurse, modeled a tentative nature. More often than not she deferred to my father in decisions.

Tall and athletic, the introverted son of a strict Victorian mother, he fought his naturally reclusive nature with minimal success. He was most at home in a faded plaid shirt sitting in the stern of a cedar and canvas canoe, paddling the calm waters of eastern Ontario.

Along with Mom's habit of putting the needs of others first, I inherited Dad's reclusive nature. And his broad kneecaps, sturdy but totally out of proportion to the petite frame bequeathed by my mother. Reluctantly, I had come to appreciate their strength and resilience.

Still fitter than many of my contemporaries, I continued to push myself to keep up with my husband, beating myself up when unsuccessful. Time after time I put myself into situations that invariably resulted in a serious blow to my shaky self-esteem.

It had taken me a long time to celebrate Barry's passion for keeping fit for adrenaline inducing outdoor pursuits. Clinging to vertical rock faces, pointing his skis over the edge of a double-black-diamond run, and maneuvering whitewater rapids in a canoe or kayak were his idea of a good time.

For years I followed along, enjoying the challenge. While I loved being fit and conquering risky expeditions, I had finally realized endurance events suited me better.

So why did I feel the need to risk travelling alone to such a remote area? Maybe because I'd spent my entire life trying to keep up; first with my older siblings, and later with the super-fit mountaineer I married. For the past few years Barry had experienced significant health issues.

It was time to discover my own pace. Time to discover a zone just for me, a milieu where I could develop personal courage, freedom from fears, and a sense of purpose.

———— * ————

While Barry loaded up the car I placed ten individually dated and sealed mountain-themed note cards on his pillow. He could open one per week, read about a shared memory, and hopefully feel less abandoned.

I removed my wedding ring, a sapphire surrounded by too much gold to flaunt in a dollar-a-day economy, and replaced it with a less obtrusive silver and turquoise band. I slipped my miniature Ganesh into my pocket.

Barry and I didn't talk much at the airport. We held hands, unwilling to let go. After a lingering hug at the security gate, I joined the lineup. Several minutes later I glanced back at the gate. Barry was still standing there, watching me. He raised his arm for one final wave. I did the same.

In my head I was already long gone.

CHAPTER 3
KEEP PADDLING

Hong Kong; April 18, 2014

G olden arches soared garishly against a smoggy brown sky. Black cabs vied for position with double-decker buses along the congested street, their exhaust contributing to the already pungent air. Two teenaged boys with spiky hair and ear bud strings draping their shoulders brushed past where I stood waiting. Under-slept and grimy, I blinked at passersby on the crowded sidewalk. Sai Kung Town inhabitants, residents of this Hong Kong suburb, bustled around me as I scanned the crowd for my first interview subject.

My fascination with Hong Kong had been frustrated by a single-night stopover on our previous trip. The respite had served the purpose of providing a good night's sleep after the thirteen-hour flight from Vancouver, but all I had seen was the hotel and a mall full of designer watches. Even so, it was a welcome alternative to trying to sleep in the Hong Kong Airport, waiting nine hours for the connecting evening flight to Kathmandu. This time my goal was to avoid the city in order to experience the green, lush locales where active urbanites escaped the shopping malls, high-rises offices, and apartments of sky city.

My thinking was as murky as the surrounding miasma, but my lips curled in a secret smile. I'd made it this far on my own.

Dave Wilson, head of Sea Kayak Academy, was scheduled to meet me at this spot. So far he was fifteen minutes late. For the past half hour, hip muscles aching I'd loitered in various spots inside McDonald's, the air-conditioned oasis of American culture. Eyeing locals eagerly devouring Big Macs with fries and Cokes, I stood on one foot then the other. With each shift my sandals squeaked off the sticky floor. Behind sunglasses my aching eyes squinted against the harsh fluorescent lighting.

When fifteen minutes extended to thirty, I'd stepped outside. The Saturday morning cacophony pounded through my head. My shoulders slumped lower than my spirit. I felt old, out-of-place and alone. My lungs cringed with each breath of the humid, scorching Hong Kong air laden with the nauseating smell of grease. My sweaty fingers clutched the waterproof plastic sack rolled and sealed at the top to keep my camera and passport dry.

Two-storey pastel cement buildings lined the narrow street. A middle-aged man in a graying undershirt and dark blue pants stepped out onto his apartment balcony. Stretching the bottom edge of his shirt down over his ample torso he surveyed the red umbrellas and green awnings shading sidewalk tables of seafood restaurants below. The scent of saltwater competed with the essence of Big Mac.

Fishermen still gathered here. Families lingered over congee and green tea before browsing in small shops for the catch of the day. Before the relocation of the Hong Kong airport, Sai Kung was a popular residential area for airport staff. Now designated as a typhoon shelter it is dominated by public housing projects.

I continued to wait, endeavoring to blend into the morning bustle.

So much for my status as a travel maverick. Had I made a mistake already? What time had he said? Last night I had set my watch to Hong Kong time. Or had I?

A husky man, his tan stretching past the top of his head

to meet a receding salt-and-pepper hairline, swaggered over. "I would never have recognized you without the dry bag," he said, in a broad Australian twang. No doubt he was expecting someone younger. I didn't know what I was expecting but this gruff Tasmanian did look the part of the seasoned kayak instructor his online ads promise. "Sorry about being a bit late," he said. "I never know when everyone will show up for sure. Hope you had time to get breakfast." He glanced in the direction of McDonald's. "We've a lot of paddling ahead of us."

Several people who looked to be about twelve but were probably in their late twenties or early thirties appeared out of nowhere. They carried backpacks and looked dressed for kayaking: shorts, T-shirts, sandals and sunhats.

Half seemed Asian, the rest Caucasian, more than half were female. All turned out to be ex-pats; an international crowd, twenty-five to thirty-five years old. They hailed from Berlin, Montreal, Iran, France, Hungary, and Wisconsin, all living and working in Hong Kong, all craving greenery and adventure. Like outdoor enthusiasts everywhere, they seemed a casual crowd, women not uptight about their hair, fingernails or fashion. All wore practical shirts constructed to protect them from the sun, not necessarily to match their shorts and wide-brimmed hats. Other than age I fit in well.

"It's a bit of a joy ride to the Wong Shek Pier," said Dave, herding me along with the rest of the ragtag group. I could hear him mumbling a count of group members as they filed by, onto the bus.

As the bus veered out into traffic I settled down and pulled out my notebook and pen eager to learn more about the itinerary for the day. Sitting sideways with my feet braced on the floor I tried not to careen off the slippery molded plastic seat as we swerved along the winding road. Were the tremors in my fingers caused by two much caffeine, too little sleep or the self-induced pressure of recording his answers correctly? Dave's accent was as broad as the harbor view. I had to keep asking him to spell and respell the Chinese names of things. "No worries," drawled Dave, after respelling one word several times. "Lots of time to talk later. I'll give you the company brochures later, too."

As we left the smog of Sai Kung, the bright azure of the sea view even through my sunglasses caused a piercing ache in my light-sensitive eyes. The rolling hills and hairpin curves of the road made note-taking impossible. Best to enjoy the scenery, make mental notes and enjoy the ride.

Forty-five minutes later we arrived at the public pier on the shore of Long Harbour beside a double-decker ferry dock serving the remote settlements of the Sai King Peninsula.

"The lineup's long," said Dave. "It's Easter weekend." It looked like most of Hong Kong had arrived for an outing. "How about we take a water taxi?" Without waiting for a vote, he negotiated a price. Then, like a dedicated teacher leading a class of teens, he called out over his shoulder, "Follow me, you lot," and shepherded all twenty of us onto two open boats.

What followed was a bone-jarring rodeo ride as the boat launched upward then crashed down, hitting every choppy wave. The young woman next to me in the front spray-soaking row seized my arm in a desperate vice grip to avoid catapulting forward off the slick wooden bench and over the bow. Her desperate act of familiarity made me feel like one of the gang. Feet braced against a ridge in the hull, I did my best to keep us both safely anchored on board. The driver, his maniacal grin protected by a Plexiglas shield, repeatedly revved the engine. The more trips he made, the more Hong Kong dollars in his pocket. Not a PFD in sight.

How cold was the water? How far could I swim if I had to? What skills remained from long ago days as a lifeguard?

A ten-minute eternity later we disembarked across a slippery

Pa and Patti model PFD's and sprayskirts.

wooden makeshift gangplank on to a crumbling cement wharf. Knees like jelly I followed the crowd up a steep pathway. With each step, deep piles of dried rhododendron leaves popped and sizzled like rows of firecrackers. At the top the trail opened onto a concrete platform in front of a row of abandoned houses, remnants of a once-prosperous fishing village. One of these pockmarked stucco edifices served as Dave's base camp.

Neon pink and orange kayak spray decks hung drying on a sagging clothesline strung along a decaying rock wall. Rows of kayaks, paddles and PFDs cuddled together under a graying event tent squished between houses. The equipment looked in good condition, but what about me? We hadn't even started paddling yet and I was already worrying about keeping up with the group. I hadn't paddled in two years. All those times I'd avoided doing pushups began to haunt me.

With what I hoped passed as a relaxed smile, I exchanged travel banter with my soon-to-be kayaking buddies. "I'm looking for the outdoor adventure side of Hong Kong," I said to the woman next to me. "I'm not much for cities and shopping."

As we giggled and wiggled our way into the required spray skirts and personal flotation devices, Pa, who turned out to be a transplanted chartered accountant from Laos, agreed. "I hated Hong Kong when I first got here. That was before I discovered sea kayaking."

I'd found a like-minded friend for the day. "Yeah, I love it, too. I've been kayaking for years," I said, false bravado kicking in.

Once on the water, we gazed back up to a kaleidoscope of rhododendron and azalea blossoms crawling up through the densely forested emerald hills. Palm fronds waved gracefully from the hilltop in the morning breeze. Ma On Shan, called Horse Saddle Mountain by the locals, towered above. This remote, windswept ridge, a popular hiking destination in Sai Kung West Country Park, was the second highest peak in Hong Kong's New

Patti excited to begin the first adventure.

Territories. Spirits of long-forgotten farmers, fishermen, and lime kiln workers shimmered on the sultry thermals.

My back straightened with confidence. I knew kayaking—lake kayaking, that is. The last time I maneuvered an ocean kayak over swells was more than thirty years ago. More used to recent paddling outings on calm Ontario lakes, I'd need to pace myself to last all day.

We paddled westward from Long Harbour around the tip of Sai Kung Peninsula into Hoi Ha Wan ("Bay Beneath the Sea"). Two hours later we beached our kayaks at the base of a rocky freshwater creek. Lacy rivulets trickled down the hillside creating an intertidal mix of fresh and salt water, the perfect environment for mangrove trees.

Others claimed shoreline spots on the sand. I wandered aimlessly away from the group, dazed, desperate for escape from the relentless sun, a sharp contrast to the snowy spring environs I'd left behind at SilverStar only two days before. Perched on a flat rock under a canopy of waxy dog-ear sized mango leaves, I felt somewhat refreshed.

Somewhere in the woods up the hill from the silvery sands, four limekilns, the remains of one of the oldest industries in Hong Kong, lay partially hidden in the undergrowth. More than a century ago locals had fired those kilns to refine lime from oyster shells or coral skeletons for use in construction and agriculture. In the1980s, with the help of Hoi Ha villagers, two of these silo-shaped coral burners, made of beach stone and crude brick, were restored to their original state. A historic lunch stop had now been created on the hiking trail above us.

When I originally booked this outing, the advertisement said lunch was provided. At the last minute, when Dave changed the trip day and location, I mistakenly assumed lunch was still part of the deal. Somehow my leisurely tourist excursion had morphed into a club trip for locals who all knew to pack a lunch. Two granola bars and one small bottle of water stared up at me from the interior of my dry bag. I munched in silence.

After downing their substantial lunches, club members decided it was time for a swim. One girl, tall and curvy, ripped off her shirt and shorts to reveal the tiniest of fuchsia string bikinis. She led the parade along the silken stretch of fine white sand into the water. Others stripped down to a variety of spandex delights worn under their clothes, donned masks and snorkels, and slipped into the tepid shallows.

"C'mon. Join us. The water's warm. The coral colors are amazing."

Not a chance. There's no way I was revealing my winter white skin in this mob, no matter how friendly they were. "Thanks, but no. I'm looking for some shade. I just left winter. The sun's too much for me." Besides, I needed to rest if I was going to make it back to base camp.

Feeling removed by at least a generation from the bikini-clad lovelies and Speedo warriors, I took a deep breath and reminded myself I was here to gather information for the articles. Notebook and pen in hand, camera slung around my neck in a quasi- professional manner, I watched them peer through pristine sparkling water to the variegated neon rainbow of hard coral and fish the area was famous for.

I could hear them chatting when they came up for air, accountants and fashion designers savoring their escape from the city. Laughter and splashes filled the air where more than one hundred years ago industrious villagers armed with long poles rowed out in small boats to break off pieces of the coral. They had harvested their catch with metal tongs attached to bamboo poles, and hauled it up the hill to the kilns. Finally, after several scorching days of tending the white-hot wood-fired kiln, they shoveled the fine white dust into sacks. Sweat must have rushed down their backs as they hefted the scratchy hand-hewn bags on weary shoulders. From there, they would have staggered back down the hill to load the lime onto the decks of waiting junks for transport to Aberdeen, Hong Kong Island.

I stepped gingerly among the rows of beached kayaks, scanning the scene through my camera lens, searching for iconic compositions. Twenty or so snaps later I sauntered over to our group leader.

The brawny long-term ex-pat organized and guided the weekly club as well as working as an instructor for Sea Kayak Academy, part of Outdoor Education Asia. I wasn't fooled by his flip manner of teasing all the women on the forty-five-minute public bus ride. His militarily close-cropped hair, thickset 5-foot, 10-inch frame and muscular calves bulging below shiny black shorts indicated he was a guy for whom outdoor pursuits and fitness loomed large.

"Not swimming either?" I said.

Dave Wilson, Sea Kayak Academy instructor.

"I'm on marine watch," he said, gaze fixed on the swimmers. Looking down momentarily from his vantage point at the top of a large rock he pulled several worn plastic containers out of his dry bag. He laid a crumpled piece of whole-wheat flatbread on the lid of one container, piled on lettuce and salami, then meticulously constructed a wrap sandwich. Envious of his substantial lunch, I unwrapped my second granola bar.

"Swim and float," he yelled in the direction of the group. "Don't put your feet down and don't touch. The coral's sharp and fragile." A true environmentalist with a passion for outdoor education.

Orsi, a recent arrival from Hungary, acted as second in command. She gracefully folded her long legs settling cross-legged in the sand beside us. Her pale, almost translucent skin glowed from sun and exertion. Although her slender arms gave her a fragile look, her athletic paddling skill during the morning had proven her to be anything but. Her straight blond hair was cut in a simple neck-grazing bob, and I admired her effortless style, a vivid contrast to my wiry white coiffure. "I've been here six months," she had told me earlier. "I'm trying to learn Mandarin and improve my outdoor skills."

This adventuresome European youngster was travelling the globe gobbling up exotic outdoor jobs and languages in yearlong bites. In contrast, I was a fish out of water, an aging neophyte journalist gasping to appear nonchalant on my first solo adventure. Except for Dave, they all seemed so young. For years I had struggled to find my niche age group for outdoor activities. I preferred to hike or ski with contemporaries but many of my friends were definitely not interested in clambering up steep rocky hills or cross-country skiing with a backpack. I often ended up in groups where most others were at least twenty years younger. I loved their vibrant, energetic company but sometimes felt disturbingly out of place. Today was no exception.

"So you haven't told me," said Orsi, after taking a few bites of her sandwich. "What are you doing here?"

"I'm on my way to Nepal. First to volunteer in a primary school, then go trekking in Upper Mustang, near the Tibet border for a month."

"On your own?" Her raised eyebrows failed to hide her surprise. "You've been in Hong Kong less than a day and already you're out kayaking?" While I shared the details of my plan, Orsi leaned in and listened intently. Despite our age difference I'd found a kindred spirit. If Orsi found me impressive, then maybe I was. When I told her I'd use the day's experience as fodder for an article she eagerly shared her newfound knowledge about the park.

She related that Hoi Ha Wan Marine Park, the only one of Hong Kong's five marine parks with direct road access, offered 230 islands to explore boasting a dazzling array of coastal and underwater natural resources.

Known for its hard coral and varied species of reef-associated fish, the sheltered square-mile bay situated north of Sai Kung West Country Park on the Sai Kung Peninsula made the wilderness of the New Territories northeast of Hong Kong accessible to travelers who longed for an escape from the city's hard-edged concrete, steel, and glass.

A haven for kayakers and snorkelers, the marine park was a hot spot in the growing ecotourism market. The Hong Kong World Wildlife Federation, formed in 1981, originally concentrated on protection of the Giant Panda and other endangered species. However in 1988 their focus turned to the establishment of marine parks and reserves. Eventually in 2003 they created the Hoi Ha Marine Life Centre for marine biodiversity and conservation. Cruises on the shallow-draft glass-bottomed boat *Transparency* were offered to educate and ensure the ecotourism boom was handled in an environmentally responsible manner.

After lunch we dragged our kayaks into the water, hopped in, and secured spray skirts around the rim of our cockpits.

We dipped blades into waters not far from Tolo Harbour, once called Mei Zhu, an area at one time abundant with pearls. Two thousand pearl divers, some living on boats in the sheltered bay their entire lives, regularly braved the depths in this once-thriving center of the pearl industry. Hunting lasted until the Ming Dynasty, when the pearls became nearly extinct.

We glided past the verdant rolling hills of Mo Chau (Moon Island) which, along with Ngan Chau (Flat Island) delineated the park boundary. Densely populated, Ngan Chau's name is apt; with an average elevation of 0 meters above sea level, the island regularly risks severe floods. Mesmerized by the multicolored rocks and sea creatures clearly visible below we

Kayak group sets out for the afternoon excursion.

paddled mindlessly along the low-lying shoreline.

In the distance we caught sight of Port Island, also known as Chek Chau (Red Island). Composed of Danxia—a land form of red igneous rock rich in iron oxide, specific to China—Port Island was designated a UNESCO World Heritage Site in 2010. We dawdled past the barren, red peaks and rusty soil glowing crimson in the eerie silence of the late afternoon. The sharp pain in my biceps downgraded from code red to manageable. Not bad for an old broad, I thought.

Dave's Tasmanian baritone interrupted my reverie. "That island, Tung Ping Chau, off in the distance is owned by Hong Kong but the shore behind it is mainland China." It looked close by. The kidney-shaped, roughly one-square-kilometer hunk of shale sitting in Mirs Bay in the northeast corner of Hong Kong had a history that included the smuggling of guns and opium. I sniffed the air for remnants of gunpowder. Smuggling was still an issue, but today the fare was more likely to be live lobsters and electronics.

Despite the warm air, I shivered as Dave described mainlanders swimming through waters teeming with sharks to reach the island, in hopes of gaining freedom in Hong Kong during the Cultural Revolution. "I heard the story of one young man who was twenty-six when he was given the job of raking out tons of cinders at a pesticide factory, where the toxic fumes made him ill. He spent months preparing, training in open water for his escape to Hong Kong."

With little warning, the sea began to move beneath us like the churning feeling the shark stories had left in my stomach. My fingers gripped the paddle shaft tighter. The pressure of new blisters forming, even through my paddling gloves, heated my arthritic thumbs. We rolled and tossed against the chop back past the northern tip of Sai Kung Peninsula. A stiff afternoon breeze blew up as we turned southeast and crossed Middle Channel toward Grass Island, also known as Tap Mun, for the return trip.

Once we reached the shelter of the fish farm community anchored along Grass Island's western shoreline, we were able to lazily meander, steering our boats through a maze of cabins floating on rafts of blue plastic barrels. At least ten kayak lengths behind the group, I lingered in the calm using my lack of speed as an excuse to take photos. A few families lived on the boats. Only one hundred resident landlubbers, mostly merchants catering to tourists, remained on the shore.

The gentle hills of Grass Island, serene but strangely melancholic in their almost-deserted state, provided panoramic views for those weary of high-rise horizons. Overnight campers regularly visited the temple complex dating back to 1788. The plight of locals no longer able to make a living here in this peaceful place, forced to retreat to the congestion of Hong Kong, saddened me.

Each time we rounded another bend of green hills, I hoped I would recognize Dave's base camp so the torture seizing my arm muscles would cease. Edith, a private maternity nurse originally from France, stopped paddling for a moment to allow me to catch up to her. "How are you doing?"

"I'll make it back," I laughed. "Barely." Slightly more mature, curvier than the others, she looked luscious in her bikini. "Follow me," she said. Wisps of long chestnut waves escaped her khaki sunhat. She pulled ahead with a smooth paddling cadence honed from years of river kayaking in Brittany. "I'm right behind you," I called, determined to mirror her effort.

Finally, Dave gathered the group. We rafted together for a safety talk. "Stay close. The corridor we're crossing has lots of traffic. We'll make one last dash across the ferry route." I hoped my sunglasses disguised my expression of terror as I edged my boat in line with the rest.

We started out in tight formation, boats three abreast, barely room on each side to paddle. Dave took the lead. The rest tucked in behind like a family of mergansers following their mother on a fishing expedition. Grains of salt from seawater seeping under my gloves all day rubbed with sandpaper-like perseverance where my fingers clutched the paddle. When I started to lag behind, Syl, an erstwhile Vancouverite who like myself learned to paddle in Howe Sound, yelled in my direction. "C'mon Patti. You can do it. We Canadians have a paddling reputation to protect." His broad smile spurred me on.

Further into the crossing the waves increased. The lining of my throat felt dry as beach sand but I couldn't stop to take a drink for fear of being left far behind. Head down in determination it occurred to me all my energy was being consumed by keeping my muscles taut and gritting my teeth. From experience I knew paddling was more powerful and efficient when relaxed. I loosened up and matched my paddle strokes to my breathing.

I squinted through the spray to survey our progress. We'd nearly reached the middle of the channel. It looked to me as if we were on a collision course with a two-tiered ferry and several speedy water taxis. Sitting at water level in a kayak can feel frighteningly vulnerable in the face of large vessels roaring in your direction. My instincts were correct. Dave gave the signal to ease up a bit. We huddled together, shivering like baby ducklings. The intimidating boats pulled ahead leaving the section we were about to traverse troubled by an angry mass of whirlpools.

Nervous laughter erupted. "Close enough," said Dave. "We're good to go now." He surged ahead at a brisk clip. Thanks to the adrenaline rush of what seemed an imminent collision a blast of energy propelled me across the final expanse of breaking waves.

Safe on the far side my shoulders lowered. I looked up and recognized the beach where we had started in the morning. The graying fishing boat shed Dave used for kayak storage filled the view.

Boats safely stowed, Orsi locked the shed. Dave led the way back up the hill past crumbling vine-covered houses and rotted fishnets. His aged gray stucco house and uneven cement yard perched like an aerie high above the abandoned village of Tan Ka Wan. Three decades ago the pathways and courtyards were alive with fishermen, limekiln workers and their families. Now spray skirts and PFDs hung next to weathered wooden filleting tables and rusted fishing gear, remnants of a more prosperous era.

Back at the hotel I fired off a quick email to Barry. By 8:00 p.m. I was in the shower. My arms ached as I washed the sand out of my hair. The blisters on my thumbs stung under the hot water. I was sunned out, hungry, and tired. But it was a good tired; exhaustion from outdoor exercise with like-minded people. Water dribbled through the saline perspiration on my face. I tasted the waters of Hoi Ha Wan Marine Park, the salty smack of independence.

I was ready for Kathmandu.

CHAPTER 4
BIRTHPLACE OF
THE BUDDHA

Kathmandu, Nepal, April 20, 2014

Well after 10:00 p.m. the next evening, five hours after leaving Hong Kong, I stepped down from the plane onto the sizzling tarmac of Kathmandu's Tribhuvan International Airport. The blast of heat and humidity conspired with the murky glow of the terminal lighting to create the air of exoticism I had dreamed of. Propelled by the crowd I was carried along the russet marble pathway through shadowy corridors toward the arrivals hall. Enviously I eyed the refreshed looking, elegantly dressed business class travelers who headed up the lengthy line at the visa desk. Men in suits came next, serious expressions brightened by the glow from their cell phones. The remainder of the unwieldy queue consisted of rumpled trekkers resplendent in logo-emblazoned quick-dry ensembles. Volunteers, like the jet-lagged troop of Canadian nurses I had met in the Hong Kong airport, stifled yawns.

When I reached the front the solemn-faced official behind the desk returned my hyper "Namaste" with a perfunctory nod, wordlessly glanced at my application papers, and accepted my American dollars. "Three months?" he said, one eyebrow raised. Square pink visa safely pasted and stamped in my passport, he handed it back true to Nepali custom with his right hand.

"*Dhanyabad*, thank you," I said, accepting with my right. He rewarded me with a weary grin.

Elbowing my way through hordes of tip-hungry, insistent porters, I wrestled my fifty-pound duffle bags onto a cart. Before heading out into the night I stopped to pay my respects to the marigold-garlanded stone statue of Buddha. Maybe if I hesitated long enough I could inhale a sense of calm. Others hurried past. I read the understated brass plaque, *Welcome to Nepal, Birthplace of the Buddha.* In spite of being the granddaughter of a minister and raised in the United Church of Canada by a choir-singing mother, I was a lapsed churchgoer. I'd heard the Dalai Lama speak, read his books and visited monasteries in Tibet and Nepal. I didn't understand it all. But what I did understand of the teachings of the Buddha made sense to me. The basic message of compassion for all sentient beings, regardless of religious affiliation, worked for me.

The statue sent shivers up my spine. I had arrived. Eyes moist, I could barely make out the exit sign, my invitation to the welcoming chaos beyond.

Steps outside, Raj greeted me with a huge bear hug, instantly quelling my foolish fears of abduction by slave traders in the late-night parking lot bedlam. He flung the red duffle onto his broad back, raised the black bag of school supplies onto his shoulder. "Follow me."

We weaved our way through a tightly woven maze of taxis, tour buses, and people to a sad beater of a vehicle. Duffels safely stowed in the trunk, Raj stuffed me—still gripping my daypack—into the back seat. "Lock the doors and don't open except for me. I've got to find another client," he said, and vanished into the darkness.

A full ten minutes later, Raj and the driver returned with a wide-eyed, rattled looking football linebacker-sized American who could barely squeeze himself in beside me. "If I had to tip any more of those porters who kept grabbing my luggage," he said, after a pause for breath, "I'd run out of money by tomorrow. All I had was twenty-dollar bills."

Guess he didn't read the email. "First time in Nepal?" I asked.

"Uh huh," he mumbled, staring straight ahead. Beads of sweat gleamed on his forehead. With a huge sigh he slumped forward over his daypack. I relaxed my sweaty back onto the plastic upholstery.

I was exactly where I wanted to be, Kathmandu, the capital city of the Federal Republic of Nepal. The fifty square kilometer city in the northwestern part of the Kathmandu Valley is home to one point five million people. An additional million and a half live in the surrounding towns of Lalitpur, Kirtipur, Madhyapur Thimi, and Bhaktapur. Kathmandu's altitude of 1,400 meters almost matched the 1,609 meters of my home at SilverStar Mountain. I breathed easily.

As we sped along the potholed road, the lack of traffic unnerved me. Late at night, the sprawling city seemed eerily deserted. Corrugated doors barricaded endless small shops. Their jam-packed interiors presented the perfect antithesis of the brightly lit commercialism of North American malls. Bargaining and laughing with the proprietors, I loved to rifle through household goods like rice cookers, brass serving bowls and the ubiquitous aluminum pots and pans favored by trekking expeditions, guesthouses and families alike. Flames from the occasional roadside fire illuminated the dark faces of men squatting in the dirt as they smoked and sipped the traditional distilled home brew, rakshi. The blatant poverty, so evident during the day in a country where the daily income barely tops two dollars, was almost invisible. Inhabitants of roadside shelters and make-shift tents melted into the night. Dogs sat up to watch us pass, stretching to prepare for their nocturnal roaming. Holy cows, having ceased their relentless garbage grazing, settled onto the warm pavement, dusky silhouettes scarcely evident through the smog. Raj and I jabbered away, catching up on news of family and friends. The American, still shell-shocked, stared through the grimy car window.

Half an hour later we turned into the narrow streets of Thamel. The racket and commotion began. A mecca for tourists, the legendary neighborhood had morphed from its beginnings as a hippie haven four decades ago to its current status as a hotspot for low budget travelers and trekkers. The assault to the senses began with myriad brightly lit shops boasting stacks of vibrant yak wool blankets and towers of folded pashmina shawls. Racks of hipster pants, loose embroidered blouses and long flowing skirts, the kind of clothes I'd been wearing since the 70s, called to me from behind huge glass storefronts. Displays of knockoff mountaineering clothing and equipment spilled into the streets. Alarming jumbles of electrical wires circled drunkenly around themselves at the top of wooden poles from an angry snarl on one side of the alley to a bewildered tangle on the other. While ninety per cent of urban areas have access to electricity, continuous service was famously unreliable. The situation was worse in rural areas, where only five per cent of villages were on the grid. Raj had told me his village now had electricity. I was soon to find out just what "unreliable" meant.

Young men, happy to be employed and able to stay at home, sat laughing and smoking, bent over sewing machines embroidering T-shirts with sayings like *Nepali flat, ukalo, oralo* (up, down) or *Everest, Top of the World*. They knew almost half of the working age population in Nepal didn't have jobs. Many of their friends had no choice but to leave their families behind and sign on for long contracts in countries like India, Qatar, Thailand or Saudi Arabia.

The swelling thunder of drums announced the approach of a Hindu wedding band. Our driver squished the car to a halt at the side of the alley. Men dressed in red jackets led a parade of family members, women in jewel-toned saris smiling and dancing at grinning men in black suits. Clarinets bleated, French horns blared and trumpets blasted in time with rapid drumbeats and joyous laughter. The chariot for the bride and groom, an aging compact car festooned with fresh flowers, squeezed past us allowing a quick glimpse of the bride, veiled in red. The groom had fetched his bride from her parents' home. They were on the way to the home of his parents where she would now live as a member of her new husband's family. Wondering if it was an arranged or "love" marriage, as Raj sometimes described the match ups of his friends, I tried to remember if I had seen a smile on her face. How would she fare with her new mother-in-law?

The spectacle faded and my excitement heightened as we neared the Thamel Eco Resort, my preferred oasis in kaleido-scopic Thamel. The driver wiggled the taxi down the slim side alley. Raj banged on the door of the lobby, already locked for the night. The sleepy night clerk stumbled to the door rubbing his eyes. His expression brightened when he saw my face. "Yes, I remember. You came before. Namaste," he said.

Raj hauled the bags up the marble steps to my third floor room. "See you at the office at eight am," he said, and was gone.

Safely ensconced between the cool sheets in my blissfully air-conditioned room and warmed by the welcome smile of the night clerk, I fell asleep instantly.

At 7:00 a.m. I lay lounging in bed, luxuriating in the magic of waking up in Kathmandu. Merchants performed ritual morning blessings for a profitable day ahead. The soothing scent of smol-dering juniper wafted through the crack where my roughly crafted door didn't quite align with its three-star hotel frame. The giggle of schoolgirls and the roar of the motorcycles jamming the lanes close to the hotel stirred me further. Dogs in the family courtyard behind the hotel let out final pathetic woofs after an exhausting night of barking and bedded down in the morning sun.

Thamel was defined not by serenity but by action. I was impatient to be immersed in the bustle. Eager for a glimpse of the hotel garden, I rushed downstairs to my go-to journal writing spot. My flip-flopped foot slid off one of the recently wet-mopped marble steps on the way down. Hobbling slightly on my sprained my ankle, I served myself at the buffet: yogurt, fruit, a boiled egg, and sweet coffee Nepali style, with *tato dudha*, hot milk. When I hesitated a moment, searching for an outdoor table not too many steps away, a solicitous young server inquired, "Anything else, madam?" Weight all on one foot, I answered, "A bag of ice, please."

Life was never predictable in Nepal. That's one of the things I liked about it. Buses ran late. Flights got cancelled. Roads washed away. That was to be expected. But an injured ankle right before a trek was not. Besides, Raj and I still had to go shopping for school supplies.

Transported to this sweltering frenetic world, vastly different from the snowy serenity of SilverStar, the surrounding sights and sounds somewhat masked the pain of my ankle during the short walk to the Ace the Himalaya office. When I arrived, I collapsed on the couch after a warm hug from Prem K Khatry, founder and managing director of the company. A recommendation from friends had steered us in Prem's direction for our first trip to Nepal. We were forever grateful. His company and our guide Raj had taken good care of us during our previous three-month long trekking adventure, especially during our ultimate unscheduled medical emergency.

Prem's story was inspirational. At fifteen, having completed Grade 10—the highest grade available in the rural school—Prem left his tiny, remote village in Gorkha, in the north west of Nepal, to find work in Kathmandu. He walked eight hours to get to a road with a bus depot. "I'd never been on a bus before. I threw up so many times during the day long trip," he said, a far off look in his eyes. "So I had to find work. I didn't want to take the bus back home," he added, with an engaging chuckle. Prem found work, first as a trekking porter, then as a guide. Eight years later, in 2006, Prem opened his own trekking company.

Around that time he had guided an Australian, Allan Waldon, in the Everest region. Both trekkers couldn't help but notice the high quality of the schools and health posts, mostly funded by the Sir Edmund Hillary Foundation. At that time there was no high school in Prem's village. He had told Allan how students from his own village, Ratmate, had to walk two hours each way to get to school by going downhill to a local market and across a river without a bridge, then back up the hill at the end of the day. "Our way to school was dangerous during the rains of the monsoon season," he explained. "A couple of my friends drowned."

After the trek Prem and Allan conceived the idea of a foundation called *Sambhav* Nepal to support education and health in the Gorkha area. "Sambhav means possibilities," said Prem. "A hopeful name."

Over cappuccino Raj, Prem and I compiled a list of classroom supplies and sports equipment. Raj and I would purchase them and later make deliveries to eight village schools in Gorkha around Ratmate, where I would be volunteering.

The rapid-fire exchange of Nepali and English taxed my jet-lagged brain. I made a silent vow to learn Nepali. While I slurped a second cappuccino, Raj disappeared briefly to exchange the US dollars for rupees.

Prem returned to his computer. I nursed my ankle, enjoyed the silence and watched Prem. He still had the boyish look of the young man I imagined leaving Ratmate. But now, seventeen years later, he had a wife and two sons, an impressive command of English, business and computer skills, and was director of one of the top ten trekking agencies in Nepal and membership chair of the Rotary Club of Mount Everest Lalitpur. Over the years, Sambhav Nepal had formed several global partnerships that provided funding for the construction of schools, hostels, toilet and water projects, and student scholarships as well as annual teacher training sessions.

One of these schools, Bhairabi School in Ratmate Village, was my destination. I'd seen a few photos. The classrooms looked small, less than one quarter the size of Canadian classrooms. The whitewashed exterior walls looked clean against the regulation royal blue tin roof. But the interior gray cement walls were bare with no colorful charts or children's artwork. Before Sambhav Nepal built the new school, only twenty students attended the original crumbling windowless stone hut. Now, about 150 kindergarten to Grade 5 students donned blue uniform shirts and walked up to two hours to attend school there, five and a half days a week. Sambhav Nepal's goal to provide better educational opportunities in rural Gorkha was one of the initiatives that had helped increase Nepal's primary school enrollment rate from seventy-four per cent in 2005 to ninety-eight per cent in 2013.

Raj waltzed back into the office with softball-sized wad of Nepali notes, secured by an elastic band. "Let's go," he said. Sustained by caffeine, we headed out for a jolt of retail therapy. Limping along, I struggled to match the Raj's brisk pace. When he abruptly turned off the pot-holed and barely taxi-width Thamel street and into the dim sepia laneway, I almost lost him.

Instantly we were enveloped in crowds and colors. It was fifty years since I had entered a similar world, the souks of Marrakech, Morocco. Then, I had been a naïve student on tour with my classmates from Neuchatel Junior College, a Canadian school based in Switzerland. That day, when I glimpsed my reflection in a window—a blond, blue-eyed high school student in a navy suit, white beret, and navy and white spectator pumps—I began to realize the magnitude of cultural differences and my position of economic privilege. Women garbed in long black *djellabas*

Patti hands donated funds to Prem at Ace the
Himalaya office, Thamel, Kathmandu.

had smiled back at me with their eyes, the only part of their
faces visible.

Now, after all these years I finally had my chance to learn
more about the so-called developing world, and to contribute.
My network of friends and family and a class of enthusiastic
Grade 5 student fundraisers led by their teacher, Steffi van Dun,
at Vernon's BX Elementary had raised and donated the money.
My mission was to ensure every cent was well spent.

For fifteen minutes we puddle-jumped along uneven streets,
dodging taxis and tourists, past endless rows of pashmina shawls,
shiny metallic Buddhas, hand knitted mittens and hats hanging
out of claustrophobic stalls. The exit into the alley, barely wide
enough for two motorbikes to pass safely, placed my sense of
self-preservation on high alert.

Three hours later, all spent in the same shop, I slumped wearily onto a metal stool. Dazed by the dusty remnants of juniper smoke, rivulets of sweat cascading down my back like a tepid waterfall, I tried to ignore my throbbing ankle. A mountain of whiteboard erasers, dry erase pens, volleyball nets, and badminton rackets lay assembled at my feet.

The shop owner, a beanpole of about four decades, stood in a dusty black T-shirt worn over sagging shoulders, his eyes drooping under the weight of the day. By then he had dutifully climbed his ladder hundreds of times to access his three twenty-foot-long walls of floor to ceiling cubby holes crammed with school supplies and sports equipment. Raj, a serious devotee of soccer and volleyball, insisted on inspecting each ball for quality and endurance. He tossed the rejects back up to the vendor who stood sweltering on his ladder at the hottest level of the store.

At 3:00 p.m. a sullen teen, the vendor's son acting as tea server, appeared with a two-tiered tray of pliable paper-thin plastic cups filled to the brim with steaming Nepali milk tea laced with heaps of sugar. He leaned precariously over our collection of goods to serve me, then offered a cup to other shoppers and staff. Quiet followed, interrupted only by sips and sighs.

While the *chai wallah* packed our haul into discarded cardboard cartons and repurposed loosely woven rice sacks, Raj discussed the tally and settled the bill. An ancient, grinning, crinkly-faced porter entered from the shadows to help us manhandle the unwieldy boxes and sacks. Eyes glued to his heavily-laden stooped back, we followed his dusty flip-flops back through the confusion of motorcycles to the street. When our search for a taxi turned out to be futile we collapsed on the boxes and pondered our options.

Sensing an opportunity, an enterprising rickshaw driver approached. He offered a double deal in concert with one of his colleagues. For 300 rupees (about $3) they would transport both Raj and me and all our goods back to the trekking office. We split up taking half the purchases each. Raj's rickshaw soon disappeared amidst the turmoil of motorcycles, taxis, and the occasional cow. The last I saw of him was one eye peeking through a narrow slit in the back of his rickshaw.

My driver, the one who had negotiated the deal, had difficulty matching the speed of his taller, younger compatriot. Calves bulging on the uphill sections, he laughed every time I screamed my reaction to the craters that pocked the street. From time to time he turned to check on me, and the packages, rewarding me with an engaging grin.

Patti arrives safely with school supplies in front of Ace the Himalaya office, Thamel, Kathmandu.

Thankful for the ragged awning shielding me from the sun, I tried to relax between jolts and not worry that Raj's rickshaw had disappeared. I had no idea of the office address. But ten minutes later my exhausted driver proudly delivered me to the A-One Business complex where a relieved Raj stood waiting on the marble steps.

After losing Raj in the streets I decided not to press my luck by venturing out into the warren of Thamel's dark alleyways in search of dinner. Instead I opted for a safe, solo table in the hotel garden courtyard.

Maybe it was the wine. Or maybe delayed jet lag. Whatever it was, after a dinner of pizza, some terrible Australian wine and a bowl of mango pudding I definitely felt fuzzy. The restaurant only sold wine in bottles, but allowed you to have a glass or two and take the rest with you. Overtired, nervous, or just not paying attention, I had a glass, or two, or maybe a bit more. After I had paid my bill, I picked up the bottle of wine and limped up the dimly lit staircase to my third floor room. When I turned down the dark hallway to my door I sensed a presence behind me. Every neuron on high alert and haunted by my inability to move quickly I stiffened, ready to defend myself. "Madame," the voice behind me said. "Madame, please."

This is it, I thought. I must look like such an easy mark, stumbling along clutching a half empty wine bottle.

I shifted the wine bottle to my left hand. Curling the fingers of my right hand tightly around the heavy metal room key I got ready to jab at my pursuer. I turned slowly to face the voice. "Yes?" I said, trying to sound self-assured.

"Excuse me, Madam. You left this on the table," said the soft-spoken gentleman who was my server in the restaurant. He handed me my camera, stepped back and bent over in a quick bow. "*Soubha raatri*, Madame, good night," he said, palms pressed together.

"*Soubha raatri*," I replied, exhaling slowly.

After I lay down on the bed I noticed the pain in my hip, a recurring souvenir of the long past T-bone car accidents. The fall before breakfast or the bumping rickshaw ride must have jolted me out of alignment. My carelessness at dinner had almost lost me my camera. Feeling foolish and unprepared for what lay ahead, I gobbled two Advil and waited for sleep. I knew the next day would be long and humid—at least seven hours on rough dusty roads to Arughat, followed by a two-hour uphill trek to Ratmate village.

Stretching my hip by hanging my right leg off the edge of the bed, my ankle now blue and yellow, I suspected this trip might be the biggest blunder of my life.

CHAPTER 5
TEACHER! TEACHER!

Ratmate Village, Gorkha; Nepal, April 25, 2014

Sunita, the school caretaker, stepped onto the second floor balcony overlooking the playground of Bhairabi Primary School. Her crimson sari glowed as brilliantly as Nepal's ubiquitous red rhododendrons in the morning light. At exactly 10:00 a.m. she raised an iron triangle in her right hand and hit it with a rusted metal striker. The clangs resounded across the valley, calling the children to school.

Like many of the women in this predominantly Hindu village, Sunita had been up for hours foraging for greens for her family's animals, milking the buffalo, and preparing breakfast over a kerosene burner. She had already unlocked and opened the staff-room and all nine classrooms. In a flurry of enthusiasm the last of the children rushed past the iron gates of the school and up the pitted concrete steps to the playground.

It was the inaugural day of my two-week volunteer teaching stint in Ratmate Village. I stood beside the other teachers in front of 155 uniformed students lined up by grade. Calming inhalations barely stilled my quivering knees. The hard-packed dirt schoolyard, about the width of a regulation volleyball court, was the widest flat surface available for morning assembly.

Nabeen, the assistant head teacher, stepped forward, towering a head taller beside me. The set of his shoulders beneath the smooth electric green fabric of his dress shirt, done up to the top button, screamed self-importance. His thin lips cut a stern horizontal line across his face. No hint of a smile escaped his brown eyes. "Attention!" he barked out in English. I wasn't sure if his use of English and his didactic tone were for my benefit or part of his usual routine. The students responded with militaristic precision. "We will sing our national anthem!"

In unison, each student raised their right hand in a two-finger salute across their forehead and sang *Sayuan Thunga Phool Ka* (Made of Hundreds of Flowers) with considerable gusto.

It was heartwarming to realize what native son Prem's NGO, Sambhav Nepal, and his global partners had accomplished here. So many local children would not be lined up in front of us ready for the school day if not for their efforts. "Seven years ago the only school in the village was a dark stone cottage with no windows, a dirt floor and a leaky roof," Raj had reminded me during our drive to the Arughat, the town below the village. "Kids had to bring umbrellas to use inside the school. Most parents kept their children home to work in the fields."

The children concluded the last lines of the anthem with particular passion, and Nabeen looked over at me. "Would you like to sing your own national anthem for the students?"

What? Nobody told me about this part!

My heart palpitated alarmingly against my ribcage. Surely the others could hear it. Eight teachers and nine rows of students stared in my direction. It was the same unsettling apprehension I had experienced as a student and then a teacher and principal since I'd started kindergarten, the exhilarating anticipation of the first day of school. All were curious about the white-haired foreigner.

I reminded myself I had vowed to say yes to all new experiences on this trip. The head teacher, Tanka, placed a *malla*, a welcome necklace of fuschia-hued azalea blossoms, around my neck. I snapped to attention, shoulders hunched, arms rigid by my sides. I drew a big breath and launched into O Canada.

The last time I had sung my country's anthem in front of an assembly I had been the principal. But then I only had to sing the first note before others joined in. This time I was on my own for the entire song. My voice wavered on the first few notes then strengthened some when my singing muscle memory kicked in. My shoulders relaxed and lowered. My ribcage expanded. My voice swelled with pride.

But partway through, somewhere around "stand on guard for thee," my throat constricted with emotion. The reality of the situation threatened to overwhelm me. I was in Nepal, starting my volunteer time—a proud Canadian eager to make a good first impression. I gazed out at the curious faces. Overcome with gratitude, I forgot the words to the next line. Who cares? Just sing on. It doesn't matter. They don't know the words.

Besides, I knew I had at least three young friends amongst the students already.

The little girl at the front of the Grade 3 line was Sharu, the first child I'd met in the village. She had come to watch Raj and our cook, Kamal, set up our camp a few days before. Curious about me, she had stood on the path one terrace level above our tents and called to Raj in a loud stage whisper to ask if she could visit our camp. "Okay with you?" he asked.

"Of course," I agreed.

She popped down the hill, her tentative nature gone, and immediately started to practice her English. "My name is Sharu."

I tried out my Nepali. "*Mero naam Patti ho.*"

"She is Bina," Sharu said, motioning to a shorter girl who had appeared out of nowhere and was now standing slightly behind her. Bina rewarded me with a smile as wide as the valley below, revealing the space where her two front teeth used to be. A faded orange short-sleeved shirt dotted with yellow apples topped her flowered cotton shorts and plastic flip-flops.

These two, along with Bina's older brother Ganesh, had rapidly become my best friends. They were eager to learn and proud to display their burgeoning English skills. Bina regularly wandered around the campsite naming items. Pointing to the red plastic wash water jug she'd say, "This is a water." Grabbing my arm she would point at me. "This is a girl."

All three regularly dropped by our camp late in the day. One evening when Raj and I were unpacking sports equipment, Ganesh had appeared in a huge green T-shirt over droopy brown

Sharu(l) and Bina welcome Patti to Ratmate village.

knee-length shorts. The girls were with him. When Ganesh spotted the badminton racquets his face brightened. "Can we play?" he asked.

"Why not," I said.

Raj counted out five racquets, grabbed the can of birdies and said, "Follow me." All five of us scuffled up to the school playground.

We arranged ourselves in loose formation. Raj and I stood on one side of the yard, all three kids on the other. The only sounds were the smashes and pings produced by the expert strokes of Raj and Ganesh, followed by the laughter of the girls as they missed shot after shot. "You guys play on your own," I said, sensing Ganesh was eager for some real competition to show off his considerable natural ability. "I'll give the girls some basic lessons."

A half hour was enough in the heat. Raj and I returned to unpacking. The kids stayed to polish off the leftover rice pudding from dinner. We repeated this routine most evenings during the two weeks I stayed at the village. Sharu, Bina and Ganesh were lonely and hungry. Sharu was a late child whose siblings were twenty years older. Her aging parents were often tired at the end of a day of working in the fields. Bina and Ganesh came from one of the poorest families in the village.

But this morning in the schoolyard, long gone were the loose tangles of hair, faded T-shirts, oversized ragged shorts and dusty feet. I barely recognized Sharu, the beautiful eight-year-old before me, her shiny black hair pulled back in a meticulous French braid, dark eyes shining up at me as she stood erect in her blue-checked uniform shirt, black tie and pants.

At the front of the Grade 2 line her friend Bina stood with equal confidence. Dressed in a similar shirt, tucked in at the waist of a black pleated skirt, she had somehow equally transformed herself from village waif clad in hand-me-down clothes to eager

Ganesh fetching water from the village tap.

student, her hair in a neat pony tail. Her brown eyes gleamed with pride, knowing she had met me before other students had. We were already friends. I marveled at the threadbare but immaculately clean and pressed uniforms. How did the mothers pull this off in such crude circumstances with no electricity and only one tap in the village? Bina's broad smile revealed the gap between her two front teeth.

Over in the Grade 5 line I spotted Ganesh. Teachers aren't supposed to have favorites, but I was in love with these three.

"At ease." Nabeen's firm command brought me back to the present. "Go to your classrooms." The children dutifully filed off in various directions.

It didn't take long to realize singing the national anthem solo was the least of my worries. From 10:15 a.m. to 1:15 p.m. I was trapped in the dismal Grade 2 classroom, a four-by-five-meter cement cell with twenty-two rambunctious, curious, demanding Grade 2 students.

The first lesson began well enough. I taped maps of the world and Canada on the wall to show where I came from. Next I read aloud the *ABC of Canada by Gurth* and *Bellfontaine*. The kids listened well, sitting quietly. The colorful line drawings illustrating m for mountains and z for Zamboni, kept their attention, even though a Zamboni was a completely foreign vehicle to them.

Then we started a review of the English alphabet. By this time the kids were getting a bit squirmy but managing okay. Raj, looking like a professional teaching assistant in a navy and white plaid shirt and long pants, sat on a student bench near the back of the room, sweat glistening right up to his slightly receding hairline. "Okay," I said. "I'll tell them what I want them to do in English, then you explain again in Nepali. Can you go around and check their printing while they are working? Encourage them to try their best."

With some trepidation I turned my back on them each time

Our campsite below the school playground.

I wrote another letter of the English alphabet on the peeling, pockmarked meter-square whiteboard. They copied the upper and lower case letters in notebooks I had provided, printed a word starting with each letter, and then drew a picture. Each student had only one pencil. Most had been sharpened down to a stub. Colored pencils were an unheard-of extravagance.

They were ready for the next letter before I could take a breath. B for ball, c for corn. I tried to keep ahead of them. These kids were smart and fast. Most completed the lesson in about twenty-six minutes, taking only one minute per letter of the alphabet.

Raj assisting Patti in the Grade 2 class.

Patti reviewing the English alphabet with students.

The second each child finished the alphabet they held out their scribbler, hands outstretched together. "Take it, teacher. Take it."

Raj and I wandered around the class giving out stickers for finished work. Rookie mistake. Canadian children are blasé about stickers. These kids went ballistic. "Sticker, sticker," they called out.

At least they'd learned a new word.

One girl was instantly given to hoarding. She valued the stickers so highly she secretly removed each one I placed on the page, hid it, and whined for another. What a resourceful kid, I thought. I couldn't blame her. I was beginning to realize that to these kids stickers were an astonishingly unusual treat.

Raj checked each student's book individually. He was the one who had brought me here to his home village. He was willing to do whatever it took for me to be successful.

I stood on the gray cement floor, surrounded by four rough cement walls. Blue, roughly hewn shutters folded open in windows on either side of the room allowing the mere hint of a breeze. I was so overheated I didn't notice. But I did notice the bare walls. The walls were not lined with the bookcases crammed with readers and boxes of pencils and erasers, crayons, and rainbow stacks of colored paper we take for granted in Canadian classrooms. No signs with alphabet letters, no word charts, no pictures of food, animals or family members—in Nepali or English. No bulletin boards displaying children's art and stories.

No wonder only fifty-five per cent of students continued to secondary school. Nepali culture dictated boys getting the chance before girls especially if there was any cost involved. What future chances were there for Bina and Sharu?

Didn't these teachers take any pride in their classrooms, I wondered in my superior North American manner.

My mind wandered back to the richness of my first Grade 2 classroom in a tony Toronto neighborhood. Classroom walls were festooned with vibrantly trimmed bulletin boards displaying children's stories and artwork. Word lists and language charts hung everywhere. Poetry books, steep piles of readers and a classroom library of more than one hundred books jammed the shelves.

Fat drops of sweat poured from my forehead, glistened and gathered on my cheeks, then slid down in rivulets, soaking my neck. The clean T-shirt I'd saved for this day was already looking as wilted and tired as I felt. It may have been culturally appropriate to cover my bare shoulders even on a humid thirty-six-degree day, but in the words of legendary American jazz singer Ella Fitzgerald, "It's too darn hot."

A call from an assertive seven year old rang out from a dark corner, jolting me out of my reverie. "Teacher, Teacher."

"Eraser, eraser," demanded another, waving her hand in the air. Sadly, I was the only teacher and there was but one single eraser for the entire class.

When I had planned for this volunteer gig, I had no idea how few schools supplies the children would have. I should have bought more in Kathmandu when I had a chance; more school supplies and less sports equipment. It was obvious these schools were desperate for both.

"Eraser, eraser," chimed the insistent voice of a third girl. In the back row, a disheveled girl with sneaky eyes and ill-kept hair hoarded the single classroom eraser in her sweaty grip. She lent it to others stingily in an attempt to gain friends. A blur of Grade 2 faces swam before me, three to a wooden bench. Tattered scribblers and grubby backpacks crushed across the narrow desks. I was adrift, paralyzed in a sea of twenty-two smiles, most missing their two front teeth, all demanding immediate attention.

Bina sat attentively in the front row. Her bewildered yet supportive expression warmed my heart. I felt the power of her gentle soul willing things to go well for me.

Clearly the year two class at Bhairabi Primary School was not at all what I had expected. For the first time in my life, I knew what it was like to be a beginning teacher struggling for my life. A natural from the get go, I had been an award winning student teacher. Engaging students and commanding their respect had never been a problem for me in Canada. But it was twenty years since I had taught a primary class, and that was to English-speaking children. I began to question my teaching ability.

Maybe I've lost my touch. Now what? They needed a break and a stretch. Hell, I needed a break and a stretch.

Right. Time for a song.

I taped up a printed chart of a simple song called "Open, Shut," meant to teach the vocabulary of opposites. In an earlier email to Canada, Prem had explained that most schooling in Nepal was done by rote learning, a memorization technique based on repetition. He had encouraged me to demonstrate more varied and modern learning techniques for the other teachers. Instinct told me this wasn't the time to introduce anything new. So, finding security in the rote learning strategy they were familiar with, I read aloud and pointed to the words.

"Open, shut them, open, shut them. Give a little clap." They repeated in unison after me. Mimicking my actions they stretched open their fingers then closed them in a fist. We clapped together at the end of the line. While I reviewed the lyrics Raj plugged in the boom box and loaded a CD of the song so we could sing along. The kids were jittery and ready for action. After reviewing the entire song again I was ready to chance singing. "OK. Press play, please," I said to Raj. He pressed the start button. Nothing happened. The one electrical outlet yielded no power.

"I'll get an extension cord and try the outlet in the next class-room," he said. I fought the instinct to escape with him. While he was searching for a more reliable source of electricity, I sang the song for them. They stood, followed my actions, and tried to repeat the words with me. Then they started to move to the beat of the song. The second time through the song, a bell clanged. I had no idea what it meant. Foolishly, I didn't ask.

Suddenly mobs of kids and teachers were peeking through the doorway and window shutters. The kids laughed. The teachers did not. Looks of disbelief clouded their faces. Singing and dancing during class time? Their wide-eyed expressions indicated this was a teaching method they'd never witnessed. Their frowns verged on disapproval. The kids from other grades squished into the doorway eager to join.

The mood in the classroom rapidly disintegrated from focused fun to unrestrained chaos. One eager boy elbowed another out of the way to get to the front row to show off his dancing skills.

Another jumped up on one of the narrow benches.

This probably wasn't one of the new strategies Prem had in mind.

A second bell rang. The spectators dispersed. If that was recess, I missed it. Sadly, so did the rambunctious Grade 2s.

Raj's tall frame filled the doorway, blocking what little light there was. "No electricity coming to the village today," he said.

"Try the batteries," I mumbled, desperation strangling my already overtaxed vocal chords. He plugged the eight D-cells into their slots. An ominous whirring sound emitted from the machine, rapidly wound to a fever pitch, then stopped.

"Out of luck," I said. "Any chance of getting more batteries?"

"None," says Raj, shrugging his shoulders. I curbed my instinct to scream.

Gorkha, a remote area comprised of terraced grasslands might be famous for producing Gurkas, the proudly fierce Nepali soldiers historically recruited for the British and Indian armies, but it didn't have convenience stores on every corner. It didn't have corners. The main center, Arughat, a town of four thousand, was a dusty, bumpy seven-to-twelve-hour ride by four-wheel drive or bus west from Kathmandu. Ratmate sat perched high on a hillside above the town, a steep two-hour uphill slog lined with banana trees, palms and hot-pink bougainvillea. Few foreigners visit this tiny sub-tropical hamlet. Infrequently, Arughat welcomed mountaineers stopping off for supplies and a rest day on their way to climb Manaslu Peak, the eighth-highest mountain in the world. But focused on their expedition, few ever ventured up the hill to meet locals. Fewer still came to volunteer. No chance of finding batteries.

Raj and I managed to calm the kids and shepherd them to their desks. I taped up a new chart. This one showed a few sentences of hand-printed English dialogue used when meeting new acquaintances. We returned to the familiar rote learning they were comfortable with. They read the chart several times in unison. Ready to try for a little active participation, I invited two students to come forward to read the parts. The class loved it. Students vied for a chance to read and act out the dialogue in pairs. "Teacher, teacher," sounded out as hands waved for a turn.

By the end of the lesson my masking tape had succumbed to the humidity. Song charts and maps were peeling off the damp cement walls, drooping as pathetically as my energy. By 1:15 p.m. I was poised to make a break for it. My songs had created pandemonium, my stickers had pushed them over the edge, and their continual calling out for pencils and erasers had left my head thumping.

Another bell sounded.

"Time for lunch." said Raj.

"Please, please, promise me you'll never, ever leave me alone with the Grade 2 class," I whined as we walked down the hill to our tent site.

I can't go back, I thought. Emotionally wrung out I collapsed into my chair.

Never one to give up, by 2:30 p.m. I was back in the classroom, Raj by my side, this time with the Grade 3 class. Having gone through the lessons once, we were better prepared. Raj explained behavior expectations. I nodded knowingly, even though I hadn't a clue what he was saying. A strong partnership was forming. We anticipated each other's actions. He handed out books. I followed with pencils and the eraser. Things went a little more smoothly.

One hour later the school day ended. "I've had it," I said. "Let's get out of here." Raj helped me haul my charts, stickers, maps and useless boom box to the second-floor staffroom. "Time for a nap," said Raj.

The outdoor iron circular staircase clanged and clattered with each step. Thunder exploded over our heads. A pre-monsoon torrential downpour soaked us completely on the way to our campsite. The weather suited my mood just fine. The rainwater diluted my salty tears. I crawled into my tent, zipped the flap closed and crumpled onto my sleeping bag.

What had gone wrong?

The idea of volunteer teaching had seemed so full of promise while preparing lessons at home and shopping for school supplies in Kathmandu.

It had started so well. I was sure I was prepared for all eventualities. Obviously I didn't take into account the limits of the language barrier. I was unable to conjure up the same kind of presence in front of the classroom I could effortlessly accomplish in Canada.

When did everything start to unravel? In my foggy brain I realized it all hinged on the lack of erasers. Sadly, erasers were the one thing those boxes we had hauled from Kathmandu didn't contain.

I had longed to prove my teaching ability to Raj, to make him proud and thankful he had brought me to his village. I had let us both down. My head hit the pillow. My sobs slackened to silent tears.

CHAPTER 6
ON (AND OFF) THE GRID

An hour later, lemony afternoon rays had dried the walls of my tent. The racket of raindrops pelting the nylon fabric had given way to steamy serenity. I rubbed my crusty eyes to clear the sticky residue of tears. The fog below had dissipated, allowing a clear valley view of Arughat. Trucks carrying goods from Kathmandu and buses transporting tourists and locals created dust clouds as they rumbled along the dirt road below. Here in camp, a chorus of male cicadas chirped from their hiding places under the broad leaves of banana trees.

I remembered the crackling calls of the electric-blue Steller's Jays at home. I could still hear the demanding twitters of squirrels that just a few days ago I had watched frolicking in the snow beside our home on SilverStar Mountain. My body hadn't yet acclimatized to the dramatic temperature increase. The thermometer registered a sweltering forty degrees Celsius inside my airless tent.

A feeling of unease churned in the pit of my stomach as I recalled my first day in the classroom. As always, the imposter syndrome reared its ugly head. What made me think I could step in and teach anywhere in the world? Was I too old for this? Why didn't I save myself a lot of trouble by asking a few questions about timetable, school routines and discipline expectations in a culture in many ways so different from my own? So what if I had once been a confident, award winning student teacher. That was in Canada, forty-five years ago. This was Nepal, and I wasn't twenty-two any more.

A rustling rippled my pool of self-pity. "Patti, are you awake?" A familiar pair of knees appeared in the arched doorway of my tent. Raj bent over and poked his head in, took one look at me and said, "You look like you need a beer. I called down to Dharapani Village. They have electricity this afternoon. That means cold beer. Let's go. Later you can meet my family."

At this point any diversion that included beer was welcome.

The fifteen-minute downhill scramble cleared my vision and my head. We didn't talk, instead falling into the companionable silence of friends who had once trekked together for months. Raj stopped in front of a small simple wooden home with a rusted tin roof. Part of the covered front porch had been converted into a store. Cans of Coke, Fanta, and Sprite lined the shelves. Bags of chips, tacos, and a twisted snack that looked like pretzels hung from clips on an interior makeshift clothesline. Raj peeked into the darkness of the shop at the miniscule refrigerator on the back wall and ordered a large beer.

From his short grey hair and trim beard I guessed the proprietor to be in his early sixties. His *topi* hat and matching loose fitting shirt were a spotless light beige. Without standing he leaned back and reached into the only electrically powered refrigerator for kilometers. From its cool interior he produced a large brown bottle of Tuborg, glistening with chilly condensation.

From the dim interior of the house his considerably younger wife, clad in a long red sari, red shirt and matching turban, stepped onto the open section of the porch. Myriad wraps of royal blue cloth bundled her slender waist.

We sat together for a few moments in the stifling slanted rays

Owners of the beer store.

of the late afternoon sun on narrow wooden bench provided for customers. "Is there anywhere else we can sit, out of the sun?" I asked.

"*Didi*." Raj called out the respectful term meaning auntie or older sister to get the attention of the lady of the house, then rattled off a few words of Nepali. "I asked for some glasses," he said, "and a cooler place to sit."

She disappeared into the house and returned with two dimpled glass beer mugs, then raised her hand beckoning us to follow her through the cool shadows of her home. The interior rooms were windowless. Fearful I would run into something or someone, I grabbed the tail of Raj's shirt to guide me. Through a low, narrow door we emerged onto a covered back porch overlooking the tin-roofed stone buildings, playground, and volleyball courts of Raj's alma mater, Dharapani High School.

Like Prem, Raj had passed his National School Leaving Certificate, going as far as he could with his education in the village. After completing Grade 10 he had left home for Kathmandu to work as Prem's first porter. Between jobs he trained as a trekking guide. Any further education, considered higher secondary, was private, costly, and limited time available for work.

We settled cross-legged on a hand-woven grass mat set on the stamped mud surface of the shady porch. Raj poured. We sipped in silence while I mentally reviewed a litany of my teaching mistakes. Raj seemed lost in his own reverie, perhaps reliving his glory days as a star high school volleyball player. My glass half empty, and desperate for advice on how to adapt my teaching techniques for Nepali children, I spoke first. I peppered Raj for information. All the things I should have asked before my first day came tumbling out.

"What did all those bells mean? Why are the classrooms walls so bare? What's up with the power outages? You told me the village got electricity two years ago," I sputtered in an accusatory tone.

Raj hunched his shoulders and fixed his gaze on the school playground below. Slowly, he raised the mug of amber liquid and took another sip. The silence was anything but companionable. Unable to contain my impatience, my voice filled the void. "Why don't they have any pencils, erasers and crayons? And why did they get so crazy when I got them up on their feet to sing an action song?"

After one more swallow, Raj shifted his position, exhaled, and turned to me. "Well, usually the kids have a new teacher for every one of the five forty-five-minute periods in the day. The kids stay in the same class and the teachers go to them. That's the way it works in Nepal."

That explained why the classrooms walls were so bare; except for kindergarten, teachers in Nepal don't have their own classroom like we do in Canada. It must be hard to not be able to decorate your classrooms with charts and stuff to enhance their learning. And even if they had their own classroom, I realized, extra paper, crayons, and colored art paper, or picture charts of birds, animals, or trees in Nepali or English were an unprecedented luxury. Each teacher specialized in one subject area and taught it to all ages, using standard government issued workbooks.

"All children of the same age are taught in the same class, no matter how large or small the number of that age group."

This concept was very difficult to fathom. It meant that year there were twenty-two in the Grade 2 class, ten in the Grade 3 class and sixteen in Grade 5. "In Canada the teachers' union would never allow that," I said. "Each teacher has to have a similar number of kids in their class within agreed-upon class size limits."

Raj explained that in Nepal there was no teachers' union. No collective agreement. None of the class-size limits elementary teachers have fought for so valiantly in countries like Canada.

"In my country teachers just feel lucky to have a good job," he said. "All the kids of one age group stay together. It doesn't matter how many there are." It seemed the North American solution of combining children of two grade levels or even three had not yet been considered in the Nepali education system.

My ignorance of even the basic timetable must have messed up the day for the other teachers. Ignoring the bells was not a wise idea. Feeling inept and more than a little bit insensitive I hung my head and listened.

As had been the case in Canada until the late 60s, young people could become teachers with only one year of post-secondary training. Called a Proficiency Certificate Level, it was the equivalent of the first year of a Bachelor of Education and allowed them to teach up to Grade 8. And, Raj explained, most departments of education paid the salaries of fewer than half the teachers needed for most schools. Other good-hearted local high school graduates without government training filled in the gaps, working for considerably less pay.

Raj interrupted my much-needed seminar on education in Nepal to wander back through the house in search of another beer. "This is the only kind that is cold," he announced, when he returned. He had chosen Gorkha beer, more for the temperature than the brand. He settled back down and refilled our glasses.

He described the ritual that began each class. "Every 45 minutes, as a new teacher enters the classroom, students stand and greet the teacher." He demonstrated in a singsong-like voice. "Good morning, teacher. You are welcome to our classroom." Returning to his normal voice, he said, "All the students in the school practiced an English version for you. After welcoming the teacher they are supposed to sit down and must stay seated for the rest of the class." So by insisting on staying in one class and plowing ahead, I had not only thrown off the schedule but deprived the other classes of showing off the practiced greeting.

"I guess it works. No one teacher gets stuck with the largest class while another breezes along with a class of half the size. But why isn't there any kids' artwork on the walls?"

"Because there's no money for paper or crayons or colored pencils. The government sends money only for pencils and notebooks, not art materials."

From what Raj described, students did show a sense of belonging in their own classroom, their home for the year. They stayed in the room perched on narrow wooden benches. Even when there was no teacher they entertained themselves. This situation happened far too often as the government didn't supply substitute teachers. When a teacher was sick, had a family emergency, or was sent away for mandatory government teacher training the children were left alone for parts of the day.

"That's your first session in Nepali education," said Raj, standing up and draining his mug. "Let's go." As we left the house and made our way through the shop, I spotted some pencils and erasers for sale. I bought two dozen and stuffed them in my pack. I planned to distribute them at the first of each class to those in need, then collect them and take them to the next class.

What a bargain: Peace of mind for only 200 Nepali rupees, about $2.30 Canadian. Two glasses of cold beer and a backpack full of supplies and I was totally relaxed.

I'd already spent a couple of hundred dollars of my own money on the supplies I brought from Canada. The money fundraised from friends, relatives, and elementary school students had been spent in Kathmandu. Time to dig deep into my personal funds. Every cent was worth it.

I followed Raj back up the hill to meet his family. A plan of action for my time at the school, how I could truly be of service, began to percolate in the back of my head.

Raj's family was gathered in their peach stamped-earth front courtyard, with a low wall around the perimeter—the perfect height for sitting. The well-maintained home was one of the largest in the village. Portions of Raj's first five years of guide's pay had gone to his parents to improve their living situation. A narrow covered porch ran along the front of the mud-and-mortar walls, resulting in the house blending with the color of the surrounding soil. Wooden benches hung suspended between the upright posts supporting the corrugated tin roof.

At one end of the porch, a bed frame covered in a skimpy mattress extended across the porch. A fragile-looking woman wearing a long grey skirt and teal blouse lay reclined on the bed. Wisps of wavy gray hair framed her weathered skin. Darker freckles dotted enviably high cheekbones. "Patti, this is my grand-mother," said Raj. He had often spoken of her when we were hiking; he saw her as his biggest fan, a source of unconditional love and support. Gently he took her hand and spoke to her in Nepali. He introduced me, telling her I was a grandmother, too. She sat up slowly, turned toward me and took my hand in both of hers, as Raj translated. "She says you are welcome here," he said. "And you have a kind face." The gentle squeeze of her hands matched the warmth of her smile.

Next I was introduced to his younger sister, an auntie, and then his parents. Raj's first nephew, a shy four-year-old, hid in the folds of his mother's red dress. The billowing material somewhat camouflaged her pregnancy. The women welcomed me with smiling eyes. Raj's dad remained taciturn. They were not sure what to do with me, and I was unsure how to act. When Raj picked up his nephew, then bounced him on his knees, the boy laughed. The rest of us joined in, grateful to have a common focus for a moment.

Raj's auntie was dressed in a gray T-shirt and pale green skirt accented by a length of brighter green fabric wrapped as a waistband, and she wore a turquoise turban-style headdress. She disappeared into the darkness of the house, then returned and presented me with a tin plate of bread formed into a stretched-out skinny doughnut and fried, and a tin cup of steaming milk. I sneaked a look past her to Raj with my eyebrows slightly raised. He knew my question without me speaking. "The milk is okay," he said. "It's just been boiled."

I took a sip then a cautious nibble of the tubular bread. It was my first taste of *sal-roti*, fried sweet rice bread. A uniquely Nepali dish, *sal-roti* is a combination of rice batter mixed with clarified butter, mashed banana and water, all deep-fried in bubbling oil. I wasn't hungry despite skipping lunch but leaving food on your plate in such a poor country, especially as a wealthy Westerner, would be unforgiveable.

They watched.

After the first bite I was hooked. I ate every bit of the delicious crispy doughnuts and washed them down with the milk. The generous buffalo stood nearby in her thatch-roofed shed under a banana tree. Huge chocolate brown eyes watched me with suspicion.

Throughout the afternoon, Raj's parents continued their daily life. Dad, a slim muscular man of medium height, was dressed in shorts and a dark shirt. His ensemble was topped with a hand-loomed pale orange topi hat. He sat on a wicker stool wielding a khukuri, a traditional Nepali knife; hands callused from farm labor, he methodically sliced thin lengths of bamboo he would later braid into rope to secure the thatched roof of the buffalo shed. From time to time he snuck a glance at me, forehead wrinkled.

The afternoon wore on lazily. No one seemed in a rush. At one point I asked Raj, "Where has your mom gone?"

"Have a look," he said, pointing around the corner. I walked over to the edge of the yard and found her sitting on a grass mat, her red sari skirt hitched up to her knees revealing shapely legs and calloused feet. A large, round flat-bottomed stone, split in two horizontally, lay between her legs. Stacks of red bangles on her wrists jangled as she scooped grains of rice from the cooking pot beside her and poured them through a hole in the top layer of stone. With both hands gripping the knob attached to the top stone, she rotated it to grind rice flour. Her smile oozed the confidence and competence of a strong matriarch comfortable in her own skin.

Raj's parents were respected leaders in their village. He was proud to be the eldest son of this prestigious family. Perhaps fearing the disapproval of his father for sitting idle, perhaps

Raj's mom grinding rice flour.

wanting to impress me, Raj got in on the action by braiding straw into a firm-handled broom for sweeping the courtyard. When Raj demonstrated the finished product, his father and I shared a smile.

No materials were wasted. No hands were idle. No one hurried in the heat of the afternoon. Everyone contributed. The only discernible sign of modernity was the cell phone his sister snuck out of the pocket of her dress from time to time to check messages. Her husband was on a two-year contract as a chef in Dubai, and she was eager to have him home before their second child arrived.

The visit to Raj's family home made me realize the wisdom of relaxing to the pace of village life, of respectfully observing in silence. Only then could I discover what I might have to offer.

By the time we climbed the path back to our campsite it early evening, our cook, Kamal, had a surprise waiting for us. He had phoned down to the storekeeper at Dharapani to order a freshly butchered chicken and sent Kopal, our camp helper, to fetch it. By the time we arrived a pot of chicken curry was bubbling on one kerosene burner and a pressure cooker of rice on the other. "You worked hard today," said a beaming Kamal. "I am making a special dinner."

I was still full from the beer, *sal-roti* and creamy buffalo milk, but the look on Kamal's face and the tantalizing aroma coming from the cook tent soon negated any doubts I had about tucking in to a bowl.

While waiting, I worked on revising my lesson plans. Lost in thought I eventually realized five women in red were now standing shoulder to shoulder, peering down from the path above the campsite. I poked my head outside the tent, smiled up at them, and called out, "Namaste." They folded their hands and nodded, returning my "Namaste" in unison. Head down, I continued my planning. Several minutes later I glanced back up. They were still there, as if patiently waiting for something.

Trying to concentrate, I was vaguely aware of some conversation between Raj and the ladies.

Almost apologetically Raj rattled the dining tent flap. "There are some village ladies on the path," he said. "They want to know, can they see inside your sleeping tent—is that okay?"

"Of course," I said. I was as curious about them as they were about me. One by one they traipsed down the path their scarlet saris ruffling the dust. I opened the flap of my tent and motioned for them to have a look.

After each had peeked in and commented to the others in Nepali, we ended up outside the tent in a loose circle. Their beauty, their radiant, open expressions of warmth and curiosity, fascinated me. From the wrinkles around their eyes I guessed their ages to range from about five to ten years my junior. Each wore a multi-strand green necklace of tiny pote beads, a *tilhari* necklace, a symbol of marriage.

"They're on their way back from a wedding," explained Raj. "That's why they have red bindis on their foreheads; Nepali women wear red for weddings, sacred ceremonies, and Hindu festivals."

Through Raj we discovered we had lots in common. We were all married and all grandmothers. I brought out my camera to show pictures of blond grandchildren back in Canada. They smiled appreciatively.

"But where is her husband?" they asked in Nepali. "Why is she alone?"

Raj told them about Barry's injury and why he was at home in Canada. He also told them that after volunteering I planned to trek for a month in Upper Mustang. They were dumbfounded that I was retired and still wanted to go trekking. "The tallest lady thinks you're crazy," said Raj. "She's tired of working in the fields all day. When she's retired, she plans to put her feet up and rest."

The women loitered around the campsite peeking into the

Ladies in red.

cook and dining tents. "Ask if I can take their picture," I said to Raj. They obliged, hands pressed in Namaste, their serenity captured by the lens. Each giggled shyly when I showed them the digital image.

I wished we had a common language. There were so many things I wanted to ask. How did they feel about arranged marriages? What age were they when they married? Had it worked for them? Where did they deliver their babies? Did they stay at home? I couldn't imagine walking the steep downhill trail to the hospital in Arughat already in labor. What did they think about the recent trend toward love marriages? What were their daily lives like?

At times like this I wished I had a female interpreter; asking personal questions might have been easier if the interpreter wasn't male and from their own village.

Kamal emerged from the cook tent and called us for dinner. The ladies in red carried on up the path, calling "*soubha raatri*," good night, behind them.

"*Soubha raatri*," I called back as their red saris mingled with the glow of the sunset.

I had no trouble wolfing down the dish Kamal had prepared. After dinner, ginger tea laced with a generous tot of Khukuri rum set me up for slumber. But as I lay stretched out on my sleeping bag, my mind raced. Images of food, friendship, and hospitality jumbled with fear, frustration, and trepidation about my teaching duties.

By their candid curiosity and kindness the ladies in red had reminded me of the power of unconditional acceptance and the shared bond of women. Maybe, I now realized, the reserved nature of the other teachers was due to my overconfident and overzealous manner. Maybe I had failed to show them proper respect by not asking to observe them teaching before I had started. And, maybe my bull-in-a-china-shop efforts needed some revision.

I resolved to retreat, to take several huge steps backward, and never to rely on electricity.

CHAPTER 7
PHERI BHETAULA,
GOODBYE RATMATE

My reflections from the evening before yielded three realizations. First, it was crucial to show respect for the teachers by observing their classes. Second, I needed to stop being a know-it-all and ask for help. And, third, I desperately needed more erasers. Even what I had purchased in the shop would not be enough.

Classroom visits confirmed rote learning and memorization as the dominant teaching strategy at Bhairabi School. Students remained seated at all times. Devi, the most senior teacher at almost my age, exuded a relaxed presence from his seat in the wide windowsill of the Grade 5 classroom. Many years of service had earned him the respect, reverence, and fondness of the students. When addressed, students met his eyes with comfort and confidence. They answered his questions, then beamed when he responded with a nod and smile. In contrast, the atmosphere in the Grade 6 class epitomized formality. Nabeen continued his militaristic manner from the morning assembly. He stood at the front of the class choosing individual students to read aloud, then asked the entire class to repeat the correct answer in unison.

One exception was the Montessori-style kindergarten. Developed by Maria Montessori, this child-centered approach had been used for more than one hundred years all over the world. Children learned concepts by discovery, observing, and manipulating materials rather than constant direct instruction.

After lunch I visited this haven for the youngest students.

I kicked off my sandals amid a jumble of tiny flip-flops and stepped into a rich learning environment created by an experienced and loving master teacher. My eyes encountered colorful displays and relaxed children. Bal, their teacher, smiled as I peeked in and, with a graceful wave of her hand, gestured for me to join the class.

"Namaste," I said. I turned to the children with the same greeting. The curious smiles of sixteen four- and five-year-olds sitting cross-legged on cushions around a low rectangular table welcomed me.

Bal reigned at the head of the class. Her expression exuded unconditional acceptance and love. Dark brown waves swept back from her face, then trailed down her back in a weighty braid. The folds of her vibrant teal top, worn over billowing red pants, hung attractively over her trim figure. She came by her shapeliness honestly with daily walks along the hilly pathways to and from her home in the neighboring village where she and her family lived, a half hour away. In the playground I'd witnessed her fitness and sense of fun. Sari scarf flying she had executed smash badminton shots too tough for even the most skillful teenaged boys to return.

One word from Bal and the group of children at her feet returned their attention to the activity I had interrupted. Bal began to sing. The group eagerly joined her in a jubilant rendition of "You Are My Sunshine." The eyes of each child remained glued to Bal's face. Each sang every English word and clapped to the beat. It was clear they adored her. When I applauded their effort the children grinned, chests puffed.

Around the room other children gathered in twos and threes,

much as they do in any Montessori kindergarten in Canada, playing cooperatively at various centers. In one corner was basket of items of discarded clothing. One little girl worked hard to wrap her friend with some sari cloth. Two boys and a girl sat at a small table with plastic cutlery, plates, and kitchen utensils, engrossed in a pretend family dinner, passing each other ears of dried maize. A third basket held bright wooden blocks. A boy and a girl took turns adding to a tower.

Bal taught the same students all day, so was the one teacher who had the luxury of decorating her classroom to enrich the school experience. The classroom walls were plastered with charts and student artwork. It seemed the staff had allocated a generous portion of the school's meager funds to give the youngest students a good start.

Raj appeared in the doorway. "Please tell Bal I think she is an amazing teacher and that I love her classroom," I said. "Also, could you ask her if she would come and watch me teach the Grade 2 class tomorrow? She knows all the kids in the school so well. Maybe she can give me some tips." Raj translated. Bal smiled in agreement. The visit was set for the following morning.

After school I swallowed my pride and asked Raj for help. The rambunctious— edging on disrespectful—behavior of the students still concerned and mystified me. "You know," I said, "when I was a principal, if students didn't behave well for a substitute teacher I would have a talk with the class about respect." I left it at that.

The next morning at assembly Nabeen, tall and imposing, stepped forward. He proceeded to chastise the students in a strident voice. His words were in Nepali but the purpose of the talk, which rapidly morphed into a tirade, was evident. The delicious lemon sugar pancake Kamal had made me for breakfast flipped in my stomach. My few words of frustration to Raj had apparently caused Nabeen's overly dramatic wrath. I felt guilty, sorry for the students, and embarrassed about my ignorance of Nepali classroom behavior standards. This scene of outrage could have been avoided had I asked questions and listened from the beginning. Students shuffled to class, their heads down. Equally subdued I followed the morose line of Grade 2s into their classroom.

About ten minutes after I started my lesson Bal wandered along the cement walkway and stood in the doorway to watch me. Raj towered beside her.

Both observed as I reviewed the printing of the English alphabet. My fingers trembled as I turned my back on the students to print both the upper case and lower case letter b on the peeling whiteboard. "Can anyone give me a word for the letter 'b'?"

Bina, sitting straight-backed in the front row, as attentive as always, raised her hand as I had reminded them to. "Yes, Bina?"

"Buffalo," she said.

"Good one. Thank you, Bina." I sent her a look of appreciation. "Let's say the word together. Repeat after me everyone. B for Buffalo." They responded dutifully.

"Now print the letter b and the word buffalo on your plastic sheets. If you have time, draw a picture of the buffalo you have at home."

Immediately they put their heads down and got to work. It felt awkward and unusual to use this method of teaching, but it was what most of the children were accustomed to. They printed the letter b and buffalo using erasable magic markers on the clear plastic sleeves containing one piece of white paper I had provided for each of them. I had brought a class set of the sleeves from Canada in order to demonstrate this quick practice technique that required only one sheet of paper that could be used many times. I hoped it would be useful and economical for them. "Now please hold up your work to show me." I held up my own page to demonstrate.

Each student held up the eight-by-ten sleeve. With one quick glance I could tell who had understood and who might need assistance. They could see mine and know if theirs was correct or not. I glanced in Bal's direction for her reaction. Two thumbs up.

Turning to the class I said, "Okay, now use the rag to wipe off your work." Bal watched each student create a blank canvas ready for the next word. Students provided English words from their own environment like corn for c, goat for g and hay for h.

Halfway through the alphabet I was getting antsy and figured they must be, too. I decided to chance a song to show Bal the vocabulary I had been teaching the kids. I enlisted Raj's help to review behavior expectations before we started. "No moving from your place, no stepping up on desks," he explained in Nepali. "Dancing in place only."

I asked the students to stand and sing. Bina and Raj held up the lyrics chart. The children belted out their new favorite.

Can you say good morning?
Can you say good afternoon?
Can you say good evening?
Can you say good night, too?

About half way through the second verse they started to dance to the music in a contained fashion dangerously on the verge of silliness. Bal twitched a few times. She was barely able to restrain herself from stepping in.

When the song was over I gestured with my arms for the kids to sit down. They did. Immediately. Ready to continue the lesson. With one ear I listened as the students volunteered words for the remainder of the letters. With the other I heard the subtle murmur of Bal asking Raj questions. What were they saying? What did Bal think?

"*Dhanyabad*," she said, when I glanced her way. Then she was gone, back to her own class. I was pleased she had come but worried about what she thought. What would she say to the other teachers? Prem, the founder of Sambhav Nepal who had arranged the volunteer gig, had requested that I demonstrate a variety of teaching techniques. I knew with Bal I was teaching to the converted. I hoped her opinion would make a difference with the other teachers.

I made it through most of the first week. As there were no substitute teachers in existence I agreed to fill in for a day for the head teacher, Tanka. He had gone to Arughat to attend mandatory teacher training. I was to follow his schedule of teaching all grade levels. Raj also had to go to Arughat on an errand for the trekking company. The prospect of an entire day of solo teaching unnerved me. I admitted my anxiety to Raj. He must have shared my apprehension with the other teachers. Throughout the day, one by one they casually drifted by the door of whatever classroom I was in to check on me.

Remnants of the self-assured beginning teacher I once was gradually filled me again. The kids responded in kind by listening during rote lessons and participating enthusiastically but respectfully in new situations. My renewed confidence allowed them to relax, too.

Still, delays continued to interrupt each class while we searched for enough pencils, erasers, and dry erase pens as well as chalk for the hopelessly scarred whiteboards and ancient ragged-edged blackboards.

The twenty-minute walk Raj and I took at the end of the school day to the hallowed source of refrigerated Everest or Gorkha beer was worth every dusty step. We debriefed the days. "I can't stand another day of kids calling out for pencils and erasers," I whined. "I can't blame them, but this is crazy. If we don't get more supplies, I'll go mad."

By the end of the week we had a plan to address my third goal, to buy more erasers. "Let's walk down to Arughat on the weekend," said Raj. "You can buy supplies."

"And check my email?"

Raj glanced in my direction. "Sure, if the electricity is working."

On Saturday I followed the surefooted Raj, who had travelled this trail hundreds of times as a child. Gingerly I picked my way down the stone steps and steep dirt sections, littered with layers of slippery rhododendron leaves.

Midway, we met a high school student climbing briskly, a brand new whiteboard hung across his back from a wide band across his forehead. "Is that one of our whiteboards?" I asked Raj.

"He says yes. He's going to Ratmate. It's for Bhairabi, our school."

"I've got to get a picture for the kids at BX Elementary back home in Vernon. They're so used to having entire walls of whiteboard in their classroom. They raised more than $500. They'll be excited to see what their money bought for the kids here."

Despite the weight, the wiry teen—not a drop of sweat evident on his lithe body—hesitated and posed for several photos. I was thankful for the chance to stop. My sprained ankle was much less painful than it had been, but walking downhill was still uncomfortable.

Every step to Arughat brought us closer to the coveted school supplies. I was determined to make my life, and that of the students, easier by buying enough supplies for the kids if I had to walk all the way back to Kathmandu.

We didn't have to go that far. Raj led me to an open storefront with shelves stacked floor to ceiling displaying a goldmine of pencils, sharpeners (or *cutters*, as the kids called them), erasers, scribblers, and sets of pre-sharpened colored pencils.

"Ask him if we can have some of those plastic jugs, too," I whispered to Raj as he bargained for our purchases. "We can use them to cart the stuff from class to class."

Third goal fulfilled, we sauntered down the main drag alternately singing my favorite Nepali tune, "*Resham Piriri,*" and Raj's preferred selection "Can You Say Hello!"

Teen carrying new whiteboard to Bhairabi School.

Halfway through town we ducked into a miniscule internet den. Three ancient computers, their keyboard characters worn almost invisible, graced a cracked wooden table. From the low stool I had to reach up to the keyboard. "Are you kidding," I said, "only 100 Nepali rupees an hour? That's about a dollar. Is that really the price for Westerners here? I'm in."

"Shhhh," said Raj. "Don't tell them you think it's cheap or they'll charge us more." In Nepal a sliding scale existed between the prices charged to locals and those for tourists. I understood and agreed; tourists and trekkers could afford to pay more. Raj went to the front counter to pay.

I composed a group email for family and friends and attached a photo of the student transporting the new whiteboard. I later learned that email had made quite an impact in a Grade 7 classroom on the other side of the world in Canada. When my friend Kevin, their teacher, received the email his students had been complaining about the inadequacies of their individual iPads. Annoyed at their first world whining he showed them the photo. It silenced their grumbles and provided the basis for an impromptu lesson on privilege and perspective, first-world versus third-world problems.

Engrossed in messages from the outside world, the hour passed quickly. One email from Lavinia Spalding, the travel journal writing guru and editor of *The Best Women's Travel Writing*, was particularly exciting. I had met her several years before at the annual Book Passage Travel Writers' and Photographers Conference in Corte Madera, California, near San Francisco. I admired her. She was half my age, had a lush mane of long curly brown hair, and outstanding expertise as a travel writer and editor. Her message said my essay describing my young Tibetan guide's experience during the Tibetan protest of 2008 against the Chinese occupation in Lhasa had made it to the long list for this year's book. I was on an adrenaline high.

At the same conference I had taken a workshop with Spud Hilton, then editor of the *San Francisco Chronicle's* travel section. That connection led to me writing twenty or so pieces for him for a column called "Five Places," a fun, tightly written weekly addition to the travel section. After that I worked on carving out a niche for my work by publishing several pieces for *Elevation Outdoors Magazine* in Boulder, Colorado. At home my articles about snow camping, backcountry skiing, avalanche safety and snowboard lessons made it into a regional magazine *Okanagan Life*. I thought I was on my way when my short travel article about Namche Bazaar on the Everest Base Camp trek made it into Canada's national newspaper the *Globe and Mail*. But the big time of national publications still often eluded me. I hoped material gathered on this trip would elevate me to the next level.

The email hour ended on a low. Barry sounded lonely and depressed. Fighting my own sadness I sent him some love. Unavoidably lengthy lapses between communication opportunities made the separation difficult for both of us.

Back on the street I squinted against the sun. "Follow me," said Raj. "I know what we need." He led me into an air-conditioned bar. We scarfed down some freshly prepared veggie momos, traditional Nepali dumplings, while guzzling frosty Everest beer.

In the heat of the early evening we sweated our way back up to the village. "Let's rest for a minute," I said halfway up, too breathless to carry on a conversation while hiking. Settled beside Raj on a large rock, I finally gathered the courage to ask, "So, what did Bal say about my lesson?"

"Didn't I tell you already?"

"Ah, no, and I'm dying to know."

"Well. She liked the plastic sleeves, the way they saved on paper and she liked the way you had the kids hold up their work to be checked."

Was that all? I was hungry for any signs of approval from

this colleague I had come to admire.

"She was also impressed you had made your own materials and was glad you were leaving things for the teachers."

"Anything else?"

"Oh yeah, she liked the song. She loves teaching English songs, too."

That night, buoyed by the endorsement of one of my new teaching colleagues, I fell asleep easily, stuffed full of anticipation for the week ahead. The jugs of school supplies stood along the edge of my sleeping bag like soldiers ready for battle.

By the end of the second week students had learned to respect my request to raise their hand instead of calling out. After listening to advice from the other teachers, I introduced my new strategies more slowly. The whiteboards had arrived from the local carpentry shop where they were being constructed, and were now installed in every classroom. Students didn't say much but one Grade 5 girl brought a basketful of freshly cut azaleas and placed a row blossoms along the top ledge of the whiteboard in their classroom. The kids, the teachers, Raj and Kamal, were all singing the English songs Raj and I had been teaching.

At lunchtime on my last day Raj explained classes were cancelled for the afternoon. The teachers had planned a farewell assembly. "Nepali people love ceremonies," he said. "It might last all afternoon." Over steaming rice and veggie curry, he schooled me on the expected protocol. "You'll have to give a speech," he said. "Might be good if it is in Nepali."

As a student of languages, I was pretty good at mimicking pronunciation. I had studied French and German and Spanish in high school and university. *Malheureusement*, Nepali was totally unlike any of these languages. I decided to keep my speech short. "Okay, I can do that. I'll tell you what I want to say. You tell me if it is okay, then you tell me the translation. I'll write it down then read it aloud at the assembly."

With my speech written phonetically, I practiced first for Raj, then for Kamal, then Raj again. I changed into my last clean shirt and climbed up the steps to the schoolyard.

On one side of the long narrow playground, all the students and many parents were seated on the cement bleachers. A curved row of red and orange plastic chairs had been arranged facing the crowd. Tanka, the head teacher, and several other village leaders stood when we arrived and motioned for Raj and me to sit in the center.

Tanka began with a speech completely in Nepali. From time to time he turned and smiled at me. The only word I understood, apart from my name, was *dhanyabad*— thank you. After about ten minutes Tanka stopped. Everyone clapped. He sat down. Raj leaned over to me. "Now it's your turn."

I stood, took one step forward, and unfolded my paper. When I looked up at the rows of smiling faces my eyes welled up and my throat constricted. I would miss these kids and teachers. They listened like they never had before to my words of thanks, praise for them, their teachers, and their parents. I hoped my pronunciation was intelligible. I made special mention of Raj's friendship and support. Then I turned to sit down. My entire speech had lasted not much more than three minutes.

"That's too short," said Raj. "You have to say more." *Now you tell me, I thought.* I rambled on in English, using teacher's names and gesticulating and smiling in each of their directions hoping my heartfelt sentiments would somehow be understood. After what seemed an eternity, in reality about five more minutes, Raj signaled for me to stop. I sunk onto the plastic chair and tugged down the brim of my hat to hide my tears.

The ceremony ended with a dance-a-thon. Thirta, the handsome but usually morose math teacher, sat amid the students. The flat of his hands and then heels of his hands alternately beat the ends of the black and red *madal*, the elongated Nepali drum. The children joined him with an enthusiastic rendition of *Resham Piriri*. Flip-flops flipping up puffs of reddish dust and my arms and fingers curving overhead, I imitated the Grade 2 students who had invited me to dance with them–Nepali style.

Then came a staff photo op. The women stood together shyly in the playground. The men remained distant. Raj raised my camera. Bal sidled up to me and slung her arm around my back. Sitala, the gorgeous young English teacher and Sunita nuzzled in behind. Tentatively the guys stepped in. Raj snapped photos. We said goodbye in a jumble of English and Nepali, several times. I turned and wandered away. My newfound colleagues, not yet

Bhairabi School staff photo.

ready to let me go, followed me to the campsite. We gathered chairs. Kamal poured tea. I passed chocolate biscuits. The staff chatted in Nepali, throwing in the occasional English word for my benefit.

There was warmth and gentle wisdom in their expressions. They made the village school a worthwhile and fun experience for their students in situations North American teachers would most surely deem intolerable. I had learned from them. They had taught me to go slowly, listen attentively, and learn by watching. I hoped in some ways I had helped them by demonstrating new teaching strategies. We had come to trust each other.

Nabeen, although gruff, was a natural teacher and leader. He was the one most comfortable speaking English. "So what do you think of our school, our teaching and our general management?" he asked.

I was pleased to be asked for my opinion. I told him I had learned from them, that they were doing a great job, and that it was obvious the children were responsive and eager to learn.

The teachers lingered into the cool of early evening. I liked to think their reluctance to leave indicated their acceptance of me. Despite little common language, we had come to understand and respect each other. I felt their support.

The sunset glowed orange, rays slanting over the Ganesh Himal. One by one they stood, placed their teacup in the washing bowl, and said good-bye. The men first, erect and formal, slightly distant, as they shook my hand. Then Sitala, chestnut eyes moist, gave me a gentle wordless hug. Last was Bal. Our embrace was long and warm. The dampness of our tears mingled where our cheeks collided. She whispered a single word in my ear: "Love."

CHAPTER 8
NAMASTE APRIK

Knees crossed in meditation pose in front of my tent, I inhaled one last look at the buttery sunrise over the Ganesh Himal. If only I could pack the view, the people, and ambience of village life into my duffel to unpack later whenever I wanted.

At 6:45 a.m. I heard the rustling of a sleeping bag. Raj stumbled out of the cook tent, red-eyed, looking grim. We had a full day ahead. We planned to leave Ratmate by 7:30 to deliver sports equipment to four village schools, then complete the six-hour drive to Pokhara, Nepal's second largest city. I didn't know it then, but Prem had suggested Raj add one extra village visit to the list we had already agreed on.

"You don't look good," I said.

"Didn't sleep. Up all night talking to my parents about my marriage and Rojina." Raj's new bride from the Solo Khumbu region in the Everest Base Camp area had arrived the day before for a visit with Raj's family. The young couple had met in Lukla, home of the Tenzing-Hillary airport. A vertical cliff bordered one end of the short runway and a drop-off of several thousand feet at the other made it the most dangerous airport in the world.

Rojina was a chef in one of the lodges. As a trekking guide

Raj brought clients to the lodge where she worked. She had come to travel with us to Pokhara and to spend a few days with her new husband before he and I set off for the month long Upper Mustang trek. "Some villagers are giving my parents a rough time because I married for love and someone of a lower caste," Raj explained. "Rojina is Gurung. They think I have let my family and the village down by marrying a Gurung instead of a Brahmin."

While the Nepali caste system, a tradition of social stratification, is still unofficially in effect today it is not as rigid as it once was. In 1962 a law was passed making it illegal to discriminate against other castes and leading all castes to be equally treated by the law. Traditions, however, die harder in rural areas.

Raj's parents' initial reservations and hurt feelings had disappeared. But while Rojina, now four months pregnant, was warmly welcomed by Raj's parents and family, not everyone in the village was of like mind. I was inwardly saddened for Rojina who, the night before, had been lying in a room upstairs in their home overhearing the conversation about how some villagers felt Raj should have waited for a marriage arranged by his parents. "I told my parents if anyone gives them trouble, I will come and speak to those people for them." A look of determination took over his face.

A few minutes later Raj's cell phone rang. He answered, listened, and then responded in exasperated tone before disconnecting.

"The car coming to get us can't get here. There's a bulldozer fixing a hairpin turn down by the beer store. The car can't get past. We'll have to walk down."

Great. For once I felt clean, dressed in fresh clothes in anticipation of the school visits. After two weeks of crawling in and out of my tent, overheated in modest shoulder-covering shirts and sleeping on a sweaty down bag, I enjoyed feeling presentable.

My aromatically pleasing state was thanks to the fact I had gathered courage to tackle the demanding art of public bathing. During our afternoon in Arughat, Raj had shown me where to buy a *lungi*, a Nepali sarong. Over the past two weeks I had observed women wearing them at the village tap. Desperate for a thorough wash, I thought I'd give it a try. I'd wrangled the slippery *lungi* fabric into a double wrap around my chest, hitched it up under my armpits, and tied it securely. The pink and black polished cotton *lungi* draped perfectly, armpits to toes.

Into a metal laundry bowl, borrowed from Kamal, I tossed a small bottle of Campsuds, the all-purpose backpacker's soap, and a few underthings. Then I wandered in what I hoped was an inconspicuous stroll to the single village tap. There was a lineup. A woman about my age and a younger man completed their washing, stood aside, and worked at wringing out their laundry. I waited for them to leave. They didn't.

I stepped forward, cupped my hands under the crystal spring water, grabbed my soap, then spread suds around my neck, arms, and armpits. Icy water dribbled down my back. A tingling shiver rose up my spine. Next I washed as far up my legs as seemed modest. I caught the surreptitious glances of the spectators. My two buddies, Bina and Sharu, had joined them. They toted buckets in baskets to fetch water.

Unsure of water tap etiquette I motioned for them to fill up. They shook their heads. Apparently they found it more fun to stand and watch. I stuck my head under the tap and squirted a generous dose of Campsuds into my hair. Suds exploded everywhere. I tried to wipe the soap from my eyes, raised my head too quickly, and smacked my head on the tap. Disoriented, I lost my balance. My left foot skidded on the slippery rocks in a spectacular *grand jeté* ballet move I hadn't attempted since dance class at age five. I landed in a soggy heap with my legs safely still attached.

When my eyes opened I was greeted by the astonished expressions of the two adult villagers and little girls. The young man extended a hand.

Upright again I massaged my hip. I'd have a bruise for sure. The extravagant dance move was bad for my hip but worse for my ego.

I had two choices: cry at this one last humiliating incident, or see the funny side. I chose the latter. The others joined in the hilarity.

I filled my bowl with water and squatted by my washing bowl to scrub my unmentionables. There was one last contortion for me to execute. Why not? The kind young man had wandered off. We were all girls. As slyly as possible I reached under my *lungi* to remove my underpants. This cunning maneuver had been demonstrated by various village women so why not me? Why not begin the next section of the trip with a clean inventory of underthings?

I pulled and tugged, casually dropped my cotton granny-style underpants in the bowl, then bowed. My audience smiled appreciatively. I almost expected applause.

These kids had witnessed my clumsy ballet tumble, my inept washing technique and had seen me at my worst in class several times, but they waited patiently to accompany me back to the campsite. Sharu insisted on carrying my bowl of laundry. Bina's small hand grasped mine. I was one slippery step closer to understanding the complexities of village life.

Now, clean and packed, I grabbed my daypack and walked down the hill to meet the car. A delegation had gathered to see us off. Sitala, Bal, and Thirta, the drummer, arrived with a *malla* necklace of fresh flowers. Tanka presented me with a certificate of appreciation in an intricately carved *Newari* frame. He solemnly smeared a red *tikka* dot on our foreheads. Raj's family formed a ragged line along the edge of the road. In front stood Bina, Sharu and Ganesh. We were all crying. Raj was leaving his parents. I was leaving the children I'd grown attached to. Rojina, who was leaving her new in-laws, heaved a sigh of relief, no doubt looking forward to private time with Raj.

I thought of my last wave to Barry at the airport. Maybe we'd be able to exchange a few encouraging words by email from an internet café in Pokhara. I was proud of how I had faced the discomforts of camping, the challenges of teaching, and the perils of open-air public bathing. I wanted to tell Barry. I wanted him to know I was safe but also managing just fine on my own.

Several miles along the road Raj introduced me to our driver. Keshar, 25, had the long, tousled, wavy hair of a disco singer. A shiny red Adidas T-shirt stretched across his slender chest above dark gray pin-striped dress pants and silver flip-flops. A driver for two years only, Keshar had purchased the 2009 Mahindra, a Jeep-wannabe truck, used, for $16,000.

Good to have a driver who owned his own car, I mused; they tended to drive more conservatively to protect their investment. The interior of the Mahindra was a study in Nepali culture, practicality, grime, and hope. Photos of serene Hindu goddesses stretched across the dashboard, leading to a frayed toothbrush in a slim pocket—for oral or mechanical use, or both, I never found out. Strips of tattered red sari fabric suspended a clattering collection of sparkling women's bracelets. They swayed in drunken circles as the truck dodged rocks, ruts, potholes, and goats. Within minutes every surface in the car, us included, was covered in a dust. "Nepali powder," said Keshar.

Each time a car approached, Keshar grabbed a pair of pliers from a pocket in the driver's side door and rotated the stubby metal post where the window handle once was to prevent further layers of Nepali powder. I took comfort in the solar Buddhist prayer wheel that spun in the appropriate clockwise direction on the center of the dashboard.

The first section of road, a scar through terraced fields of corn and rice, was barely wide enough for one vehicle. As the only person other than Keshar who knew how to drive I focused intensely on his technique. Like a rally driver, he switched effortlessly from the regular gearshift to the separate four-wheel drive controls on the floor.

We rarely got out of first gear. When we had to back up to execute an eight-point turn near a dizzying drop-off, Keshar's fuchsia-shirted side-kick hung his head out the back window, peered down at the rear wheels, and slapped the side of the truck to indicate it was safe to proceed. When the wheels were too close to the drop-off, he yelled. No seat belts. I closed my eyes and held my breath. Keshar always stopped just in time. My thoughts vacillated between enjoying a great adventure and wondering if I'd remain alive to tell about it. I considered walking but then gave the prayer wheel an extra turn. My fate was sealed.

At one terror-inducing corner, slate rocks about four feet high and two feet wide formed a hastily adapted guardrail. They looked like headstones, predicting the fate of those who missed the turn.

The ride continued with two hours of bumpy rut-riding downhill to Arughat, an hour of rolling with the flow alongside the boulder strewn Istul Khola riverbed, then three hours uphill in slippery dirt tracks which would be impassable in monsoon months.

Each school visit followed a similar routine: speeches, Hindu marigold *malla* necklaces, Buddhist white *kata* scarves, and the lengthy speeches that were *de rigueur*. Each time we stepped out of the car, curious uniformed students surrounded us shouting Namaste and hello. Teachers, administrators, parent council, and village development committee members shook our hands.

We visited classrooms with tin roofs, dirt floors, dilapidated wooden student benches, and ancient, peeling chalkboards. Scarred wooden tables, faded word charts and photos of past members of the royal family haphazardly decorated staffroom walls. Bhairabi School in Ratmate seemed palatial in comparison. After black tea and biscuits, we brought out the donations of sports equipment. The inadequacy of our gifts embarrassed me. A volleyball net with three balls and six badminton racquets with birdies would never accommodate the needs of the students or match the kindness of the villagers.

Once back in the truck an idea began to form: It might be wiser and more efficient to choose one school to support instead of spreading the funds so thinly.

En route to our last stop, Raj's surprise destination, we passed two long-legged teenaged girls dressed in navy skirts and blue blouses with bulky school bags slung over their shoulders. Walking for an hour to get to school, they carried umbrellas for protection against the punishing thirty-five degree Celsius sunshine.

Village rooftops layered with thin slabs of dark gray slate outlined an amphitheater of warm taupe one and two-storey homes built of traditional mud and stone. Lush green terraces of rice and corn extended to the steeper slopes of the Himalayan foothills.

The Mahindra rattled up to a single lane leading to Devi Jal Kumari School. I stepped down onto the patchy grass, rarely flattened by vehicle tires. A slender man about forty years of age extended his hand. "Namaste. I am Hari Sharma, school principal."

A younger man slipped forward, eyes crinkled against the searing sun. Ballpoint pens, one red, one blue, in his plastic shirt pocket protector suggested official educational status. "Welcome. My name is Kumar," he said. "I will escort you to our school." Later introduced as the vice-principal, Kumar extended his arms over my bowed head and placed an intricately woven grass *malla* necklace around my neck.

Patti welcomed to Aprik village.

I was the first foreigner to visit the school. Since 1961, Sir Edmund Hillary's Himalayan Trust had supported schools in Nepal's Solu Khumbu, the area leading to Everest Base Camp. Monasteries of Buddhist organizations from all over Asia have sent financial assistance to educate young monks in various Buddhist regions. Most of these schools and monasteries are on popular trekking routes, so have received throngs of international visitors and large donations.

In Gorkha, however, villages were off the major trekking routes. Isolated from the outside world by roads impassable during the heavy rains of the monsoon season, passageways often plagued by rock and mudslides, many schools have been forgotten. Devi Jal Kumari School in Aprik Village was one of them.

Aprik is located in the region of Manaslu Peak, the highest

summit in the Gorkha area, and eighth-highest mountain in the world. Despite its proximity to this famous trekking and climbing destination, the area doesn't entertain much international traffic. Manaslu circuit trekkers and mountaineers going for the summit of Manaslu have no need to pass through Aprik.

Adventurers spend time in Arughat Bazar, the rubble street town of raggedy shops and restaurants Raj and I had visited to access the internet. Home to about four thousand people, it was the starting point for expeditions. Aprik remained remote, a four-hour drive away.

Kumar led me along the alleyway between high stone walls defining the narrow stamped-earth pathway to the school. A river of students dressed in sky blue school uniform shirts and blouses heaped fresh blossoms on my cupped hands. This must be how Queen Elizabeth feels, I thought. But, why me? Don't they realize I don't have huge pockets of money to help them?

We continued along a series of well-swept dirt trails between simple homes, and emerged into a small, open square. A young woman with the visage of a Hindu goddess and an obvious innate sense of style greeted us from her small front porch. Her shiny black braid hung over a form fitting black T-shirt, tugged down over her dirt-length sari skirt. She wouldn't have looked out of place in a Bollywood dance number.

Metal retro Coca Cola signs decorated the porch, indicating her home as the one store in town. An ancient metal pop cooler sat beside the front door. It received electricity from a small hydroelectric power plant designed, built and maintained by the villagers.

Kumar ushered us into a low-ceilinged room at the back of the house with just enough space to accommodate two three-seater school desks with attached benches, a double bed festooned with mosquito netting, and a stairway to the second floor. The dirt floor, covered with sackcloth and flattened cardboard boxes, exuded a cool, earthy odor. Mindful of the fact that the best house in the village was elected to host us, I wondered about the state of the other homes. All look well-cared for from the outside, but living conditions must certainly be basic.

We were each presented with a tin plate containing a pile of steamed white rice, a hearty dollop of steamed spinach, and two scoops of *dahl* lentils. The lady of the house placed a few pieces of curried chicken on each plate.

Ravenous from our busy morning we dug in. The curry was delicious but spicy hot. My lips began to burn, but in order not to offend my hosts I cleaned my plate. The weight of representing Westerners in general and my country specifically hung as heavily as it would on any Olympic athlete.

I leaned to Raj and whispered, "It's kind of spicy. I'm out of water."

"*Didi*," he called in the direction of the kitchen. "Could we have something to drink, please?" Clanking and gurgling noises came from the porch. Raj reappeared with a chilled glass bottle of Mirinda, Pepsi Cola company's syrupy sweet version of Fanta orange drink. I caressed my sunburned cheek with the cool bottle.

Fortified from lunch we set out to tour the school. The original two-storey mud and stone school building had been financed and built by the villagers fifty-three years earlier, and was falling down around the students. We climbed a rickety ladder to the second floor where I stepped onto the rough loose boards of the makeshift balcony. Through the cracks I could see patches of blue shirts below. A row of five door-less rooms about a quarter the size of a typical Canadian classroom opened onto the narrow balcony. We peered into one used until recently as a staffroom. The once substantial beam stretching across the room now drooped ominously under the heavy slate roof. Mud plaster had flaked from the walls, revealing jagged, gaping cracks between the stones. Rays of dusty sunlight streamed down through gaps in the roof. Wisely, the school management committee had condemned the second floor. Out of necessity some rooms on the main floor were still being used. Kumar explained monsoon rain poured through into classrooms on the main floor. Umbrellas were essential school equipment.

We visited several classes. In one, kindergarten students were forced to join a Grade 4 classroom, inappropriate for five year-olds. There was no primary play equipment or learning materials—nothing but benches, reddish dirt walls and floors. Eyes wide at the sight of a foreign guest, the younger children sat squished between their older siblings, their legs dangling off benches built for nine-year-olds.

Old Devi Jal Kumari School before the earthquake.

My years in spacious classrooms with ten-foot ceilings over huge windows in hundred-year-old Vancouver inner-city schools had done nothing to prepare me for this educational nightmare. Despite the fact schools where I worked as a teacher and principal were situated in one of the lowest socio-economic neighborhoods in Canada, they were full of well-trained teachers and ample teaching materials. Word charts, posters and children's art and stories adorned bulletin boards. Colored paper, glue and scissors for every child, and a multitude of paints were available for daily use. Stacks of library books were piled high on the shelves. With stomachs full from hot breakfasts and lunches provided by the Ministry of Education and local businesses, children were happy and ready to learn.

The children in Aprik and similar villages all over Nepal deserved the same opportunities. A parade of parents from the school management committee followed us, classroom to classroom, silently encouraging their children to put their best foot forward, to stand when questioned and show off their limited English. I was struck by the respect and eagerness of these attractive, well-scrubbed, and well-mannered students.

Community members had maintained the school for more than fifty years without government assistance. In Nepal, villagers must build their own schools. The government supplies only three teachers, minimally trained by Canadian standards, for 225 students. Five local untrained teachers with only a Grade 10 education were paid for by the local Gorkha District and subsidized by villagers. Devi Jal Kumari School was by far the most forlorn school I had visited. I asked questions and took notes, all the while wondering what I was doing there. I felt guilty taking up so much of their time, raising their hopes. Were they under the impression all Westerners were wealthy?

Kumar knew how to work the room, as I had done when raising funds. But his charming smile didn't quite cover his sense of urgency. He seemed desperate to make a good impression and to will me to grasp the needs of the children. I recognized his look. It was the exact expression I used to have when I welcomed potential donors and corporate sponsors to Admiral Seymour School in Vancouver's Downtown Eastside. Thousands of kilometers and continents away I had found in Kumar a like-minded colleague.

His hopeful countenance dug its way into the recesses of my brain. But why me? Why at this stage of my life had I come upon this village in need of a school? How could a person like me make an impact on this community? Made to feel so welcome, valued and honored, I longed to discover a way to contribute to their lives.

A deep melancholy welled up in me, sadness for the cavernous contrast to education in Canada. Haunted by the part I played in raising their hopes, feeling hollow and decidedly inadequate, I stepped back into the waiting Mahindra. Like Scarlett O'Hara in *Gone With the Wind* I decided I couldn't think about it now. I'd think about it tomorrow.

Still within sight of the village, I was ashamed to admit my mind had already catapulted ahead to the creature comforts of Pokhara: an air-conditioned hotel room, Mediterranean pizza, and a glass of red wine.

CHAPTER 9
LONELY IN LAKESIDE

Pokhara, Nepal; May 12, 2014

By day's end my world had been transformed. The red earth homes of Ratmate had faded into the mist over the Ganesh Himal range. And, with them, the pleading expression of the vice-principal from Aprik.

In their place the delights of Nepal's second-largest city materialized before me. Until the end of the 60s Pokhara, the burgeoning tourist town 204 kilometers west of Kathmandu, was accessible only on foot. At that time, because of its inaccessibility it was considered to be even more captivating than Kathmandu. Now a popular destination for tourists it can be reached in from six to twelve hours by car or bus. That is, depending on traffic jams, accidents, landslides, washouts, spontaneous roadwork, and unruly herds of highway-blocking goats. When the Siddhartha Highway was completed in 1968, Pokhara grew as quickly as the population of garbage-eating holy cows that dot its streets.

Since the early 70s Lakeside Pokhara, bordering Phewa Lake, had morphed into a major tourist hub. As gateway to the Annapurna Circuit Trek, most months of the year its streets are chock-a block with hikers either shopping for pre-trip gear or nursing weary post-trek muscles in fifty-dollar-a-day three-star hotels.

Adventure seekers from around the globe crowd storefront businesses in search of adrenaline-inducing activities like white water kayaking and rafting, paragliding, bungee jumping, canyoning and bouldering. Mountaineers and armchair adventurers visit the International Mountaineering Museum. Yoga classes and twenty-five dollar ayurveda massages soothe muscles strained from sightseeing or outdoor pursuits.

I swooned in anticipation of three-star luxuries: clean sheets, hot water, café lattes, red wine, and pizza, in that order. Leaning back against the dust-free faux leather seats of the private car, I stared at the passing scene. Nepal was in a constant state of disrepair and repair, tearing down and rebuilding. Just like me. I had put my heart and soul into getting the teaching gig right. My aching muscles and overtaxed emotions were in need of refueling and relaxation before the next challenge.

Trucks rattled noisily through the industrial outskirts, in and out of potholes and over curbs. Local franchises, soon to be shuttered for the night with weighty corrugated steel, boasted signs like "Shivani Cement" and "Pashupati Paints Colour Bazaar."

One out of five buildings lining the lake view promenade bustled with construction workers. Sari-clad women, hems scuffling through dirt, hefted baskets of newly baked bricks to building sites. They unloaded their cargo, then filled their baskets with discarded rubble and hauled it away. Barefoot men roamed high bamboo scaffolding like agile rock climbers. They slipped past puzzled tangles of electrical wires, lithely slalomed through jungles of rooftop rebar, then dangled precariously above mounds of gravel hand hewn by local families for five dollars a bag. Outdated lodges were being torn down, then reconstructed and modernized. Old, valued bones were evolving into fresh-faced hotspots supervised by entrepreneurial owners wisely reluctant to give up prime locations in order to compete for foreign currencies.

Old buildings, limp with fatigue. My sentiments exactly. Two weeks in Ratmate tenting, public washing and climbing wonky cement steps to the only Western toilet in town had left me ready for creature comforts. Roughing it was fine, for a while. Those forays made the rest breaks, comfort food, fine wine and a comfortable bed all the more sweet. If camping was the only route to first-hand experience of the everyday culture then bring on the tent, sleeping bag and pit toilet. If surviving rustic conditions was the only way to provide volunteer service and forge friendships with kids like Bina, Sharu and Ganesh, then I was all for them.

The threat of squat toilets had provided conclusive inspiration for pre-trekking gym workouts to keep my aging knees flexible. Discomforts were tough, but well worth the trade-off of visiting magical, otherwise inaccessible places. Knowing just days from now I would be setting out on a month-long trek to one of those places, I planned to take full advantage of what Pokhara had to offer. Besides, tourism created employment for locals. I didn't mind being a tourist, temporarily.

In the hotel lobby, a man of elegant stature and bearing appeared from an alcove beside the lobby desk with a silver tray of glasses. "Namaste," he said, with a quick bow. "Welcome. Cold drink, Madame?" The cool, velvety mango juice soothed my throat. Minutes later, safely behind the locked door of my room, I luxuriated under the warm shower. The red dust of Ratmate streamed down into the drain.

———— * ————

I was happy to be in Pokhara. Barry and I had loved our time here in 2011. With him in mind, I started the next day at our favorite coffee shop, the Black and White Café. From my wooden bench at a sidewalk table I sipped a steaming latte, forced myself to exhale slowly and mindfully, and enjoyed the ambience. Couples and groups of tourists strolled past along the lakeside promenade. A pang of loneliness caught in my throat. Most foreigners came to Pokhara seeking adventure. Days were spent searching for trekking items in the myriad stores blatantly selling North Face and Mountain Hardware knockoffs, or rewarding themselves with post-expedition Western-style culinary delights. Pokhara offered countless diversions. Reunions of long lost friends or friendships forged only weeks before in some remote location happened every few feet along the street.

"*Guten tag*, hello," a strapping blond man in shorts and a T-shirt called to a petite female. "How was the Annapurna Trek?"

"Bonjour," she said, dark bangs barely masking the flirtatious look in her eyes. The epitome of French chic and simplicity, she had draped her swanlike neck with Nepali pashmina. "It went great. Good to see you again."

Across the street I spotted a couple closer to my age conferring with a fruit vendor. Their practical khaki clothing, scruffy wide-brimmed hats, and worn backpacks hinted at seasoned-traveler status. Both had binoculars slung around their necks. Perhaps they belonged to a growing flock of birdwatchers attracted to Pokhara. As they sauntered away her hand slipped into his in an effortless gesture refined by decades of familiarity. Involuntarily my fingers twitched. I remembered how warm and comfortable Barry's hand felt in mine.

On my stroll back to the hotel I passed shops bulging with multi-colored shawls, T-shirts emblazoned with OM signs, and sandwich boards advertising today's "best exchange rate" from American, Canadian, Australian and Hong Kong dollars, German deutschemarks and French francs: all to Nepali rupees.

Like Pokhara and these various currencies, I was in a state of flux. Ready for renewal, I also needed scaffolding to build my confidence for my imminent transition from teacher to trekker. Deep excavation was required to mine my journalistic skills as well as the physical stamina for trekking. I hoped the emotional strength built by teaching would give me the courage to continue. A few nights in a comfortable bed would take care of the rest.

The evening was warm enough for short sleeves. Machhapuchare, the Fishtail, towered above town in the pink evening alpenglow. On the patio of Cafe Concerto I hovered over slices of pizza dripping with gooey cheese and chili oil across the rickety wooden table from Raj and radiantly pregnant Rojina. Raj sweated as he sipped his "quarto" of whiskey. His other hand rested proprietarily on Rojina's knee. On the sidewalk a tourist parade wound languidly through the heaviness of the humid air.

The last time I had sat at this table I was with Barry. Tonight I missed him more than ever. Was he at home, missing me? Was he struggling to cook for himself? Had he figured out the controls on the washer and dryer?

He'd graduated from a prestigious private school and was valedictorian of his class at UBC. Maybe that was part of the problem. I saw him not only as stronger, but also smarter. I had voluntarily placed myself in his shadow. It was time to come out in the sun, by myself. Maybe that's what this trip was all about.

Being alone was most difficult during transitions from one portion of trip to the next. Not only were Pokhara and I in transition. My relationship with Barry was also in flux, in need of rejuvenation, some rekindling to keep the fires burning. We needed to get past the present doldrums. I wasn't sure how things would be when I returned home. Would we feel more distant or end up closer than ever? Still, there was no way I was going to give up and go home. I had a strenuous month long trek ahead. I was determined to complete every step.

After dinner I stopped in at an internet café. The first email I opened was a romantic, missing you type message from Barry. We were both better at expressing tender feelings via email than face to face. Maybe we would learn to appreciate each other more after some solitude. Had we become complacent, taking each other for granted? Or were we both trapped in our own separate bubbles of sadness, unable to burst through the surface to reconnect?

On the way back to the hotel the guttural utterances of monks chanting Om Mani Padme Hum drew me to hole-in-the-wall Tibetan shop. The familiar mantra, *Hail to the Jewel in the Lotus*, a reverence to the Dalai Lama, shifted my focus to the next section of my journey. This simple phrase created the aura of Tibetan Buddhism and the centuries old monasteries dotted throughout my next destination. For three years these sounds had been calling me to return to the arid hills of the forbidden kingdom of Upper Mustang.

Drifting off to sleep I revisited the day we had spent three years ago in Lo-Manthang. One brief encounter with King Jigme Palbar Bista and conversations with shopkeepers had left me hungry for a deeper connection with the residents of Lo-Manthang, Upper Mustang's capital city. One of those shopkeepers, Pema Bista, had recently completed construction of the town's newest hotel, The Lotus Holiday Inn. I wondered how success was influencing Pema's life. Narcissistically I hoped he might remember me, somehow distinguish me from the thousands of tourists encountered every year. The journalist in me was eager to discover how the lives of locals had changed since the rudimentary road to the capital was completed the year before.

———•———

Almost seven decades of experience had taught me never to underestimate the restorative power of a good night's sleep. Weariness and melancholy had engulfed me at bedtime. The next morning I was up early, fresh and ready for my first urban school visit. From Canada I had arranged to visit a school where in winter classes were held on the outskirts of Pokhara. In summer the children travelled to Chhoser, a village outside Lo-Manthang, 109 kilometers north and almost 2,500 meters higher in elevation.

Though separated by formidable geographical features, the lives and educational opportunities of the inhabitants of Pokhara and Upper Mustang intertwined. During the winter months sixty boys and thirty girls from tiny villages in remote corners of Upper and Lower Mustang attended school and boarded free of charge in Kaski, a pastoral area a thirty-minute drive from Pokhara. For the summer session, students journeyed over high mountain passes and treacherous river gorges to Chhoser, the small village closer to their cultural home, providing the chance for immersion in local language, religion and tradition. Our visit coincided with the end of the winter term.

Our driver turned off a bumpy road at the black iron gates of Pal Ewan Namgyal Monastic School in Kaski, and we left the predominantly Hindu milieu of Pokhara and entered a bustling enclave of Tibetan Buddhist culture. Sixty young monks in burgundy robes scurried back and forth across the stamped-earth courtyard, spreading their laundry to dry in the sun. A senior monk broke away from a basketball game with young monks. "Namaste and welcome. I am Lekshey Lama, principal." Glancing back at the playground full of boisterous monks, he smiled the gentle smile of one who breathes true calm and compassion. "No classes today. Buddha's birthday. Boys doing washing before travel to Chhoser."

In the spacious assembly hall over traditional butter tea and finger-length twists of *khapse*, fried Tibetan bread, Raj and I were formally welcomed by the English teacher who acted as translator. A native of Pokhara, the young scholar held a degree from the Central University of Tibetan Studies in Varanasi, India. Well-schooled in public relations, fluent in five languages, he deftly explained the curriculum offered at this location and at a nearby home, where thirty young nuns lived and attended classes. "We provide a modern education as well as the study of Buddhist philosophy. Lessons are taught in Nepali, English and

Tibetan. Children study social studies, science and computer use but also religious *Thanka* painting and music with traditional ceremonial instruments."

I wondered if the price paid for a free education was the promise of becoming a monk or nun. "Not all the boys become monks, nor the girls *anis*, nuns," he said, as if reading my mind. "The students decide for themselves in their teens. Some leave for other professions. Whatever their decision, we are happy to have provided them with a good start."

The abbot, or *khenpo*, the Venerable Tsewang Rigzin of the Namgyal monastery, who oversaw the school programs, was absent. He had recently returned from a five-month tour of Singapore where he had offered Buddhist teachings to raise funds to operate both the summer and winter schools. He was already in Chhoser, preparing for summer school. I hoped I'd get a chance to meet him there in a few weeks.

I mentioned my disappointment in missing Khenpo. I explained how I was interested to hear how he continued to finance free education for so many. The visage of the Aprik Village vice-principal appeared like a flickering candle in my conscious-ness. Was there a possibility I could learn a few fund raising tricks from Khenpo and help the children of Aprik after all?

"Don't worry," he said graciously. "I will contact Khenpo and let him know you will come to visit. He will be expecting you."

The following morning Raj picked me up at 5:00 a.m. for the twenty-minute drive to Pokhara airport. Through the security gates by 5:30, we were first in line for Yeti Airlines' eighteen-seat Twin Otter to Jomson, the starting point for the Upper Mustang trek. My first thought was, can this plane get enough altitude to miss the jagged Himalayan peaks between here and Jomson?

Raj and I led the parade of heavy-eyed travelers across the tarmac and into the plane. First in, I snagged a single front seat right behind the open cockpit door. A beautiful hostess in traditional Tibetan dress doled out candies and bits of cotton batten, presumably to stick in our ears. She nonchalantly called out something about fastening seatbelts. I mumbled a few rounds of *Om Mani Padme Hum*. The exterior door closed. The pilot's door remained open. I watched the pilot turn the ignition key. The engines roared to life. We ascended steeply into the splendor of the Himalaya.

Twenty-five minutes and 146 kilometers from Pokhara we landed in Jomson. Thunderous winds growled like freight trains, barreling along the parched expanse of the Kali Gandaki River Valley, said to be the deepest gorge in the world. Every day around noon, due to the incessant, catastrophic winds, flights ended for the day.

We exited the tiny airport through an archway draped with prayer flags. The variety of faces and regalia of locals, trekkers and pilgrims signaled a crossroads of Hindu, Buddhist and Western cultures. For trekkers, Jomson was the gateway to the Annapurna and Mustang Circuits. For pilgrims it was the road to the sacred city of Muktinath. Vacillating between thoughts the trek ahead and the children I'd left behind, I was as much at a crossroads as anyone else.

Vendors edged the narrow flagstone street, sitting behind blankets resplendent with tender mangoes, ripe bananas, huge cabbages, milky cauliflower and white potatoes. Ruddy-cheeked Tibetan matrons peered through dust-caked shop windows. A young boy in a blue hoodie, brown jeans and flip-flops perched on a spiraled wicker stool, a book open on his lap. A sign behind him read "Feel Like Your Own Home, Thakali Home Stay Hotel."

Two bearded Hindu gentlemen in traditional *dhoti* wraps, father and son status hinted by matching profiles and posture, loitered on the other side of the street. Gingerly, they popped out of the way of a cadre of stampeding soldiers. Large backpacks and weighty rifles slung over their brown camouflage fatigues,

the military trainees jogged down the street, heavy boots rhythmically pounding the stones. Gasping in the thin air of almost
3,000 meters, stern faces focused, they thumped past on their
way to the Nepal Army High Altitude and Mountain Warfare
School a kilometer out of town.

———•———

Through the back window of my room at the Himalayan Hotel,
the breathtaking spectacle of the Nilgiri Himal, a range of three
peaks that are part of the Annapurna massif, dominated the view.
That is, until a flash of colors in the primary school playground
below commanded my attention. Under a cerulean sky they
jumped, laughed, and executed calisthenics in the crisp morning
air in time with the drumbeats of one of the senior students. On
a final directive they bowed to the head teacher, hands together
in Namaste. Dressed in warm jackets and hats they filed off into
tiny, windowless, unheated classrooms. Everywhere I looked the
contrast between the state of education in the Western world and
Nepal was magnified, taking me back to that face, the concerned
expression, the beseeching gaze of the vice-principal and the
villages I had left behind.

What was I supposed to do about Aprik?

CHAPTER 10
GATEWAY TO THE FORBIDDEN KINGDOM

Upper Mustang; May 15, 2014

A rmed with fresh clothes and a clean attitude I was restless, eager to start trekking. A day in Jomson taking photos, reading, and napping had helped me to acclimatize after the 1,343-meter elevation gain between Pokhara and Jomson.

Our team gathered on the pocked cement steps of the hotel. Our two porters had arrived directly from Kathmandu by bus the night before. Raj introduced the two men who would carry our loads for the next month. Resham Rana, a boyish but quietly confident twenty-four-year old, stepped forward with an out-stretched hand. His smile seemed oddly familiar. "I met you at the tap," he said. "At Ratmate."

Inwardly I cringed when I realized it had been Resham who had witnessed my inaugural foray into public bathing; he had stood by silently when I banged my head and did the spectacular grand jeté ballet move, and offered a considerate hand up. His discreet handling of that situation boded well for our future. "That was you?"

"Yes," he said, with a conspiratorial nod. I suspected secrets would be safe with him.

Our second porter was Tika Ram. Older than Resham by at least thirty years, he had the muscled calves and the wiry frame of a seasoned carrier. His face showed deep crinkles from years of sun exposure and laughter, and I took comfort knowing one of the crew was closer to me in age. Tika's job would be to carry emergency tents in case guesthouse rooms were unavailable, or unsuitable.

Raj led the way out of Jomson. Tika and Resham smoothly lifted their loads, settled them on their backs, and placed the wide attached strap, what Canadian voyageurs termed a tumpline, across their foreheads. Childhood responsibilities had prepared them with strong neck muscles. They grew up carrying water, greens for the family animals, vegetables, and firewood in *doko*, hand woven baskets carried by a strap they called a *namlo*.

My trekking poles clicked on the flagstone streets as we passed the barbed wire fences of the military training base. We turned right and crossed a wooden bridge, almost obscured by layered lengths of prayer flags, to the pathway on the far side of the river. The muffled crunch of gravel punctuated every step. In loose formation we leaned into the increasing howl of the late morning wind. I raised my neck buff to screen my mouth and nose from the swirling grit.

Resham and Tika, both from Gorkha, had never set foot north of Jomson. Resham, not much taller than I, carried my embarrassingly heavy duffel with ease. They frequently walked ahead then stopped to wait for Raj and me, perhaps as an excuse to rest and adjust their loads. Both seemed fascinated with every boulder, pebble and rock formation in this environment so unlike the green terraces of their homeland. The next month would not be easy. Challenges of altitude, winds and sun lay ahead, along with—for me—the joys of renewing past acquaintances, making new friends, and deepening my understanding of an ancient culture. I was both excited and apprehensive. Despite my three jovial trekking buddies, part of me was lonely.

It took three hours to reach the Kagbeni, the entrance to the

restricted area of Upper Mustang. Officially the transition into
the regulated territory would happen the next morning when
we showed our permits at the Annapurna Conservation Area
office. My crew could probably have reached Kagbeni village
in half the time but were, I realized with gratitude, adjusting to
my pace. We arrived at The Annapurna Inn by noon. Raj scored
me a large bright corner room with two single beds covered in
six-inch foam. The Western en suite toilet looked good but the
flush lever was broken. A bucket had been provided for flushing
purposes. The tap and shower nozzle worked with both hot and
cold water. My lower back was already cranky from the first few
hours of carrying a pack, and I craved what could well be my last
hot shower for a month. Besides, I stank from the morning's effort.

After the shower I rinsed and hung the offending quick dry
shirt, dressed, and headed to the dining area. Red geraniums lined
the perimeter of the sunny room. Fierce, mesmerizing winds
rippled like ocean swells through surrounding green fields of
barley. Dry-stone walls protected the fields from wind erosion. I
devoured a plateful of fried local Kagbeni potatoes with tomato,
spinach, onion, cabbage and cheese. My crew ate, as is the custom,
in the guides' and porters' lounge. Most trekkers wouldn't arrive
until dinnertime, so I ate alone.

After lunch I grabbed my camera and notebook and set out
with Raj for a reconnaissance walk. Computer-generated posters
of a nearby ancient red-painted monastery and school were
evident in all the local shops. "Kag Choede Thupten Samphel
Ling Monastery – our door is open. Come visit us," the posters
stated. "See how we're expanding our ability to help young monks
become educated religious leaders, ready for the future." Three
years before, I had learned about the monastery school. But when
Barry and I had tried to visit, it was evident visitors were not
expected. The courtyard had been guarded by a ferocious barking
Tibetan mastiff whose mammoth shoulders strained against his

chain. Now, signs that would make a New York advertising agency proud hung from every available vertical surface in the village.

This time I'd come prepared. I'd made an appointment online to meet with school principal *Khenpo* Tenzin Sangpo, and tour the site. When we entered the courtyard we were immediately thrust into the center of a gang of boisterous junior monks wielding cricket bats. Burgundy robes flew in all directions. They barely noticed our arrival.

Two pudgy late-middle-aged Asian men in floppy sunhats and brand-name outdoor attire, necks slung with two impressive looking cameras each, approached one of the pre-teen monks. They inquired about tickets to tour the monastery. He handed them tickets in exchange for rupees, never looking up to meet their eyes. Raj bought us two tickets. The young boy pulled a large metal key adorned with a red, yellow and blue fabric braid, from the pouch of his robe.

As we wandered around the main assembly hall, the young monk waited silently by the door. The men with cameras told us they were also en route to Lo-Manthang. As we exited the monastery they motioned to the young boy to stand in the doorway to have his picture taken. It wasn't long before I felt uncomfortable with the way the two men almost manhandled the compliant youngster. By the number of angles and postures they demanded, the constant switching from one camera to the other, it seemed they considered themselves expert photographers. The young monk remained patient. His flickering gaze told a different story. With a final sigh he accepted a Polaroid of himself, then ran off to join the cricket game.

Feeling troubled about taking advantage of their aggressiveness to get good shots myself, I recalled an unsettling incident in Lo-Manthang during our previous trip. The experience I witnessed had led me to renew my vow to never photograph a person without their permission. On that occasion I had joined a throng

Young monk in monastery doorway.

of tourists and locals to witness Duk Chu, a celebration marking the beginning of winter in Upper Mustang. I had been standing on a hill looking down at twenty monks twirling their vibrant costumes to the beat of drums and cymbals. Heads covered in gargoyle masks, they swayed to the wailing sounds of the *dungchen*, the long horns used in Tibetan Buddhist ceremonies.

Closer to the action, leaning on the wall of the monastery courtyard, a stunning young local mother garbed in traditional attire held a toddler. She was almost edged out of her place by a tall, blond European tourist jockeying for position to photograph the event. At one point he turned and noticed the attractive pair beside him. Without a word, he pointed his camera toward them, inches from their faces. The young woman, posture stiff and angry, raised her hand to cover her child. He laughed and turned his lens back to the dancers.

A minute later I watched as a woman from the same tour

group approached him from the other side. Without a word she raised her equally large lens inches from her fellow tourist's face and started clicking. It took only a second before he started waving his hands in protest, yelling about intrusion of privacy. The female tourist and the young Tibetan woman shared a knowing glance and a laugh, and I vowed to ask permission before taking photos of people.

My reverie of photography etiquette was interrupted by the shouts of the young cricket players. We watched the game, waiting for my interview time. The reclusive side of my personality, the side inherited from my dad, started to take over. Like him I was most comfortable alone, reading, writing or enjoying the outdoors in solitude. My stomach flipped as it always did at the thought of interviewing a stranger, especially someone of a different culture.

From a balcony above the courtyard, a monk summoned us upstairs. We were ushered into a small reception room and invited to sit on a bench covered in Tibetan carpet. Twenty minutes later the smiling *khenpo* entered. Thankfully, my mom's side of me, the social butterfly, took over. My focus had easily shifted from myself to the fascinating man beside me who was explaining his plans to combine medieval beliefs with practices of the modern world.

"How are the internet, computers and mobile phones changing life for your students?" I asked.

"I cannot ignore them. We must try to use them to our best advantage," he said, in surprisingly fluent English. "And, we encourage the boys to embrace the positive aspects of technology while also keeping traditional values." He leaned forward as if to accentuate his point. "There are six monasteries in Upper Mustang. The message of His Holiness the Dalai Lama, who appointed me, to all of the *khenpos* in Lower and Upper Mustang, is to embrace the responsibility of preserving the Tibetan language, culture, Buddhist traditions and practices as free Tibetans." As he mentioned the Dalai Lama I detected a glimmer of pride and warmth. "I believe in a balance between the modern world and ritual, culture and traditions of the past. Students need to embrace the good parts of the modern world. Take advantage of modern conveniences and comforts, while preserving their own culture and traditions."

He crossed one leg over the other, revealing long burgundy socks. The toes of his brown running shoes protruded past the dusty hem of his robe. He removed his glasses and rubbed the bridge of his nose. Dark circles shadowed above smooth cheeks. It was mid-morning for me, but he had been up since 5:00 a.m.

Patti with Khenpo Tenzin Sangpo.

to lead the morning *puja* prayer session and had already taught two classes.

"What about the posters?" I asked. "Why so many?"

"We need money to reconstruct the ancient monastery and increase the size of the dormitories so we can serve more students. We have raised the price of a visit from one hundred to two hundred rupees," —from about $1.50 to $2.50— "developed a website explaining the various levels of donations, printed posters to encourage foreigners to visit, and printed a brochure about the monastery reconstruction." Spoken like a true entrepreneur.

I tucked away bits of his wisdom to be dusted off later when considering the possibility of helping the people of Aprik.

"I have to keep up with the times," he said. "The village is changing. Not so friendly. People are tired of tourists. Many local people are confused. They have lost their way."

I marveled at the myriad opportunities afforded the children educated in Buddhist monastery schools. These *khenpos* spent half of the year travelling, giving teachings and fundraising. Were there any leaders out there to advocate for the Hindu children of Gorkha? Had my visit to Aprik been a serendipitous challenge to me to be their champion?

———— * ————

Kagbeni had recently changed from a sleepy village to a bustling metropolis. Progress was inevitable. But electricity remained intermittent at best. Solar ovens, large metal bowl-shaped reflectors that focused light directly to convert sunlight to heat energy, provided a healthy alternative to smoky indoor cooking fires. Motorcycles and mountain bikes now sped along the narrow flagstone streets once frequented only by livestock and villagers.

During our last visit, Barry and I had loitered at the end of the narrow dead-end street gazing apprehensively at the northward route we were about to take toward the snow crowned mountains of Upper Mustang. Across from the checkpoint office we had watched locals sorting rocks for the construction of a small building.

Now, in the exact spot just down the flagstone path from the local McDonald's and the 7-Eleven, a spiral staircase led to the newly opened Café Applebee's. It looked as trendy as any European sidewalk bistro. Drawn by the buzzing whine of the Illy Espresso machine, Raj and I followed the aroma of freshly roasted coffee beans. We placed our orders. They arrived at our table on the rooftop deck. My fork sliced easily through moist double chocolate cake. I sipped an Americano and took in the panorama of pebbles, boulders and mountains. There it was again, the route north along the expansive Kali Gandaki River valley. For the past three years those gentle tones of coffee, russet and tan had summoned me.

What changes lay behind those far off peaks glistening with spring snow? The route that once frightened me now seemed totally doable. I knew there would be lots of uncomfortable days and nights. But the people and experiences ahead would more than make up for the screaming back muscles, dust storms, sweaty days and chilling nights. Unconcerned about my physical ability to complete the trek, I remained apprehensive about the effect the road may have had on the culture. In Kagbeni, there was a definite air of progress, of industriousness. Sadly, there was also a coolness toward strangers not evident before.

An unexpected downpour soaked us on the way back to the hotel. I changed into my dry fleece sweater for the first time since leaving home. Elated by my interview with *Khenpo* Tenzin Sangpo I bought a bottle of wine, a generic export from Australia. At 2,250 Nepali rupees, more than $25, it was appallingly overpriced but likely the last time I'd taste wine for the next month.

Raj had a glass with me then headed to the guides' lounge. Alone again, I sipped wine in the glow of my tiny travel candle.

Gateway to Upper Mustang.

Barry and I had been apart for a month, the longest time ever in our relationship. I felt sad for both of us. His latest email had seemed cheerful enough. He reported keeping busy with swimming, mountain cycling and even piano lessons. But he also said it was doubtful he would ever return to Nepal again. What did that mean? Would this be my last chance to trek in the Himalaya? A lump stuck in my throat. What was I was trying to escape? Being responsible for others? Putting myself second? Always being at the end of the line, trying to keep up?

I felt his presence. I hoped on the other side of the world he could feel mine.

How would things be between us when I got home?

CHAPTER 11
MERO SATHI, MY FRIEND

Early the next morning Raj and I ambled somberly through the sleepy streets of Kagbeni. Opposite the Applebee's Café we ascended stone steps to the Annapurna Conservation Area office, the checkpoint for Upper Mustang trekkers. Resham and Tika sat down to wait. A single trekker, I was still worried about being allowed past the checkpoint. Permits were only issued to groups of two or more. And, the usual time limit for the visit was two weeks. My plan was to stay for a month.

Since reading anthropologist Michel Peissel's book *Mustang: Lost Tibetan Kingdom*, I had been fascinated by the vast rugged terrain and unspoiled Buddhist culture of the area. My idea was to travel at a leisurely pace, mornings only, leaving the afternoon for exploration of villages and interviews with locals. The distance from Jomson to Lo-Manthang was only forty-nine kilometers but I knew from our past visit it could seem far longer because of the rocky up and down "*ukalo, oralo*" trails, altitude over high passes, unrelenting winds, and high-altitude sun. Leaving the forests of Jomson behind, we would be approaching the sparse vegetation of the edge of the Tibetan Plateau. This vast, elevated area lying in Nepal and in the Tibet Autonomous region of China was sometimes called the Roof of the World. It stretched mostly across Central and East Asia, but some parts continued south into Upper Mustang.

Every step toward this authentic stronghold of Tibetan culture was worth it. Mustang is one of seventy-five districts of Nepal. Located in the northeast of the country, its territory spreads over eighty kilometers from north to south and forty-five kilometers at its greatest width. Much of Upper Mustang's history is based on legend rather than documented facts. Though the people of Upper Mustang—the northern third of the Mustang area—live within the geographical boundaries of Nepal, their history is closely tied to Tibetan religion, culture, geography, and politics. Originally referred to as Lo, it was incorporated into the Tibetan empire by Songsten Gampo, the most famous Tibetan king. Because of its strategic position, from the fifteenth to the seventeenth century Mustang had control over the salt trade between India and the Himalayas. In 1380, Upper Mustang became an independent kingdom under warrior Ame Pal, who oversaw much of the building of Lo and the capital city Lo-Manthang.

The walled city has changed surprisingly little. Prior to the introduction of tourism in 1992, Upper Mustang's relative isolation made it one of the most preserved areas of the world. The majority of the population still speaks traditional Tibetan languages.

Until 2008 the Kingdom of Lo (now Upper Mustang) was an ethnic Tibetan kingdom and suzerainty, a technically independent kingdom, part of the Kingdom of Nepal. In 2008 the monarchy of Nepal was overthrown by civil war, and Nepal became a republic. Mustang became a district of Nepal, losing its status as tributary kingdom. Jigme Dorje Palbar Bista, king of Upper Mustang, the twenty-fifth generation descendent of Ame Pal, was reduced to the level of Raja. We'd met the king briefly on our last trip. I hoped to meet him again.

Raj and I wandered around the checkpoint office. A huge photo of the Kali Gandaki river valley covered the back wall. I longed to get trekking directly into that mesmerizing view. From its source near the Tibetan border, the Kali Gandaki flows south through a sheer-sided and deep canyon south of Lo-Manthang then widens as it approaches Kagbeni. It continues on to Jomson and beyond. We would follow the river much of our way north.

"What are you going to tell him?" I whispered to Raj. "Prem did tell them I am a journalist and need a special permit, didn't he?"

"Give me your passport. Leave it to me. Don't say anything."

A rather sour looking official presided. Raj handed him my passport and proceeded to tell him a long story, in Nepali, from time to time gesturing in my direction. Keeping my expression neutral, serious but innocent, I explored the displays. I spotted a

Raj signing us in at the checkpoint.

printout of statistics reporting the number of travelers admitted to Upper Mustang during the past year.

The official limit for tourists to the restricted area was 1,000 per year. The sheet on the wall showed 3,443 tourists visited last year, the largest groups from Australia, Russia, France, Germany, and Switzerland. That number counted only foreign visitors. It didn't mention guides, porters, and kitchen staff with ponies that carried the gear of those camping and cooking. Some rules were strictly followed. Campers were required to produce a list of supplies, equipment, and fuel; wood was scarce in Upper Mustang. Campers must be self-sufficient and carry out all of their garbage.

Other rules, like the number of permits issued, were neglected. No wonder the locals were becoming jaded.

Raj called me forward to sign the book. Fingers trembling, I signed.

"Okay. Let's go."

We scurried down the stone steps in silence. Once out of earshot I asked, "What did you tell him?"

"I said your husband has a stomach bug and needs to stay in Kagbeni to rest for a few days and will catch us up later."

"Do you think he believed you?"

"Probably not. But they don't care as long as you pay."

One of the things I hoped to discover was where the money collected at this checkpoint was going. Did the locals ever see any of it? Was it only hotel and restaurant owners who benefitted from this massive increase in tourism?

Sienna Craig, anthropologist and author of *Horses Like Lightning, A Story of Passage Through the Himalaya* and a regular visitor to Upper Mustang since 1993, wrote that from 1992—when the area officially opened for tourism—to 2008, tourists paid seventy dollars a day, for a minimum of ten days, for the privilege of visiting the area. By 2008 the fee had dropped to fifty dollars a day.

After nearly two decades the government's promise to remit sixty per cent of royalties for local community development projects remained unfulfilled. Since 1992, more than fifteen thousand tourists have visited Upper Mustang, generating more than seven point eight million US dollars in revenue. Little was returned to Upper Mustang.

Packs shouldered, we passed the barrier and descended down a rocky trail into the wide expanse of dry riverbed. Raj explained that Prem had purchased two permits, one for me and one for my absent husband. The second would allow me to stay the additional two weeks. Would one more indiscretion be noticed? I'd hired three Nepalis and paid the full amount for two permits. Would that help quell my guilt and angst?

Villages along the rubbly trekkers' route north to Chhusang appeared relatively unchanged since my last visit. We passed the red, white and black *chortens* on the approach to Tangbe, a Gurung village, our halfway point for the day. Women and children stood up from their backbreaking fieldwork to look at us. Smiles stretched across their faces when I waved and called out "Namaste" and "*Tashi delek*" (good day). Only a few kilometers north their response was much warmer than those offered by the tourism-weary inhabitants of Kagbeni. "The villages have changed," said Raj. "Many lodges have new rooms, cleaner dining rooms and even Wi-Fi."

Wi-Fi? How reliable was the Wi-Fi likely to be? It must be solar. We had passed workers erecting poles and stringing electrical wires yesterday. They weren't moving too quickly. It would be a while before electricity reached Lo-Manthang.

Neophyte visitors, Resham and Tika continually paused to pick up and examine pebbles and rocks. They were in awe of the increasingly barren landscape. The prevailing ochre and beige hues provided a stark contrast to the fields of barley we had left behind in Kagbeni.

Towering red sandstone pillars soared over seas of burnished scarlet rocks. Ten-meter-tall spires of pebbles dwarfed low mounds of delicate black flinty spikes. Gray pebbles and smooth brown stones haphazardly rested alongside Volkswagen-sized boulders.

As our morning unfolded, I reminded myself to keep my pace to a relaxed ramble; bistari, bistari (slowly, slowly). Today's interior pep talk: Stop feeling lonely and sorry for yourself. Definitely stop wasting rupees on overpriced wine. But don't waste the burgundy elixir still sloshing around in your water bottle. Enjoy what you can before reaching higher altitude.

The single trail expanded to the width of the roughly completed road. It led directly to Lo-Manthang and the current main tourist draw, the Buddhist Tiji festival. The original name of the festival, Tempa Chirin, tells of the hope that the Buddha's teachings will prevail in all places and among all people of the world; the three-day festival is considered a harbinger of hope and peace.

Other trekkers passed. I eavesdropped on conversations in French, Italian, Russian, and broad Australian English. I recited the motto learned from a ninety-five-year-old cross-country skier I once knew: "Stay positive and keep moving, baby." The relentless high-altitude sun rapidly scorched the thin skin on the backs of my hands. My pack straps dug into my shoulders. The highest pass this morning had been just over 3,000 meters, the altitude at which headaches often started for me.

By early afternoon we had reached our overnight stop at Bhirkuti Guest House, Restaurant and Camping in Chhusang Village, a shady desert oasis cooled by apple orchards. While waiting for my room to be ready in the newly constructed wing I sat and opened my sketchbook. Under a grove of weeping willows near the Buddhist chorten marking the north entrance of town, local women and children gathered round to watch. A toddler in squeaky running shoes plopped herself down beside me. I handed her a new toothbrush. She examined it carefully, still in its clear plastic sleeve. In pantomime I asked the women for permission to take photos. They nodded, then erupted in giggles when I showed them their images and those of their children.

Five men riding handsome steeds Upper Mustang is famous for raced by, their horses' hooves clattering like thunder on the flagstone street. Heads swathed in scarves topped with Western ball caps, they blasted northward across the solid parched riverbed into the full brunt of the afternoon winds. They would reach Samar, over the next two high passes, in much less time than it would take us to walk there the following day.

My room had two single beds with a small wooden table between. A faded blue flowered curtain partially shaded the room from the late afternoon glare. A dusting of fine sand whistled through slits between the window frame and cement wall. I propped my boots and wool socks against the wall outside my room to dry in the sun, then slipped into the tiled bathroom next to my room. Raj had chosen carefully. He knew I often had to get up to pee in the night.

At happy hour Raj met me in the dining room with a freshly popped bowl of popcorn and a 400-rupee (about $5) Lhasa beer to share. He'd forgotten I still had half a water bottle of leftover wine. I said nothing. No need to worry him with unimportant details.

"Tomorrow will be a hard day," he told me. "Samar is just below 3,600 meters. Two high passes and lots of climbing." He paused to take a sip. "Enjoy the cold beer while you can. No more electricity after tomorrow."

Sliding his chair back along the linoleum floor he stood, picked up his glass, and disappeared down the stairs into the guides' room to watch one last match of the India Premier League cricket match on TV with the guys.

After dinner I met the hotelier, Urken Lama Gurung. He spoke Nepali, the local *Lhoba* language, Tibetan, and a smattering of English. When he learned I was a journalist, the diminutive Nepali offered me the unusual backpacker privilege of an invitation into the family kitchen. Raj came with me.

Urken smiled, said hello and patted the bench beside him. In a flurry of Nepali, Raj explained I would like to ask a few questions about changes tourism had brought to his life.

Before 1992 the area was virtually off limits to outsiders. There were two notable exceptions. Swiss explorer Toni Hagan dropped by in 1952 during one of his journeys across the Himalaya. French ethnologist, author, and explorer Michel Peissel became the first

Patti with Urken at Bhirkuti Lodge.

European to be granted an extended stay in Lo-Manthang, in 1964. Peissel, who spoke Tibetan, became close friends with many inhabitants, and my reading of his adventures had inspired me to try to get to know some of the locals.

Urken and I sat cross-legged, knee-to-knee in front of a white coffee table where he had placed his cell phone. Behind us a glass-fronted cabinet contained plastic containers of Eveready batteries, a jug of Aunt Jemima Maple Syrup, rolls of coconut biscuits wrapped in yellow plastic, jars of peanut butter, and Nescafé instant coffee. A shrewd businessman, Urken stocked what many backpackers considered necessities. He made them available at his own inflated prices.

His deeply lined, wind-leathered face glowed with grandfatherly kindness. Born in Chhusang, Urken had spent most of his fifty-nine years in his home village except for occasional trips to Kathmandu. Circumstances changed for Urken—once a subsistence farmer—and his family when Upper Mustang welcomed foreigners. "I built the lodge twenty years ago," said the hotel titan. "More tourists come every year. I earn good money. Grow better crops. Three hundred fifty people live in Chhusang. The Nepali government school, thirty-five students. Goes to Grade 7. Paid for by villagers. All my children gone there. Learn only Nepali and English. With money from lodge I send to schools in Kathmandu and Pokhara after Grade 7."

There it was again: Only those who could afford extras could give their kids a superior education.

I asked if he noticed any negative effects of tourism. "Nothing. No bad effects from tourists coming." He held up his right hand and touched his index finger to his thumb, forming a zero. "And now, road. We send garden produce to Pokhara on somebody's truck. That cheaper way than porters or donkeys." The journey from the northernmost capital city of Lo-Manthang to Pokhara, cities separated by the Himalayan Range— a distance of a mere

112 kilometers—once took thirteen days by horseback.

"ACAP [Annapurna Conservation Area Project] sent solar panels twenty years ago," he said. "Ten years ago I bought TV in Kathmandu. I get seventy-two channels, mostly from India." He gestured to the thirty-inch TV at the other end of the room. Raj perked up, hoping to catch more of the IPL cricket finals later. "We got electricity six years ago."

Urken's cell phone rang. He picked it up and turned away.

I exchanged a smile with Urken's mother-in-law. Dressed in traditional Tibetan *chuba*, a long dress decorated with a colorful, hand-woven striped apron, she hummed contentedly as she scoured greasy tin plates and milky coffee mugs left from backpackers' dinners. What did she think of me, a woman travelling alone, dressed in grubby hiking pants, white hair cropped short and boyish, so unlike her long dark silken braids? She must have had as many questions about me as I did of her. If only we could have had a frank, unfiltered conversation. I loved Raj, but this was another time I longed for a female translator.

Urken rambled on, making deals for more cases of peanut butter, Nescafé and coconut biscuits. He stayed silent for a few moments then put the phone down and turned back to me, picking up where he had left off. "But, children forgetting traditional songs. Western dress now usual. They losing traditional culture. Only my mother-in-law," he said, glancing toward the smiling matron, "remembers old songs and dances. When the children home from school we follow Buddhist rituals and practices. We have *tsampa* and butter tea at seven a.m., lunch at ten a.m., more tea at noon, a meal at three p.m., then dinner at seven p.m. with more butter tea. Later, adults drink *rakshi* we ferment from millet. No Everest beer. No sugar. Very healthy."

His mention of *rakshi* reminded me, alcohol and altitude don't mix; I had better finish that wine tonight. Prem always advised trekkers headed for altitudes over 3,500 meters, "No beer on the way up. Beer on the way down." I had looked into it, and learned the presence of alcohol in the blood interferes with the normal use of oxygen by the tissues. It's called histotoxic hypoxia. Because of reduced pressure at high altitudes and the reduced ability of the hemoglobin to absorb oxygen, the effect of alcohol in the blood is much more pronounced than at sea level. Not a good thing when climbing in oxygen thin air.

The next few days would be my first go at trekking alone at altitude. I had no desire to succumb to the debilitating headache, lack of appetite, and nausea I had experienced at an altitude of 3,500 meters in Manang on the Annapurna Circuit, and I wanted to avoid taking Diamox as I had for three days on that trip. The remainder of our time in Upper Mustang would be at an average of more than 3,500 meters in altitude, often trekking over 4,500 meter passes. It was serious business.

I'd been to the Travel Medicine Clinic in Vernon before the trip. All my shots were updated. I had taken a pre-trip booster dose of Dukoral, the drinkable vaccine to protect against diarrhea. My small drug kit included Imodium (anti-diarrhea medication, in case the Dukoral wasn't one hundred per cent effective), a dental kit for gluing on displaced dental crowns, and Diamox. I didn't like taking medication, though, and hoped I wouldn't need any.

I returned my attention to the gracious man beside me. "My grandfather followed traditional ways. He was bigger, healthier," said Urken, straightening his back, sitting a bit taller. "We used grinding stone to make *tsampa* barley flour. Now we use electric mill. It makes flour hot," he said, wrinkling his nose. "Doesn't smell good. Goes bad too quick. Must use right away. Now we follow more Western schedule. Breakfast at seven a.m., lunch at noon and dinner at seven p.m. And eat more sugar. Not healthy."

"So, what help do you receive from the government?" I asked. "How much of the extra money each tourist is now charged for a ten-day visit do the lodge and restaurant owners, like you, and other locals receive?"

"No permit money comes to us," he said, his tone guarded yet resentful. "Money goes to district office in Jomson, and then, I think, goes to Lower Mustang."

Our interview completed, I stood and shook his hand. As I headed upstairs to bed he called out, "*Tapai mero sathi.*"

"What did he say?" I asked Raj

"He said you are now his friend. "*Dhanyabad*," I called, waving back. "You, too." Two successful interviews down. I had stories to tell about *khenpo* in Kagbeni and Urken in Chhusang. Maybe I could make this travel writing thing work after all.

More stories lay ahead. So did a dramatic increase in altitude.

CHAPTER 12
REACHING NEW HEIGHTS

T he next morning I sat with my face hovering over a bowl
of oatmeal, steaming enough to provide a desperately
needed facial. I sipped Nepali milk coffee, down jacket
zipped to my chin. I hated eating early. Though fully aware of
the energy needed for the day ahead, it took as much courage to
eat porridge this early as it would to tackle the two high passes
of today's route.

Our daily trekking schedule followed a mix of Western and
Nepali style. We rolled out of sleeping bags at 5:45 a.m., stuffed
the puffy bags into compression sacks, splashed water on our
faces, dressed and tried to appear presentable. The latter became
an increasing challenge as we headed north into the wind, dust,
and single tap towns. For me, two cups of Nepali sweet milk,
dudh, coffee and journal writing at 6:15 a.m., a bowl of muesli
with powdered milk at six-thirty, teeth brushed by six-fifty and
hit the trail by seven.

We trekked rubbly roads and trails, past treeless arid vistas,
resting on the pebbly ground to gulp water and munch melted,
misshapen Twix bars every couple of hours. By early afternoon
we escaped the roaring winds in the guesthouse destination for
the night. After lunch I ventured out to meet locals. Our schedule

being more leisurely than that of most trekkers allowed time to visit schools, meet children, and talk to entrepreneurs like Urken. In the evening, after our usual happy hour of popcorn and beer (replaced by lemon ginger tea at higher altitude) I ate alone, recorded interview notes, and then cocooned in my sleeping bag to read eBooks. I had no firm plan for all my notes, just wanted to make sure I had lots of information for article topics. The guys retired to the guides' quarters, often a communal room with mattresses on the floor. They ate *dal bhat* every night, played cards, and phoned their wives. Periodically Raj phoned Prem to report our progress.

Today began with a stroll along a pebbly path edging the Kali Gandaki River. Raj led the way, head down. "Looking for something?"

"*Saligrams*," he said. "Seashell stone fossils. They're in round black stones. You have to break them open to see the design. This is the only place in the world to find them."

"How did seashells get to 3,000 meters?"

Always happy to teach me more about his home country, he reminded me the Himalaya was formed when the Indian plate collided with Asia. The mountain ranges on either side of the river valley, Dhaulagiri and Annapurna, were more than eight kilometers high, making the Kali Gandaki one of the deepest valleys in the world.

"Are they easy to find?"

"Probably not," he said. "But I've always wanted one. They're important to my religion. Each stone is a manifestation of the Hindu god Vishnu."

We wandered ahead for a while, each of us scanning the riverbed.

"Got one."

"OMLB," I said, using the phrase "oh my lord Buddha" I had invented to replace the overused OMG. "You have not." I laughed.

We gathered round to look. There it was. The imprint of a seashell was evident in the black rock cradled in his palm.

Two hours later we came to a place where the river veered sharply right. Rapids disappeared into a weathered hole in the red sandstone. Rows of openings, said to be ancient cave dwellings hovered high on the cliffs. Straight ahead, across a steel footbridge, past the flat delta formed by river floods the trail zigzagged up almost vertical switchbacks toward the village of Chele.

Sensing trekkers might be intimidated by this abrupt change in the route, an entrepreneurial family had set up a makeshift restaurant in a grey nylon tent. Reminiscent of astronauts gathering on a monochrome lunar landscape, a multicultural mélange of clientele milled around, hungry for tea and biscuits.

Sitting on a boulder at the base of the hill we watched, sipped water, and ate cookies. Once refueled, we forged up the slippery scree trail. We faced a rapid elevation gain of almost 600 meters from the river to the first of the high passes, Taklam La. A steep descent would follow. After that we would face another sudden ascent to Dajori La. At more than 3,700 meters it was even higher than Taklam La. We had to top both before we reached Samar, our destination for the day.

———— * ————

The ramble along the riverbed had been easy. The steep climb to Chele heralded a wakeup call. The route up to the first pass, Taklam La, opened a floodgate of memories. Carved out of peach toned sandstone, it wound its way up the edge of a steep grade. On the left, a sheer drop. On the right, a wall of rock curved back over our heads. Thigh-high rock steps challenged me at every turn, followed by short, less-steep sections of slippery pebbles.

How would I ever manage the huge downhill steps on the way out? Was this the spot where I had dreamt of being squashed against the rock by an overloaded yak?

But I'd hiked this trail three years before. I could do it again. Each time we approached a blind right turn I expected to see prayer flags that would signal the top of the pass. Time after time I was faced with another series of giant steps.

At several points rockslides had destroyed the trail. At these spots the path narrowed to a width of less than a foot, shored up by carefully placed rocks covered with precariously placed, unfixed planks.

The tinkling of bells and the shrill whistle of a pony driver jolted my senses. "Ponies," shouted Raj. "Go to the high side." Frantically I searched for the widest bit of trail and plastered myself against the overhanging wall to avoid a downhill line of twenty ponies. Laden with bulky packs, they picked their way down the treacherous trail, hooves clicking on rock.

While waiting for the parade to pass I noticed long suspension bridge leading to village high on the hill on the opposite side of the river valley. A long, blue-roofed stone building stood on the outskirts of the village. I asked Raj what it was. "A village school. Built by the Japanese." The image of a new school in Aprik Village popped into my head. If I had the stamina and determination to make it up and down this trail a second time at my age, maybe, just maybe, I could fundraise enough to build a village school, too.

Distracted by daydreams of fundraising dinners, I found the next high pass less daunting than expected. The distant view of strings of fading prayer flags, flapping in the constant winds, helped explain a bit about the route ahead. From them I could discern whether the trail would be up or down, and predict about how many hours it might take to get to the highest point. It's a control thing. For me, the worst thing was to reach what seemed to be a high point only to arrive and find out it was a false summit with more vertical to gain. Prayer flags are strung from posts above rock cairns at the highest point in the trail over each pass; if I can't see the prayer flags, I'm not at the top. And when all else failed I held on to actor Dev Patel's comforting words of wisdom from *The Best Exotic Marigold Hotel*, "Everything will be all right in the end. And, if it isn't all right, it's not yet the end."

We reached Samar four hours later. I inhaled a bowl of veggie chili with rice, then gulped down a mug of lemon tea with slivers of fresh ginger. Maybe it was the altitude, the fact I'm no longer a kid, or four hours of *ukalo, oralo*; no one needed to persuade me to have a nap. I woke up half an hour later and ventured out alone.

The deeper we travelled into Upper Mustang, the more Tibetan the culture. The narrow flagstone trail through the center of Samar first passed a rough eight-foot-high stone wall, a *medong*, both sides adorned with flat *mani* stones carved with the traditional Buddhist message *Om Mani Padme Hum* (Hail to the Jewel in the Lotus). A second wall housing thirty randomly dented copper prayer wheels gleamed in the morning sun. Both walls were painted with vertical stripes of white, grey and dark red to signify Sakyapa, the red hat school of Tibetan Buddhism.

Prayer wheels still spinning from my touch I stepped gingerly around two black horned bovines, carefully avoiding the trickling stream of urine. White-washed vertical walls of the Tibetan houses towered above me. Livestock, fodder and salt took up the ground floor, allowing heat to rise to warm the house above. Balconies across the front of second floor living quarters displayed riots of cheerful red geraniums planted in rusting tin cans, plastic tubs, and discarded boots. Vertical poles dressed with *Dar Cho*, house prayer flags, reached skyward from the four corners of every roof. Between them, rows of firewood lay along roof edges, ready for the winter.

The switch from the rectangular shrines to the Hindu god Shiva to the rounded Buddhist memorials indicated our arrival into a predominantly Buddhist area. In the middle of the widening trail I passed a row of three white dome-shaped Buddhist *chortens*, monuments to lamas. In deference to the possibility of the relics of monks buried inside I kept them on the right, respecting the traditional clockwise walking direction. The scent of juniper smoke drew me to a small orange fireplace on the side of the hill beside a rectangular tower. A shimmer of gold flashed from the dark interior. Inside I found a giant red prayer wheel three times my height, circled with rows of raised Sanskrit letters and gold embossed Buddhist designs.

Homes in the village seemed deserted with no children in sight. There was no school in this village. Some children attended school in Chhusang but few families could afford to pay room and board for their children there. And the Chhusang school was a government school; all lessons were taught in Nepali. If parents wanted their children to learn the local *Lhoba* language or Tibetan, extra teachers had to be paid by villagers.

The need for foreign aid was endless. My thoughts returned to Aprik, the village that had for some reason chosen me. Maybe I could find a way to raise awareness and funds to support an entire village of kids.

———— · ————

The next morning we left Samar by way of the northern village gate and descended a steep pebbly path to the river and back up the other side for the long, gradual climb to the first of four passes on the agenda for the day. To quell my growing apprehension about the increasing altitude, I counted steps. For thirty steps I stared at my dusty boots, then stopped and looked up, trying to sight prayer flags. Seeing none, I would gaze back down and start counting again.

To amuse myself I tried to discern the different prints in the dust of the trail. With concentrated observation I learned to tell the difference between marks made by mules and horses. Goats were easy. Then I noticed the tread patterns made by the soles of trekkers' boots, the running shoes of the porters or the flat footfall indentations of flip-flops. And, finally I could discriminate among the v-shaped scratches of various birds. When the hikers' trail matched the route of the road all prints were obliterated by the lines of mountain bikes, motorcycles, four-wheel drives and trucks.

I tried everything to mask the weighty indentations of my pack straps. Twenty or so pounds didn't seem like much, but as the day wore on it was enough. Because of altitude and possible changes in mountain weather even basics like a sunhat and another for warmth, wind buff, mitts, rain jacket and pants, down jacket, camera, journal, Band-Aids, headlamp, spare batteries, and first aid kit all had to be with me. My memory of the day in the 80s when I completed the Black Hills Half Ironman Triathlon in Washington State came to mind. What got me through that race was a lesson learned from Dave Scott, the six-time champion of the Hawaii Ironman Triathlon in that same era. "When you're tired mid-race, concentrate on what you have accomplished so far, how far you have already come, instead of worrying about what lies ahead."

However, there was no forgetting the weight of the real culprit, the two full liters of drinking water required every day. Sweat evaporates quickly in high, dry mountain air. The lower oxygen levels also cause us to breathe faster and more deeply, so more water is lost through respiration. High altitude can also make you need to urinate more often and can blunt your thirst response, putting you at even greater risk of dehydration. Not only is dehydration risky on its own, but it can mask or worsen the symptoms of altitude sickness.

I stumbled ahead in a meditative state, mesmerized by the grandeur of the vast moonscape. When we saw prayer flags, we celebrated. At the top of each pass each of us grabbed a stone. We took turns chucking the stone as high as possible on the

Raj, Tika and Resham resting at the top of a pass.

cairn of rocks anchoring the pole that marked the pinnacle. I'd heave my pack in the dust and collapse. Water first, then mini-chocolate bars all around. I'd dole out the individually wrapped blobs that had melted weeks before in Ratmate.

After that we inevitably dispersed in four different directions in search of the best boulder or scrubby juniper bush to pee behind. Raj and Resham would seek out the high places with the best phone reception to call their brides. In only a few days we would be beyond cell reception. Barry seemed farther away than ever in this captivating wasteland. I hoped to send him an email from Lo-Manthang if the solar powered computers in the community library still existed.

"How many hours until the next pass? And how many until lunch?"

"About two hours, Patti Maam. *Ukalo, oralo.*"

Bhena La, Beg La, Yamda La and Syanboche La, four high passes, each measuring more than 3,800 meters. We knocked them all off before lunch at Syanboche.

"The afternoon walk to Ghilling is easy," said Raj "Quite flat."

"English flat or Nepali flat?" Trekking tourists in Nepal rapidly discovered that Nepali flat meant more up and down than flat. After Namaste, *dhanyabad* (thank you) and *bistari, bistari* (slowly, slowly) the next words new trekkers learned were *ukalo, oralo*.

True to his word, Raj guided us along the flat and gradual downhill of the trail, still challenging because of relentless winds. We rolled in to the New Kung Hotel in Ghilling at about 4:00 p.m., ending the day at a slightly lower elevation than where we had started.

In the common area hallway I found Jelmer, a mountain biker from the Netherlands, slouched on one of the carpeted benches. We had swapped travel stories in Samar a few days earlier. This was his second time in Nepal. In 2008 an extensive cycling trip through Thailand, Cambodia, Vietnam and India had ended in Nepal, and ended badly. He had aborted the trip because of altitude sickness. Diamox hadn't worked for him. He had headaches, nausea, and a lack of appetite.

Altitude affects people differently no matter their age, fitness or general health, and it can affect the same person differently each time. Except for my one three-day bout on the Annapurna Circuit I'd been lucky so far. Drolma La, the 5,670 meter pass on the three-day Mount Kailash circumambulation, or *kora*, in Tibet, had caused me no problem, due to our cautious ascent, gaining altitude slowly on the road trip west from Lhasa. Now, thanks to our mainly half-day walking schedule, my body was having no trouble acclimatizing.

Six years after his first bad experience, Jelmer had considered a second excursion to altitude, this time to Tibet. "But the Chinese wouldn't allow me to cycle from Kathmandu to Lhasa alone. You must have a guide. It was too expensive for me." Thirty-one, tall and tanned, with a mop of curly blond hair, he looked fresh out of college. "I wanted to experience Tibetan culture. I couldn't go to Tibet so I came here."

"Who are you travelling with?"

"I'm alone."

"How did you get past the checkpoint?"

"I paid a mountain bike guide to take me through and show me the beginning of the way until we were out of sight of the checkpoint. He snuck back to Kagbeni. The first day was rough. He gave me bad directions. I had to cross a couple of sections of the river in waist deep water. I still feel cold."

The lure of one of the highest roads in the world seemed the draw for him. Apparently he didn't realize exactly how high it was. In Samar he had looked fit and healthy. Now his skin was an alarming gray. His eyes sunk above hollow cheekbones.

As afternoon tea morphed into dinner, Jelmer lounged in the corner, his head propped against the wall.

"Try some lemon ginger tea," I said. "It may help you feel better. How much water have you been drinking?"

"I'm trying for two liters a day but it makes me pee a lot."

"That's good. It helps get rid of the excess fluid."

He leaned forward and almost in a whisper said, "My pee is milky white." I began to get worried. Milky pee can signal a urinary tract infection or dehydration.

I knew from past experience how rapidly a body could succumb to altitude sickness. In 2009, two days after completing the three-day *kora* around sacred Mount Kailash in Western Tibet one of the group Barry and I were travelling with had became drowsy, nauseous and confused. Our guide had sent him back to Lhasa by car. Despite the non-stop day and night drive to reach the hospital the sixty-three-year-old fell into a coma. A day later he died of altitude sickness; pulmonary and cerebral edema, the abnormal accumulation of fluids in his lungs and brain.

As I went to the kitchen to order the tea, two European women joined us. Their high tech Gor Tex clothing, full shank climbing boots and ice axes hinted at serious mountaineering. The faded tricolor flag of green, white and red sewn onto the worn backpack of the taller woman told me they were Italian. Grey streaks in her brown hair led me to guess the age of the first at somewhere north of forty. The other appeared less seasoned, probably in her early thirties. When I returned with the tea they were engaged in deep conversation with Jelmer.

"Have you taken any Diamox?" asked the more petite woman, an expression of concern creasing her forehead.

"Yes," he said, stretching out his large hands and wiggling his slender fingers. "But now my fingers are tingling."

"That's not unusual with Diamox. Maybe drink more tea and more water," said the taller woman. "Do you have enough clean water?"

"Yes, I guess," he said, indicating a half-full Nalgene bottle.

"When did you last eat?"

"Yesterday. I don't have much appetite." I listened in, remembering my nausea and my total lack of appetite in Manang.

"Plain broth and mashed potatoes might be okay."

Jelmer sipped the lemon ginger tea and water. Half an hour later he forced down more tea, some broth and potatoes. Like a bunch of mother hens caring for a lost chick, we escorted him to his room, gave him a full bottle of purified water and closed the door.

"He doesn't look good," said the taller woman.

"And he's by himself. He needs to get to a lower altitude. There's no way he can ride back over those high passes. He told me he doesn't have money to hire a Jeep or insurance to pay for a helicopter."

"Nothing we can do right now. Have to wait until morning.

Even if he did have evacuation insurance a helicopter couldn't land until daylight," said the older woman.

Over dinner the two women shared details of their fifteen-day trek of the challenging, high altitude Dhaulagiri Circuit.

"We've had enough for now. We'll hire a Jeep in the morning to get us back to Jomson."

The distraction of helping Jelmer had made me forget to settle into my room. The good news was that Raj had thoughtfully snagged me a single room on the main floor next to the toilet. That, however, was where the good news ended.

Most nights I couldn't wait to snuggle into my sleeping bag. I don't mind being uncomfortable, but this windowless room—part bedroom, part storage—made monk's cells I'd imagined seem as spacious as the Taj Mahal. One thin bunk lined the side of the room with just enough space to side-step to the end, where sacks of grain were piled against the foot of the bed. The ceiling was fashioned from hand-hewn poles spaced about a foot apart. Rough wood slates haphazardly completed the ceiling above them. I gathered my bag around my head and zipped it, allowing just a slit for my eyes and a breathing hole. I vowed to keep my mouth closed. I fell asleep counting the number of insects dropping out of the ceiling.

The next morning I shook off the insects and packed and left the room as quickly as possible. The Italian women were in the dining room.

"How's Jelmer?"

"I'm going to check right now," said the older one.

It heartened me to witness how strangers, trekkers far from home could take care of each other. "He isn't any better," she said, when she returned. "Maybe worse. We'll take him with us in the Jeep. There's room for him and his bike."

Raj came in to go over the plan for the day. "How was your sleep?"

"Don't ask. All I can say is, thank goodness for Italians. How many hours to Ghami?"

Thankful for Raj's guidance, wise pacing, and friendship, I was happy to be heading north on foot, not suffering from altitude sickness and heading south in a Jeep.

CHAPTER 13
THE GREATEST
LIBRARY OF LO

Raj had promised the first ninety minutes of the trek to Ghami village would be English flat—truly flat. However, what Raj had failed to highlight in his evening briefing was the 500-meter elevation gain to follow. The steep trail we would climb to Nya La reached 4,010 meters, making it the highest pass of the entire trip.

The lush green barley fields of Ghilling gave way to glorious desolation, the semi-arid Himalayan climate that defined Upper Mustang. The Dhaulagiri and Annapurna Mountain ranges blocked the passage of rain producing weather, casting a shadow of eternal dryness. Musings about Jelmer were replaced by another pressing concern: the debilitating high-altitude sun. My head soon dampened with sweat and, despite the practical sun-shading fabric of my sensible wide-brimmed hat, my cheeks were rosy from overheating.

Not wearing a hat in Ratmate had been unwise; my nose, lips and forehead still felt aggravated, downright angry. Even with daily doses of SPF 40 sunscreen, trekking at high altitudes exacerbated the situation. The higher the altitude, the quicker sunburn happened. "I've got to stop," I said, under siege of heat-induced frustration. "Too hot."

I felt like a well-roasted turkey: hot and juicy on the inside, crispy on the outside, as if trapped in a parabolic solar cooker like the ones in the courtyards of Kagbeni. When the rim of my water bottle lightly grazed the widening fissure in my bottom lip, my shoulders stiffened with pain. The backs of my hands shone as pink as steamed lobster.

Deep in my pack I found my sunglasses. *Visions of Mustang*, a video I'd seen at the Banff Mountain Film Festival, haunted me. Due to sun exposure at altitude the people of Upper Mustang had the highest rate of cataracts in the world. The documentary recounted the journey of eye doctors from the USA's Dooley Foundation who collaborated with doctors from the Himalayan Eye Hospital to perform free cataract surgeries in Upper Mustang. One scene, where an elderly woman sees her grandson for the first time, had stayed with me.

Sunglasses perched amidst the scabby peeling skin of my nose, I swallowed a few sips of water. I tied my turquoise cotton handkerchief to the front strap of my pack, ready to wipe salty moisture from my face. I turned the collar of my shirt up to protect the back of my neck, rolled down my shirtsleeves, and pulled on my fingerless rag wool gloves.

One sweltering hour later we reached the base of the climb to Nya La. Thirty minutes more, my spirit of perseverance reinforced by murmured mantras, we arrived at the summit. I slumped against the rock cairn at the base of the prayer flag standard. "That was a tough one," I said, lungs raspy from the effort. "This is the altitude where I start getting headaches."

"Don't worry. It's all downhill from here," said Raj.

"Right," I said with a smirk. I was fully aware we had two more days of *ukalo, oralo* ahead of us, with a couple of spots close to our present altitude before reaching Lo-Manthang.

"Just decide you're not going to get a headache and you won't," he added.

"Right." Secretly I remained skeptical.

The roar of a four-wheel drive engine straining to gain the height of the pass disrupted the serenity. A white Toyota Land Cruiser skidded to a dusty halt several meters from us. A stocky woman, in her sixth or seventh decade, stepped out. Loose gravel crunched under her brown, perfectly polished hiking boots. Silver hair spiked above her tanned, squared, weathered face. Beige cropped pants stopped high above her boots to reveal socks as white as the snow on the surrounding peaks. She marched around, taking long, confident strides, hands on hips, the sleeves of her red and white checked shirt pushed up to the elbows. Her tall, middle-aged Nepali guide followed several paces behind.

Patti at the summit of Nya La.

Great. Another rich tourist. Stops for three minutes and later brags she's done Nya La Pass.

She ran one hand through her hair and walked in the other direction. As if crossing at a busy intersection, she gazed down both sides of the pass, directed exclamations accompanied by bold, sweeping arm gestures to her guide, presumably about the grandeur of the Annapurna range, then lumbered back into the vehicle.

"When was the road finished?"

"Last year."

"It was quieter before," I grumbled. "Now anyone with enough money to hire a four wheel drive can get up here."

A trekking snob, my intention was to blend in with local culture. That meant consuming *dal bhat*, lentil soup with rice, and veggie curry; doing my own laundry in local creeks; and, above all, walking every meter of the route. I hoped to gain respect and trust from locals. I wanted them to be at ease with me, comfortable enough to give their honest opinions on how the road and tourism were affecting their culture and their homeland.

The Land Cruiser disappeared down the parched road. She would reach Lo-Manthang that evening. We would walk for two more dusty days.

Well before noon we reached Ghami, our endpoint for the day. We made a right turn down a shady alley to the fortress style edifice known as the Royal Mustang Hotel. Built more than one hundred years before, the whitewashed three-storey house in the heart of the village was the home of Thari Bista, niece of the king of Upper Mustang, and her husband Lopsang Chhompel Bista, known as Raju.

The ground-level cement courtyard entrance to the hotel also served as the kitchen. Three women bent over low concrete sinks washing recently harvested wild greens. I dropped my pack on the third floor beside a roof garden with a mesmerizing vista of the Himalaya, and then descended to join the guys for tea.

The palatial dining room whispered understated royalty. Benches draped in plush Tibetan carpets lined three sides of the room. On the fourth wall a magnificent Tibetan cabinet topped with glass-fronted cupboards stretched across the end of the room, dominating the space. Intricately carved gold accents shimmered over the red background; I'd seen similar cabinets in Vancouver's upscale Yaletown design shops priced at $20,000. Photos of the king and queen of Mustang and the Dalai Lama hung side-by-side, draped with *khata*, the filmy white scarves symbolizing purity and compassion in Tibetan Buddhist culture. Raj, Tika and I settled back on velvety cushions. Resham removed his shoes and socks, padded to the center of the room and wiggled his toes in the plush yak wool rug.

I hoped to speak with Raju about the disappearing tourist dollars. As past chairman of the Upper Mustang Youth Society and treasurer of the Lo Gyalpo Jigme Foundation, a non-profit affiliated with the American Himalayan Foundation, he was the most reliable and up-to-date source of information. Thari told us Raju wouldn't be home until dinner time so Raj, Resham and I settled in for a leisurely lunch.

After devouring a plate of freshly prepared *momos*, Tibetan dumplings filled with the spring greens harvested that morning, I decided we had time for Resham to practice his English. Raj and I tried to include him in daily discussions. He longed to be promoted from porter to the better-paying and more prestigious position of trekking guide. He knew proficiency in English was key. That afternoon Raj and I encouraged him to share the story of his marriage and family. A recent newlywed, he had married a girl from a neighboring village. The three of us had already hashed over Nepali marriage customs, the merits of modern love marriages versus traditional arranged marriages. Raj had shared his story of finding Rojina. I was keen to hear what Resham had to say.

"So was yours a love marriage or an arranged marriage?"

His face flushed faintly.

"I saw her at my cousin's wedding. And, she saw me. We knew we liked each other. We asked our parents to arrange it."

"Sounds like it was both arranged and love. Do you have any children?"

"One son." Smile lines creased the corners of his eyes. Then his expression darkened. His tale of his pregnant teen-aged wife, carried on a stretcher down a steep 300-meter pathway from Ratmate to Arughat was frightening. The story became even more terrifying when he explained how the doctor in the local hospital was not equipped to perform a Caesarian. Tears glistened as he described their chilling five-hour Jeep ride over bumpy roads to Kathmandu to find, just in time, a doctor who could perform an emergency Caesarian section. Both mother and baby were saved.

"No more children. One is enough."

I was honored he had shared his story after only knowing me a short while, but that was enough English lesson for one day for all of us. We each claimed a spot on the comfy dining room benches and stretched out for an afternoon snooze.

A few hours later I looked up to see the tall and ruggedly handsome Raju. His height, posture, and broad face signaled his position as a member of the high caste Hill Brahmin Bista clan of Upper Mustang. He welcomed me with the confidence of someone comfortable dealing with Westerners.

"Do you have time to talk to my client about what happens to the tourist permit money?" asked Raj.

"Of course," said Raju, motioning toward a corner bench. "Come sit here." His smile put me at ease. "When the tourists started coming, the Nepal government said sixty per cent of the permit money would go to Upper Mustang. We needed to repair bridges, improve trekking routes and restore monasteries. At first we received twelve per cent of the funds. In 2010, after consultation with Upper Mustang people, we threatened to close the borders until the government lived up to its promise." Raju shifted in his seat with a faraway look of frustration and hopelessness. "We staged protests. I went to the newspapers in Kathmandu to ask them to write articles to pressure the government. Finally, they promised to pay sixty per cent." He heaved the weary sigh of someone fatigued by constant battle with the government. "After a few years it ended up to be about thirty per cent."

"And what about schools?" I asked. More and more I realized how deeply I had been affected by time in Ratmate and my visit to Aprik. My original focus of researching the effects of tourism in Upper Mustang in order to write travel articles was gradually being crowded out by a more personal focus on the discrepancy of educational opportunities. I cared about the effects of tourism and the allocation of trekking permit money, but now, particularly after my conversation with Resham, my emphasis was shifting to how these changes affected education as well as health services.

In his role as treasurer of the king's trust—the Lo Gyalpo Jigme Foundation, an NGO headquartered in Lo-Manthang—Raju had collaborated with the American Himalayan Foundation to improve educational opportunities in Upper Mustang in order to preserve culture and language.

I knew a bit of the Foundation's history; in 1992, American investment banker Richard Blum was one of the earliest outsiders admitted to the once forbidden kingdom. As founder and chairman of the American Himalayan Foundation he worked tirelessly to create daycares in fourteen villages and to supply Tibetan language teachers in Nepali government schools. "He also sent money for us to build a hostel in Chhoser, near the Tibet border, to allow seventy-four students to board there so they could complete high school," said Raju, radiating satisfaction. "Foreigners make donations. The American Himalayan Foundation then gives money to the Jigme Foundation. Before 1992, there were few primary schools and only one high school, up north in Chhoser, too remote for most students."

The American Himalayan Foundation, led by one determined man, had made a huge impact of the lives of the people of Upper Mustang. Blum had demonstrated the powerful influence of an outsider willing to work with consideration and respect to benefit the lives of locals. But what about children in Gorkha? Maybe I could learn from Richard Blum's initiatives.

My conversation with Raju fortified my resolve to become involved in educational reform. The families of Aprik village had chosen me. The call to make a difference was strengthening every day.

———— * ————

The next morning I woke up to the sickly sweet aroma of smoldering juniper drifting from the roof top altar. The pervasive odor wafted freely through the wide crack in the door of my room. Was it the smoke or the altitude? I definitely felt nauseous. Afraid it was the onset of altitude sickness I crept down the ladder-like stairs thinking a cup of hot, sweet Nepali coffee might help. Journal open I scribbled, shivered, and waited for Raj.

Our route turned out to be a perfect combination of cultural enlightenment and physical challenge. Leaving Ghami we passed a magnificent tribute to Buddhist culture: a *mani* wall 308 meters long. Reputed to be the longest *mani* wall in Upper Mustang, it was constructed of countless sections of mud and prayer stones. Its vertical stripes of charcoal grey, ochre and whitewash, sandblasted by relentless winds, mirrored the hues of the surrounding cliffs. Tall *chortens* embedded in the wall interrupted its length at intervals.

A sharp right turn at the end of the wall led to an ascent

of more than 300 meters, topping out at the grainy grandeur of Tsarang Pass. From the prayer flag pole marking the height of the pass we continued downhill. Three hours later we were rewarded with a view of the Great *Chorten* Gate, the entrance to *Tsarang*. I had spent so many hours at home, curled up in front of the fireplace, poring over the pages of Michel Peissel's book, the enormous chorten gate seemed like an old friend.

Perched on the edge of a crag of rock, hence the name Tsarang, cock's crest, the village hovered above dramatic Tsarang *khola* or river. It had taken six days of trekking to reach the fabled, fortified village of Tsarang, the fourteenth century capital of Upper Mustang. We were still a day's trek from the present capital Lo-Manthang. The village was at the same elevation as we had slept at the night before. My bout of nausea abated, and now my goal was to investigate the Greatest Library in Lo.

Housed in an abandoned palace, the library contained shelves of ancient Buddhist scriptures. My pre-trip reading briefly mentioned this treasure-trove of sacred literature guarded by monks from the adjacent monastery. I wanted to see for myself; two years before the fortress had been locked, off limits to tourists. While Raj went ahead to secure rooms at the Maya Guesthouse, I wandered off in the direction of the palace.

Tsarang Dzong, the heavily fortified five-storey Tibetan style palace, had been built in 1378 by Ame Pal, the first king of Upper Mustang. I suspected photos of the ochre, grey and white vertically striped monastery, Tsarang Gompa, would be more dramatic from a higher vantage point, namely the palace window two floors up. But inside the main door a sternly worded message sign lay disintegrating on the dirt floor at the base of a rickety wooden staircase. Hand-scribbled in black ink on soggy cardboard, it read: "No enter."

The ascent to the second floor was strictly forbidden.

Rebar, stones and assorted lengths of ancient tree trunks rested in a pile of rubble beside the stairs, as if poised for a century old repair job. The elm handrail, smoothed by generations of venerable palms, shone a golden patina in the dim afternoon slit of light descending from an open skylight.

I glanced around. No other tourists. I listened for a few moments. No footsteps.

Not one to break rules, I hesitated. Dark gaps in the staircase showed missing steps. My muscles tensed. Was it safe to climb higher? Headlines in The Morning Star, my hometown newspaper, flashed before my eyes. "Foolhardy tourist falls to death in ancient fortress in Nepal," or "Traveler Ignores Rules: Imprisoned in remote monastery in Upper Mustang."

I was determined to see more. My eagerness to find a high window with a commanding view of the monastery was fueled by my desire to get a magazine-worthy photo. No turning back.

My fingers felt the warmth of the wood as I grasped the railing and stepped onto the first thin hand-hewn rung of the steep, ladder-like stairs. Slowed by awe of the surroundings, or maybe by the thin air of the high altitude, I inhaled a measured, meditative breath before each footfall. Halfway to the second floor platform a low, guttural buzzing sound reached me.

I waited. Took another few steps. A haunting voice resonated through the dancing dust motes to my sternum.

Tentatively I slid one foot, then the other, onto the rough, loose boards precariously placed on floor joists forming the second floor. Here, the mud that once held them together had crumbled away, and the planks lay far enough apart to allow a clear view to the ground floor. Several paces further my feet reached solid floor.

The eerie sound beckoned me along a spidery cave-like mud and stone corridor. At the end of the hallway I turned the corner and peered into a dimly lit room. I felt untethered from present reality, as if this day, this moment, had dissolved around me and left me in this dusty, holy monks' cell hundreds of years old. The room was square under a low, darkly-sooted ceiling. A monk sat cross-legged, perched on a thick mat, chanting, looking as though he had been sitting in that same place since 1378. The holy man's hunched frame leaned slightly against an iron cot, sparsely covered by a thin straw mattress. A rough spun woolen shawl tightly swaddled his shoulders. Toes cocooned in thick, earth-toned anachronistic woolen socks peeked from under his robes. Tiny wisps of gray escaped from his coral toque, high-lighting his brown, wind-leathered face. I guessed him to be somewhere in his eighth decade.

Close to his elbow, juniper branches smoldered in a blackened kerosene stove, surrounding him with the hazy sweetness of traditional Buddhist offerings. A battered tin kettle rested beside a wooden tea bowl, hinting at a fulltime living arrangement.

Although worried my snooping was disrespectful or inter-ruptive of his meditation, I was mesmerized, boots firmly rooted to the floor, soles grounded in the stamped earth. Involuntarily I began to breathe in a rhythm matching the rise and fall of his chest. Seemingly oblivious to my presence, he continued the deep, throaty sound, accompanied by hand gestures and finger snapping. From time to time he reached for a small Tibetan *damaru* hand drum, twisting it back and forth, punctuating various phrases with its light snapping sound.

An eternity later, following a sliver of silence, he placed the drum on the mat at his side. He looked up with lively eyes, lips bowed in a benevolent grin, as if he had known I was there the entire time. He unfolded his legs with a few crackles, stood, shook out his robes with a cloud of dust, and stepped toward me. Palms pressed together, we exchanged Namaste greetings.

I guessed he was a long time resident of the monastery, a relic of an era when Nepal and Tibet border lines wavered across the Tibetan plateau indicating no real cultural barriers. I greeted him in my few words of Tibetan, "*Tashi delek*." It was the closest greeting I knew to his native *Lhoba* dialect. I hoped he would appreciate my nod to his heritage. Our means of communication exhausted, I held up my camera and raised my eyebrows asking permission to take photos. He shook his head vigorously but indicated with a broad sweeping gesture of his arm the antiquities hanging haphazardly on the wall behind me. I took this to mean it was fine to have a look.

Against a dark grey mud wall I could make out a makeshift museum comprised of artifacts hung by worn and cracked leather thongs. Several angry-looking beetroot-tinted masks, displaying jagged rows of yellow fangs, stared down at me. Below them was an arsenal of medieval-looking daggers, swords, mallets and ornately silver-trimmed wooden helmets, reminiscent of a time when the palace acted as a fortress. When I spied something looking like a petrified body part I drew in a poorly stifled gasp. Hanging at eye level were several withered fingers, looking like charred breakfast sausages, tied to a palm-shaped lump of the same substance. Later I learned this was touted to be the wizened 500-year-old hand of the master architect of the palace.

Curiosity more than satisfied by the intriguing yet somewhat creepy museum, and not wanting to disturb his solitary existence further, I turned to leave. The revered ancient stepped past me, then turned and waved his hand, motioning for me to accompany him. I paused. Where was he taking me? No one knew where I was. How long would it be before Raj started looking for me? Oddly, I didn't feel nervous. Surely a Buddhist monk could be trusted.

As a solo traveler, I knew the only way to a full experience was to trust my heart, observe carefully and reserve judgment. Placing my trust in others, no matter how different and distant their life from mine, was the key to discovering more about this ancient land. Still, it was a constant struggle to find balance on the tightrope between blind acceptance of strangers and naïve foolishness. My heart wanted to honor the good in others. My head held me back. My head also told me reaching beyond my reservations and letting others understand my intentions was the only path to forming true bonds.

Puffs of dust rose from the hem of his robes as the tattered hemline scuffed the dirt. My eyes never left his silhouette. He led me back along the same gloomy hallway to the open stairwell. The ladder trembled under his weight. Our steps took us through a shaft of dust motes to a higher, equally derelict platform at the base of a massive, intricately carved wooden door. He reached deep into the folds of his monastic garment and produced a hefty-looking iron key. Its frayed rainbow tassel swung back and forth as he wiggled the key into the lock, then leaned his shoulder into the door. It swung open without a sound. He vanished in the shadowy interior.

Should I follow him or not? What did he want to show me? Was this dark room the Greatest Library of Lo? I felt privileged this holy man trusted me enough to allow a glimpse at his culture and religion, wanted me to understand his position of responsibility. But, what about his fellow monks from the adjacent monastery? Would they accept his decision to display sacred texts to a Western woman, or be angry with both of us if they found me here?

I stepped over the raised threshold. My eyes adjusted quickly in the glow of the butter lamps he was lighting. A fascinating array of statues, deity-embossed *thangkas*, religious paintings, and contemplative Buddhas returned my gaze from the back wall. Floor-to-ceiling bookshelves lined the side of the room. Fragile foot-long tomes of sacred scriptures crammed each cubicle.

I was standing in the original location of the legendary library. The thickness of dust layers on each masterfully carved wooden cover made it impossible to estimate when monks had last carried

Tsarang monastery from upstairs window.

these sacred texts, written in gold, to the adjacent monastery.

My thoughts turned to Ekai Kawaguchi, a Japanese monk who in 1899 lived on this cold and desolate plateau for nearly a year. He had come to study the Tibetan language and religion before continuing to his ultimate goal, a secret journey over a high pass into Tibet and an audience with the 13th Dalai Lama, Thubten Gyatso.

Had he once stood where I was standing now?

How much had Tsarang changed by the time French explorer Michel Peissel visited the abbot of Tsarang sixty-five years later? What would the two early adventurers think of the present irrigation ditch running along the main street of the village? Could they even have imagined the micro hydro-electric plant, established in the 90s with the assistance of the Annapurna Conservation Area Project, would mean the monks in the main monastery no longer needed to squint at scriptures by the sooty flickering light of butter lamps?

We left the library of ancient manuscripts and descended to the second floor. There, I held up my camera again, raising my eyebrows. My tour guide pointed to a window along the hallway, a prime location for a shot of the monastery, then turned and shuffled off to his cell.

Almost without breathing I watched as he returned to his reclusive existence. I willed the moment to last, mindfully cementing his image in my memory. My encounter with him had raised my hope for understandings between disparate cultures, people lacking common language but tied by a willingness to communicate the essence and purpose of their lives. My confidence to trust others, take risks, to be a leader instead of defaulting to my usual position of last in line, was bolstered. Silently I thanked this vessel of contemplation and inner peace for acknowledging my trust in him and repaying it with his own trust in me.

CHAPTER 14
RETURN TO LO-MANTHANG

Like running a marathon, a day's trek sometimes feels best when it's over. "Easy walk today. We'll be in Lo-Manthang by mid-morning," said Raj, as we ascended from the deep river gorge outside Tsarang to cross the grassy gradual slope that led to Lo-Manthang. We forged ahead, both certain we had made it from Tsarang to Lo-Manthang in about three hours last time. It's curious how we humans tend to remember only the best of past experiences. Perhaps it was the excitement of finally reaching the legendary kingdom. I remembered it as a pleasant, short stroll.

Some trekking days seem short. Some seem to go on forever. This turned out to be one of the forever days. If either Raj or I had consulted the map we would have more precisely predicted the expected walking time. But we didn't. We lumbered on.

"This seems a lot longer than last time," I said.

Raj shrugged his shoulders and continued, humming a Nepali folk tune.

We shuffled along the meadow edged trail through a sea of ankle-deep silt left by hundreds of truck tires now eating into the road previously indented only by the hooves of horses, donkeys and goats. Under persistent sun, we felt as though we were inside an oven set on convection bake. When our dust coated boots made a final uphill left turn, we spotted the silver grey cliffs bracketing the gorge of Lo La (Windy Pass). Under rows of threadbare prayer flags we stood still as statues, mesmerized by our initial glimpse of the medieval city.

Raj and Resham clambered up the bordering cliffs for their last chance at cell phone reception. Once we reached Lo-Manthang the only source of communication, three aged solar-powered computers in the community library, would be intermittent at best. Groups of trekkers converged with the main trail from alternate routes, their bright packs and jackets garish against the dominant landscape shades of russet, tan and auburn; crowds of visiting Nepalis and eager foreigners were headed for Lo-Manthang for the Buddhist Tiji Festival.

Not only had I forgotten how many hours it took to reach the mystical city, my mind had completely blocked out the steep descent from Lo La and the resulting precipitous climb back up the other side of the canyon into town. My head was brimming with other, more vibrant memories.

———*———

The two-day visit to Lo-Manthang in late October 2011 had teased Raj, Barry and me with a brief glimpse into a culture concealed for centuries. Isolated and untouched, hovering at 3,840 meters on the high desert of the Tibetan Plateau, the city of one thousand residents rested close to the northern border of Nepal. Surrounded on three sides by Tibet and politically part of Nepal, Upper Mustang and its capital Lo-Manthang remained geographically and culturally Tibetan, an enclave of Buddhist rituals and tradition.

This ancient walled city fascinated me. It was different from any place I'd ever been. By November the streets would be almost empty, deserted by sixty per cent of the population, entrepreneurs who escaped to Kathmandu and cities in India when the harsh climate became unbearable. Only the elderly, eyes clouded with cataracts from high altitude sun, bones too brittle to walk over the high passes, or manage several long days in wooden Tibetan saddles, and the monks, caretakers of the monasteries, would remain.

Other than a seventeen day canoe trip on Canada's Yukon River, where we had an emergency satellite phone stashed deep in waterproof container, I had never been in a place so distant from what most consider civilized. Yet, considering the age of the local monasteries, it was obvious an ordered civilization had flourished here since the fifteenth century. Although I felt somewhat isolated, I welcomed the experience.

On that trip in 2011 Barry and I had arrived in Lo-Manthang late in the afternoon, been granted a somewhat unsatisfying audience with the king, and had only one day to meet locals and hear their tales of survival in this remote land. I'd had so many questions. How did they make a living, feed and educate their families? How did they feel about dramatically increased tourism? And, most of all, how much of the tourist trekking permit money did they see?

With only one day in town, we had ventured out for an exploratory walk. Barry had shoved open the heavy scarred wooden gate leading from the fenced in courtyard of the family home where our tents were pitched to the street. Right outside the gate a tall, imposing silhouette loomed over us, his shadow stretched long across the arid dirt of the narrow street. Clothed in a style shouting poverty combined with Tibetan Wild West, he stared. Wealth was measured here, as it was in the old West, in horses and land, and this man didn't appear to represent either. Tourism was well on its way to trumping horse-trading.

Apparently word had travelled with the speed of the swallows darting through the shadowed alleyways of the walled city: strangers in town. He had been waiting for us, two of the last tourists of the season.

Silently, the stately figure stepped forward. Dry, calloused fingers reached into a tattered pocket to quick draw a dog-eared business card.

"*Tashi delek*," I said, because, to me, he looked Tibetan. His broad countenance and high cheekbones recalled the faces of the Sherpa people who also resided near the Tibet border, dominating the Solo Khumbu Everest Base Camp area. Unusually tall for a Nepali man, I imagined him to be a descendant of the Khampa warrior class that had once defended this area against Chinese insurgence. He looked to me as if he had been born around the time of the first moonwalk, shortly after peace was restored to this remote border area.

"I am Pema from Lo-Manthang."

"Are you Tibetan?" I didn't suggest Khampa; locals preferred to be seen as trustworthy shopkeepers rather than descendants of unpredictable Khampa guerilla fighters.

A gentle smile warmed his weathered face. I liked him instantly. Khampa ancestry or not, his gray eyes projected warmth. "Come to my shop. Inside the wall. Close to king's palace. I sell you things from Tibet. Here, take card, please." When he handed me his card, I noticed the frayed cuffs of his gray winter jacket. A string of wooden prayer beads circled his sturdy wrist.

I recalled stories of thousands of tall, nomadic Tibetan Khampa warriors, renowned for their horsemanship and marksmanship, who strode these streets in the 60s, signature red wool woven into the long braids wound around their heads. Guerilla forces with links to the CIA, they struggled to secure Tibet's freedom from Chinese oppression. Taking refuge in caves hollowed out of the surrounding sandstone hills, guerilla units began as support for the 1959 Tibet uprising, then continued making raids inside Tibet. Thousands were massacred. US support had dwindled by 1965, leaving an aging and barely armed guerilla force in dire straits. Few survived.

Inside the medieval walls, close to the palace entrance, we followed Pema Bista into his shop. In the doorway of the shop a traditional white door curtain filled the entrance. In its center a royal blue endless (or eternal) knot design indicated Buddhist treasures within. A fading sign hung above. Red letters spelled out "Lo-Manthang Souvenir Shop." Underneath, smaller green script proclaimed "Visit us for collection of Mustang and Tibetan Handicrafts, old thanka, carpet, Tibetan tea-cup, bel, etc. Local postcards available here."

Dim solar wands illuminated the tiny shop. His wares, almost exclusively Tibetan, stood displayed on dusty narrow shelves: prayer wheels, statues of deities, and prayer beads bought during the annual August trading market at the Tibetan border.

Pema, a *Lhoba* of Upper Mustang, had married a Tibetan woman he met twenty years before at market. She was seated behind a small glass cabinet, forearms resting on a frayed square of black cloth, stringing brown yak-bone beads into bracelets. We exchanged *Tashi delek* greetings, her whispered response almost inaudible. Long ebony tresses spread down her back, partially covering her traditional Tibetan garb—a dark sleeveless wrap dress over a long-sleeved turquoise blouse. Over her dress she wore a *pangden*, the striped woven wool apron signifying her status as a married woman. Most married women still dressed in traditional clothing, even while riding their own motorcycles. Men have adopted Western dress. Pema's gray jacket, layered over a collared shirt and crew-necked sweater, was zipped up against the chill of the unheated shop.

Though originally on the hunt for locally made treasures, I was a seasoned shopper of Tibetan artifacts. Our visit to Lhasa had taught me the differences between Chinese and authentic Tibetan art. I wanted to support local artisans as much as possible. In the dim light I noticed a small green jade tea bowl, its lip rimmed in smooth, slightly tarnished silver, its hammered silver base dotted with coral and turquoise. Two carved dragons chased each other around the perimeter of the bowl. I rubbed my index finger along the smooth interior, worn silky by countless cups of butter tea. The dancing dragons on the exterior raised themselves roughly under my fingers. It would add almost imperceptible weight to my backpack.

"How much for the bowl?"

"One hundred dollars."

Whoa. That was way beyond my budget.

I continued perusing the shelves. I hoped to purchase one small, inexpensive, backpack-friendly item.

But a second never-before-seen object derailed my good intentions. A solid brass thirty-centimeter tall dome-shaped lamp with intricately carved leaves dangling from its base hung suspended from the ceiling. Reminiscent of Kathmandu's iconic Boudhanath temple, the lamp boasted an individually postured Buddha at each of four compass points representing protection, meditation, medicine and earth grounding. Before each, a scooped indentation provided a shallow receptacle for butter lamp oil. I had admired black, rudely fashioned lamps hanging in hotel courtyards in Kathmandu. This was far more delicate, yet oddly bold and mysterious. I asked the price.

"What would something like this cost?"

"I traded it for a *Mustangi* horse at the Tibetan border. I sell for seven hundred dollars. But last day of season. I give you bargain."

Noticing my interest, my husband chimed in. "That's far more than we can spend."

Pema took it down from the ceiling and handed it to Barry. His arms sank.

"It must weigh about thirty pounds. It's way too heavy for our porter to carry."

Pema assumed Barry's statements were a bargaining strategy.

The usual expectation was to pay half of the originally stated price, but corruption was rampant in some parts of Nepal. We had absolutely no idea of Pema's integrity or the true value of the piece. Time wore on, along with our discussions.

Pema's broad-shouldered bulk filled the doorway, shoulders hunched humbly, forming a barrier to the outside world. Barry stood opposite, straight-backed, his Western sense of self-confidence firmly intact. I watched, perched on the edge of a hard bench, palming the jade bowl and examining the lamp, and took the opportunity to ask Pema what he thought of all the tourists.

"Tourism changes good. Small businesses starting, like camping and supplies. More outsiders come to build schools and a hospital. My children learning Tibetan, Nepali and English."

Barry continued chatting with Pema, trying in vain to explain our goal to keep to a budget. Pema countered with lower prices. Barry reminded him of the restrictive weight of the *stupa* lamp.

"No problem. I send Canada."

From behind the counter he produced a tattered scribbler with names and addresses from Australia, England and France.

"I send many countries. Free shipping. You trust me. I am Buddhist."

"But you are so tall. I assumed you to be Khampa," said Barry, wondering if he could trust the possibly unscrupulous descendant of a guerilla fighter.

"No, I not Khampa." Pema's eyes shone with steely certainty.

A long discussion of Buddhism and meditation practice ensued between the two men. Pema listened to our stories of meeting the Dalai Lama in Vancouver. Finally when the topic was exhausted, Pema artfully brought Barry back to bargaining, producing a calculator to assist in communication.

"My brother take lamp to Kathmandu by horseback. My friend there will send. We wrap carefully. You see. I am honest."

Finally we settled on what we considered to be a ridiculously low price for both the jade bowl and the brass *stupa* lamp. The total included shipping to Canada. Haggling complete, the deal sealed, I squished the bubble wrapped bowl into my daypack. This treasure would get to Canada, for sure.

Namastes and handshakes all around, we thanked Pema and headed to the open field at the end of the village to witness Duk Chu, the Buddhist ceremony honoring the coming of winter. Chilled by fierce afternoon winds at the Duk Chu extravaganza, we were enchanted by not only the demon-chasing ceremony but also the ruddy, wind-calloused faces of the locals. Twenty years of foreign influence were evident. Married women wore traditional *chuba* dresses, but some younger women wore form-fitting jeans

Pema's hands as he watches the Duk Chu festival in 2011.

and down jackets. Monks reigned resplendent in maroon and saffron robes. Local men, like the king, wore Chinese brocade jackets, lined with snowy sheep fleece. Most children sported Western-influenced logo jackets, ball caps and tracksuits.

When the three-hour ceremony wound down, we returned to our tents to prepare for the six-day return trek. Snuggled into sleeping bags we dreamt of prayer-flag-bedecked mountain passes ahead. Too soon we would catch the plane from Jomson to Kathmandu, leaving the ancient kingdom, like Shangri-La, protected from outside influence, at least until the following spring.

During the months ahead, Pema's face had often appeared to me. I wondered how he and his family would survive the long winter months. He was, I finally realized, a family man, not an outlaw but a fledgling entrepreneur desperate for a chance at tourist dollars to feed his family and educate his children.

Whenever I thought of him, I vacillated between worrying we paid too much for the lamp and been ripped off, or paid too little, cheating Pema. Barry was honest with Pema. We were saving to buy a carpet in Tibet. I questioned if we would ever see the *stupa* lamp again. Then, I decided it didn't matter. Whatever we paid was fine. The memories of our audience with the king, our visit with Pema and his wife, and the magic and mystery of the Duk Chu festival remained priceless.

Now, three years later, Raj and I had again reached Lo La and my entire being buzzed with excitement. Through the opening between the cliffs we marveled at the imperial seat of the former kingdom of Lo, the medieval village of Lo-Manthang. I could see the distant white-walled five-level palace of the king, the red walls of the monasteries, and flat roofed homes topped with twigs stockpiled for the harsh winter ahead. House prayer flags, *dar cho*, soared on vertical posts. Blue, white, red, green, and yellow flags indicated sky, wind, fire, water, earth.

So many times, poring over photos, I'd wondered if I'd ever see it again. There were moments I was sure I'd never stand in this place a second time. Yet, here I was. Tears of joy pooled behind my sunglasses. I had met no other solo women travelers on the trek, and few women my age. I stood still on the sun-bleached earth below the sapphire sky and wept.

———— * ————

Curious to find out how things had altered since my last visit, I was also apprehensive about what I might find. I'd come to witness the atmosphere of the town during the Tiji festival but also to discover what it would be like when the mobs of tourists departed.

From the pass we made our way downhill, crossed a dry, wide river valley, and began the steep climb into town. The first changes were evident close to the outskirts. The newly developed capitalist spirit marred the once pristine boulders on the hill leading up to the fortress city. One large rock, painted bright royal blue with white handwritten letters, advertised the Lavazza Coffee and Bakery. A few steps further, the spirit of competition showed on a white boulder scrawled with red and blue script. It invited the weary traveler to sample Illy coffee in another establishment.

"None of those signs were here last time, were they?" I asked Raj.

"I don't think so."

The main street outside the walled city was bustling with back-packers, horses, and Jeeps. The occasional pony waddled through the crowd, its back laden with kerosene jugs. Blaring horns competed with bleating goats. Vehicles vied with meandering cows for street real estate. The usually sleepy town was busy dressing itself for what promised to be the largest crowd ever for the Tiji festival. Maroon clad monks scurried along the street, orange flip-flops stirring up puffs of dust. Others wrestled with a large red welcome banner being erected to lead guests to the inner square of the medieval city. Women dipped plastic watering cans into the shallow open viaduct running along the side of the street, then swiveled the cans back and forth in front of them as they walked, sprinkling the road to dampen the dust. Military men in blue Nepali combat camouflage uniforms, here to control crowds and protect the king, swarmed out of trucks and jogged toward the gate.

Feeling proud of making it this far unscathed by altitude sickness, I strolled into town with my posse. I'd come a long way from the night that had brought an abrupt end to my previous Nepali adventure with Barry. That night had ended in the wee hours of the morning as I lay in bed alone at Kathmandu's Thamel Eco Resort Hotel, wrapped in a thick duvet, fully-clothed, shivering and frightened. Barry and I had experienced a harrowing 24-hour misadventure. That terrifying episode had begun one night after dinner near the end of the fourth trek of our three-month stay in Nepal. We had been trekking for fifty-one days when Barry experienced a bout of indigestion that rapidly developed into uncharacteristic chest pains.

Dr. Ang Gelu Sherpa, sweats and flip-flops belying his professional manner, came to the hotel. Raj arranged an early morning helicopter evacuation from Namche Bazaar to Lukla. Bad weather and *baksheesh* (bribery) by tourists wanting to get out of Lukla had delayed our flight to Kathmandu until 4:00 p.m. By the end of an agonizingly slow ambulance ride through Kathmandu's smoggy rush hour, a drop-off at the wrong hospital, cab to a second hospital, then finally an angiogram, it was 9:00 p.m. And so, at midnight, on the eve of Barry's 64th birthday, Dr. Bharat Rowat, a renowned Indian cardiologist, installed a stent in one of Barry's arteries. Happily fit again, his heart presented no further issues—until the ruptured Achilles. It had been a discouraging two years for him.

Now here I was, on my own, back in this ancient city. At

times I was lonely, but with each interview I grew in confidence.

At the end of the street I spied a royal blue sign above an open archway: Lotus Holiday Inn. We had arrived at Pema Bista's new hotel. Pema, beaming with pride, appeared even taller than before.

The first thing I said was, "Thank you so much for sending the *stupa* lamp to Canada for us. It arrived in perfect condition." Yes, the lamp had arrived intact, meticulously bubble-wrapped. It now held a place of honor in our home.

Pema was no longer the shy, humble shopkeeper Barry and I had met in 2011. My intention was to discover more about him, and about some of the other shopkeepers I had met on our last trip. I was looking for details about how the completion of the road had changed their lives. Handsome in a fresh haircut, clean jeans and fashionable pewter down jacket, he told me more about his background and his new hotel. "I only went to class one and two at school. Then I worked in mixed farming. In 1993 I opened my first small shop, then two years later I start trading horses. Now I have ten horses. I buy in Tibet, sell in Nepal. Some money left from father and savings paid for land. We opened our hotel August 2012."

He gestured toward the walls around the dining room. "Paintings of eight auspicious Buddhist symbols done by an artist from Chhoser, nearby, north of walled city. Carpets for benches from Tibet. We have big kitchen, electric stove and generator."

At forty-seven, Pema and his wife had three children; the eldest had graduated from Grade 10 and was working at the hotel, the younger two were in boarding school in Pokhara.

The hotel overflowed with tourists. A few tourists and guides set up tents in the walled back courtyard. His expanded souvenir shop on the main floor opened onto the street. Pema had become the go-to guy in the rapidly expanding business of Jeep transportation, horseback excursions and guided walking tours.

A newly arrived group of tourists stomped into the dining

room demanding attention. "Wait, please," he said. "I speaking with old friend."

My heart swelled. I felt a close affinity to this gentle giant, a sense of mutual trust. Feeling part of two worlds, I was becoming more comfortable with the locals than with other tourists. It felt like a homecoming. I had two weeks to soak up the mystical ambiance of this medieval culture. Sleeping in the same location for a while would be a welcome break from the routine of packing up and walking to a new destination every day.

Pema stood to greet the new travelers and show them to their rooms. As he left the dining room he turned and, ever the salesman said, "Go to new shop downstairs. Take a look. Lot of good things. Come for tea later. I show you."

CHAPTER 15
MEDIEVAL MONARCH

Despite my good standing with Pema, I ended up not in the best room of the hotel but tenting in his courtyard. "Sorry I didn't book earlier," said Raj, "but Pema promised you the only room with the en suite Western toilet for the entire week after Tiji." I had one tent all to myself; the guys shared the other. The luxury of sleeping in one place for two weeks, having time to rest, do laundry, meet locals and explore the nooks and crannies of Lo-Manthang and its surroundings far outweighed any disappointment at not scoring a room. Tenting was private and quiet. It was on the periphery of the action, observing from the outside—a lot like me.

That evening an international mix of multi-aged Tiji groupies packed Pema's hotel dining room. I had loved being on my own for the past six days with Raj, Resham and Tika, but it was time to overcome my natural shyness, stop being so reclusive and make an effort to meet some fellow trekkers. Saying I was a journalist made it easier. It gave me the license and confidence to approach people. The role provided me with a new persona. All I needed was a notebook, a pen, and a smile and I could ask whatever questions I wanted.

I loved the excuse to be nosy. Reticent at first, once I started asking questions I enjoyed the easy connections. People loved to talk about themselves. Not on assignment for a particular magazine or newspaper, I was, to be honest, not certain what I would do with all the information I was gathering. My morning and evening journal scribbles and interview notes were rapidly filling notebooks. And, remembering the maxim that hundreds of photos might only result in one printable image, I was filling my camera memory cards at a blistering pace.

In an effort to clarify my own motives for visiting Lo-Manthang, I started by asking others why they had come. I hoped their answers might help me work out why this trip was so crucial to me. Was it the lure of the mountains, the Tibetan culture, the mysticism of Buddhism, or a wish to investigate and embrace a culture so radically different from my own? Or was it as simple as proving to myself I was not too far over the hill for the kind of trekking I hoped made for engaging travel stories?

A trio of fair-haired, well-scrubbed kids in their late teens to early twenties, dressed in throwback hippie garb, was gathered in one corner of the dining room. They seemed a good place to start. "So, why did you guys come to the Tiji Festival?"

"Oh, we're not here for Tiji," said the tallest boy, who seemed to be the leader. "We're leaving tomorrow." Turned out they were American students in a program called Youth with a Mission—an evangelical, interdenominational, non-profit Christian missionary organization based in Kona, Hawaii. They introduced themselves as Victoria, Caleb and Zach.

"We're part of a team of seventeen youth based in Kathmandu," explained Caleb. "We're here for Discipleship Training School."

"We've been here for two weeks," added Victoria, blond waves haloing a beatific smile.

"So what have you been doing?"

"Just talking to people," said Zach. "Playing with the children and telling families about our relationship with Jesus. This trip is our outreach to share our beliefs."

I wondered how successful they had been with their proselytizing in this staunchly Buddhist culture. Based on centuries of history and tradition, it was the home of three ancient monasteries. Their intention seemed pure but their actions made me uncomfortable. What originally attracted me to Buddhism was that its teachings were not entwined with worship of a particular being. I also liked its acceptance of other beliefs. Heaven help me, as a lapsed Christian, aspirant Buddhist, raised by the choir singing daughter of a United Church minister, all I could think of was Dan Aykroyd's recurring line, "We're on a Mission from God," delivered from behind the darkest of dark glasses in the 1980 classic film *The Blues Brothers.*

These kids seemed harmless enough and no doubt some would go on to do good in the world. And they seemed happy.

At the check post in Kagbeni, I had noted Australians were high on the list of travelers to Upper Mustang. So it was no surprise to meet four Australian women, all from New South Wales, all in their forties, travelling in pairs.

Leanne told me she had heard about Tiji from a friend. "I'm here because I'm a Buddhist."

"And I'm here because I'm a friend of the Buddhist," said her companion, Sue, in a cheeky Australian drawl.

Sandy, who I had noticed earlier striding ahead with her guide on the route into Lo-Manthang, offered her explanation. "I'm a student of Buddhism. I saw photos of the festival so wanted to see for myself." Her friend Kate, a psychologist from New South Wales walked well behind her. "The trip was graded moderate, but it's been challenging enough for me. The timing fit my work schedule so I came along."

A strikingly beautiful, young dark eyed woman from Argentina sat next to them. "I'm a hobby dancer. I travel alone to festivals to study costumes, movements, gestures and eye contact. When

I googled folkloric and traditional dances in Nepal, Tiji popped up. And, I love to trek." Valeria was the only other solo female trekker I met during my entire trip.

I recognized two familiar faces in the opposite corner, the Asian doughboy pair I had met at the monastery in Kagbeni. Setting aside my annoyance at their intrusive photography style, I decided to give them another chance. Both in their fifties, they hailed from Kuala Lumpur. "This is my fourth trip to Nepal," said Wong, "My second to Upper Mustang. I missed the Tiji festival last time so decided to come back."

Leaning forward to join the conversation, his friend Robert chimed in, "If Wong was willing to come a second time, I thought it must be good. So I came along."

"You have a lot of camera gear. What do you plan to do with all the photos?"

"We're taking photos of the Tiji festivities," said Wong. "We hope to capture images of locals preparing for Tiji, like backstage sessions we have done at the Chinese opera." I stored that photography tip for future use. "I am drawn to Tibetan culture. I am a Buddhist. We also love to visit monasteries and make donations to support them."

Their warmth and sincerity prompted me to reconsider my inexcusable habit of making snap judgments of other travelers. Hearing French spoken, I approached a group of three women and one man chatting *en français* with their French-speaking Nepali guide. They looked to be almost my contemporaries.

"*Est-ce que je peut parler avec vous?*" It took a lot of nerve for me to speak French. Despite years of education I wasn't at all confident. I hoped my accent and grammar would reflect at least a nuance of my long ago studies in Switzerland.

"*Oui. Asseyez-vous.*" The man in the group gestured to a spot beside him. I had seen him on horseback on the way from Tsarang earlier in the day. He confirmed my suspicion he was suffering from the altitude. Veteran trekkers, the women in his party appeared to be faring better.

The only Canadian and oldest in the room, I felt oddly out of sync in this genial assembly of world travelers. While a notebook and a pen opened the door, when I ran out of questions I was at a loss as to how to continue the conversation. I felt distant from fellow trekkers—closer to Raj, Resham and Tika and the locals. In reality I didn't feel completely at home in either camp, lost somewhere in a lonely wasteland. Lack of internet access for the past week seemed to increase the distance from Barry and home.

Because of my age and awareness my time on earth was finite, I felt increasingly curious to discover what my contribution could be to this country. I was searching for a way to reciprocate the kindness of people who always welcomed me so warmly. Tourist dollars were not enough. Some sort of lasting legacy would be more appropriate. What could it be? Memories of Gorkha and the importance of quality local education swirled though my brain.

In an effort to be part of the group, I mentioned I had been in Lo-Manthang before and had been lucky enough to have an audience with the king. My fellow travelers perked up, ready to listen. All eyes on me, they urged me to tell them about the mysterious monarch hidden behind medieval barricades. Their request took me back to that chilly October day in 2011. As I described the encounter, the scene played as clearly as a movie.

———— * ————

Barry and I had come to reconnect with the Tibetan culture that had seized our souls during a visit to Lhasa two years before. We wanted at least a glimpse of what was left of an ancient civilization no longer forbidden to the outside world.

We had walked alongside and often through the ankle breaking pebbles of the Kali Gandaki riverbed, all the way from Jomson, for this opportunity. Six days of blasting winds, sand grains biting at bits of skin, swathed like bandits by buff neck tubes, hats, sunglasses and long-sleeved hiking shirts. Six nights of camping in dusty packed-earth courtyards, our tents protected from fierce afternoon sandstorms by rudely constructed mud brick walls. By day we communicated with hand signals, our words snatched by noisy gusts; by night we mined sand from our ears, caked on the sweaty interior of our sunglasses and deep in our wool hiking socks.

We had set up camp on the fenced packed earth backyard of a large house on the outskirts of the walled city. Rumors abounded that the legendary Jigme Palbar Bista was not well and might not grant audiences after today, and we decided to jump at the chance to meet this twenty-fifth generation hereditary ruler, this legendary Lo-Manthang titan of horses and land.

Raj had gone to make arrangements and, after five hours of hiking that morning to reach Lo-Manthang, Barry and I were sprawled in our sleeping bags, trying to escape the daily afternoon dust storm.

I had read accounts of the loyalty felt by the people of Upper Mustang to their hereditary king. His wealth in land and horses and his wisdom in settling local disputes made him an imposing character. I had thought knowing my own family history back six generations was special, but he knew his for twenty-five. I couldn't wait to meet him. An interview with him would be personally captivating and, journalistically, a prized scoop.

"We have an appointment to meet the king at 4:00 p.m.," Raj called past the open flap of our tent. "Better get cleaned up. Try to find something clean to wear. We must look respectful to meet the king. I asked the bodyguard if we could ask questions and take photos. He said he would give the king your card. You will be able to interview him."

We rifled through our filthy duffle bags, searching for the most presentable of our grimy trekking clothes. Eating lunch in the dining room of the family home, we peered out past frayed curtains secretly observing the comings, goings and gossiping, feet washing and water gathering at the village tap under our window. But I couldn't sit still.

Anxious to meet the fabled sovereign, we entered the inner medieval walled city through tall wooden gates and crowded into the only small circle of late afternoon sunlight in front of the palace. By the time the sun disappeared over the wall we were shivering with nerves. The king's bodyguard stepped down the flagstone staircase and called us inside. He paraded the three of us through the murky interior, up the wooden ladder, past a raggedy stuffed red mastiff hanging piñata-style from the ceiling—"The kings' first dog," he said—then invited us to follow him along a dreary narrow hallway into the royals' private chambers.

The king slouched silently on a carpeted bench at the end of the audience room. His eyes, clouded by cataracts, perhaps the result of seventy-nine years spent in dim kerosene-smoked rooms at the end of long days in high altitude sun, revealed a haunted soul. Those brown eyes, witness to countless changes during his reign, at first radiated boredom and defeat, but flickered with warmth when his interpreter reported we were from Canada. Though obviously exhausted from being on display yet again, he maintained a regal posture.

His faded burgundy brocade jacket, gray wool pants and toque offered a testament to the proximity of the Chinese border and Western influences that had steadily infiltrated his kingdom. Turquoise earrings, a classic sign of Tibetan wealth, drooped from his freckled earlobes. Head slightly tilted, he seemed anesthetized by the daily audiences demanded by an endless stream of foreign trekkers.

The bodyguard ushered in five Swiss trekkers and sat them on a bench on the opposite side of the room. They were introduced to the king. Barely a blink marred his regal expression.

Through the palace walls we heard the din of cymbals, whining trumpets and the rhythmic pounding of drums. Buddhist monks were preparing for Duk Chu, the next day's festival of dances and prayers marking the coming of winter. Our host, king in name only, was Mustangi Raja Jigme Dorje Palbar Bista. After the Duk Chu ceremonies he, like sixty per cent of the one thousand resident Lhobas, would depart for warmer climes. For now, he had grudgingly agreed to entertain the presence of the last few foreigners of the season. This once tall, proud royal knew each guest paid for the privilege, an extra source of income to fill the kingdom's coffers.

In Upper Mustang, a kingdom where wealth has long been measured in land, horses and social standing, the king controlled the majority of the holdings. Each day he supervised the harvesting of barley, wheat and mustard crops; settled local disputes; granted audiences to visitors; and graced festivals with his presence.

The three of us had boosted the local economy, as well, by purchasing white *khata* scarves at a shop across from the palace. Each of us in turn was called forward. The king sat with arms folded across his chest, a gateway closed against the intrusion of the outside world. When it was my turn to approach, I followed Raj's instructions. I bowed humbly, palms together, the folded white scarf held in my hands, close to my forehead and presented it to the king in the traditional Tibetan manner. His tanned weathered hands reached forward to accept it. His eyes met mine, then clouded over as he looped the silky white strip around my neck. I had been blessed.

We waited in silence as the bodyguard left to prepare tea. My survey of the room revealed majestic red pillars supporting the roof of this formerly grand residence. The five-story mud-brick structure, built around 1400, stood proudly inside the walls of the once isolated city.

A photo of the king's son, crown prince Jigme Singi Palbar Bista, and his family held a place of honor above the smoky butter

Barry, Patti, the king of Upper Mustang and Raj in 2011.

lamps of the family altar, next to the portrait of the Dalai Lama. The crown prince spent most of the year in Kathmandu where he ran a travel agency. The king's grandson attended university in New York City. His youngest brother was head of Lo-Manthang's Choedhe Monastery in Tsarang. The queen, now Rani of Upper Mustang, a Tibetan daughter of a Ladakhi king, was absent, said to be not feeling up to any more audiences.

The bodyguard, an overbearing figure reminiscent of the Khampa guerrillas, demonstrated an officious manner. After a drawn out, increasingly uncomfortable interlude, he returned to the chamber and served jasmine tea in chipped Chinese porcelain cups. With the king since childhood, his attentiveness proved the rumor he was devoted to and extremely protective of his boyhood pal. We drank quietly, unsure of protocol. Tea finished, the other guide ushered his five Swiss clients from the room.

I whispered to Raj, "Ask the bodyguard if I can ask some questions now."

Raj and the bodyguard exchanged a few words of Nepali. It didn't sound good.

This was not the first of many experiences with the Nepali cultural tradition of not wanting to say no, not wanting to disappoint others directly. Their kindness and compassion or perhaps intense dislike of confrontation often led Nepalis to wishy-washy answers that encouraged hope but inevitably resulted in a negative response.

"He says no questions. The king is too tired."

Photos, however, were still allowed. Barry used both cameras in hopes of getting a good portrait in the dim single solar bulb lighting. The bodyguard beckoned us to a place on the floor at the feet of the king. He snapped one photo with each of our cameras, and hustled us out of the room.

During the entire episode the king never uttered a word.

Disappointed, yet entranced by our meeting with the mythical leader, we wandered back to our tent.

With that, my story ended.

"You were so lucky," said Wong, an expression of awe on his round face. "I've been here before but I never got to meet him. I heard he is now more than eighty years old and no longer grants audiences. They say he may not even attend the Tiji festival this year. I hope we get to see him."

Sharing the story of my encounter with the king seemed to gain me a bit of celebrity. Still, I felt disconnected, apart from the rest of the group. A concerted effort would be necessary to prevent my solitary status clouding the days ahead. I had wanted to do this alone. It was up to me to enjoy it.

CHAPTER 16
AGE-OLD RITUALS, CONTEMPORARY CONNECTIONS

The morning of the Tiji festival dawned cool and gray. Festival-goers packed the dining room of the Lotus Holiday Inn, simultaneously munching omelets with freshly grilled chapatti, tinkering with camera equipment, and vying for position in the lineup for the meager number of charging outlets.

The tourist booklet described Tiji as the triumph of good over evil, based on the myth of a deity named Dorje Shunu, reborn to defeat the demons and evil forces that created hell and suffering on earth. Through the power of dance and the variety of forms Dorje Shunu would take over the three days, he would supposedly defeat the demons and restore peace and prosperity to the country.

Now a major tourist attraction, Tiji is believed to have begun in the 1400s in the time of Lama Lowo Khenchen, the son of Mustang's second king Amgon Sangpo. During this era the acquisition of immense fortunes from the salt trade made Mustang a prosperous kingdom. Lo-Manthang blossomed as an important transit point on the salt trade route. Men in long sheepskin *chubas* led herds of heavily laden yaks between the dry saline lakes of Tibet and the large salt markets on the Indian subcontinent.

During the reign of the fifteenth king of Mustang, the country witnessed unrest and economic downfall. The queen was unable to bear a son. In these desperate times, Tiji was almost forgotten. To appease the gods and remove obstacles to the Bhuddist religious traditions, a great Sakya master was summoned from Tibet. He visited to perform masked dances in the monasteries. The Tiji ceremony regained popularity.

Then toward the mid-nineteenth century many age-old traditions, including Tiji, were abolished due to political changes in Nepal. The main ceremony in the city square no longer took place, but the monks of the Choede Gompa, the central monastery of Lo, still secretly celebrated within monastery walls.

The most recent revival of Tiji happened when an apparition appeared to a local layman prophesying that if the Tiji festival was not practiced, great evil, plagues and poverty would befall the people. King Jigme Palbar Bista met with the head lama of Choede Monastery. The decision was made to reinstate Tiji. By the 1970s the festival was once again celebrated annually in the square in front of the king's palace.

With the decline of the salt trade, agriculture along with animal husbandry and horse breeding became the most important occupations of the people. But survival in this harsh, windy Himalayan desert was not easy. The average size of a family herd of mountain goats, kept for their meat, milk and wool, had declined greatly in the last two centuries from 200 to twenty or thirty. In low-altitude areas of Nepal, subsistence farmers might produce a yield of three to four crops each year. In the high, inhospitable climate, barley, the main crop, yielded only one harvest. Wheat, mustard, potatoes and buckwheat followed the same pattern. Climate change allowed hardy vegetables like peas, spinach, cauliflower and cabbage to grow in some fields. Alternate sources of livelihood arose with the 1992 tourism boom. Hotels, restaurants and art shops now squeezed between derelict open storefronts stocked with kerosene and aluminum cookware. Lhobas studied English and offered services as local guides and laundry maids.

While we perused pamphlets over second cups of coffee, monks offered the first prayers of Tiji within the wall of the Choede monastery. "Anyone know when things will be starting in the main square?" asked Wong, from the corner of the dining room.

"My guide said around 11:00 a.m.," said the Argentine dancer.

"I heard nothing is happening before noon," said Leanne.

Finally, around 1:00 p.m., Raj came to get us.

"You'd better come now or you won't get a good spot to watch. There's a big crowd in the square."

Following the noise, we made our way through the enormous main gates into the walled city. The crowd was backlogged at a booth run by the Mustangee Youth Group. Local teens in yellow festival T-shirts, who would have looked at home at any North American summer festival, huddled under a tent making their bid for tourist dollars. Mostly boys, they sold festival photography permits. Bits of English, French, Italian and lowland Nepali danced in the air among snippets of the ancient *Lhoba* language. Prayers and festivals such as Tiji, a time of religious pilgrimage, formed an integral part of the lives of the people of Mustang. They flocked to Tiji, one of the annual events that helped to keep their Buddhist culture alive. Families came from neighboring villages, sometimes walking for days, in the belief that simply attending Tiji would bring merit.

Amidst the blare of *dungchen*—long copper horns—and the beating of drums and cymbals, tourists and pilgrims crammed shoulder to shoulder. We watched in reverence as an enormous 400-year-old *thangka* (a hand-embroidered scroll painting) was unfurled from the top of a towering flat-roofed building at the end of the square. Pilgrims waited patiently, then stepped slowly forward, some in tears, for their turn to touch their forehead to

The ancient thangka is unfurled. Tiji begins.

the lower hemline of the ancient silk. Then the *tsowo*—the main dancer, a head taller than the others because of his elaborate headgear—started the ceremony. For the next two hours he and twenty other monks dressed in scarlet, gold and blue, swayed and swirled in their interpretation of *Tsacham*, a gentle, slow dance in the form of a circular *mandala*. The stylized arm movements of the dancers with their long crimson and gold sleeves swinging overhead were said to invoke the protective deities to ensure the purification and preparation of the soil on which the dances were performed.

On the second day of the festival the crew at our hotel adhered to a lazier brunch schedule, knowing the morning prayers would again occur privately in the monastery. "Our guide said the king is here staying in his palace," said Robert. "Do you think he will make an appearance today? I hope we get to see him. I heard it is traditional for him to arrive on the second day of the festival."

By noon, tourists formed tight rows with locals and pilgrims, creating a pathway from the palace steps into the main square in anticipation of the royal appearance. When the tall carved wooden doors of the palace swung open, onlookers surged forward. Like frantic paparazzi they held video and still cameras high, struggling to capture perfect images of the aging ruler as he made his way down the steps.

Members of the royal family, dressed in flowing, long-sleeved white shirts, brown *chubas* knee high leather boots, and golden brocaded fur-lined Tibetan style hats surrounded him, providing protection as well as physical and emotional support as he was paraded into the square. His full-length shimmering gold Tibetan coat embellished with a rainbow of embroidered flowers brushed the top of his royal blue and red boots. A wide-brimmed, red and gold dome-topped hat, decorated with a shiny medallion and tall horsehair plume, completed his ceremonial ensemble. A black cord strung snugly under his chin held the ancient

The king of Upper Mustang at Tiji 2014.

headdress in place.

As he painstakingly shuffled across the rough flagstones, leaning forward heavily on the strong arm of his niece's husband, Raju—the tall and powerful hotelier from Ghami—locals and foreigners alike pressed palms together and bowed. Despite his status having been officially reduced by the Nepali government to the level of Raja in 2008, many still sought his advice on property rulings and local disputes. Finally reaching the other side of the square, he settled onto a carpeted raised seat, backed by government soldiers flashing blue camouflage uniforms. After arranging his long coat over his legs, he folded his hands inside his voluminous sleeves. This once great monarch now appeared fragile and unsure. Dark sunglasses masked his expression, concealing his inner dialogue.

There he sat for the rest of the afternoon.

Occasionally he looked left or right. From time to time he made a comment to his bodyguard, who had positioned himself on a cushion close to the king's feet. He appeared rather uninterested in the swirling dances and drumming. At one point he produced a grand, barely stifled yawn, then sank back heavily on his throne. It was hard to discern whether he was awake or not behind his oversized sunglasses.

The high point of the afternoon was the unfurling of another *thangka*, a near replica of the earlier one, but much newer in age. The masked dances of day two became more active, more aggressive in style. Weapons and animal forms represented various means to drive away evil. In mid-afternoon a straw effigy depicting the demon made an appearance.

As on the first day, the dances continued all afternoon. Several troupes took part, and as one group finished their sequence, another bunch would seamlessly appear. A veteran of many elementary school Christmas concerts, I had witnessed the smooth transition of hundreds of young students. When one class leaves the stage and exits the auditorium another enters from the other side. I wondered how the dancers in this situation knew when to leave the square, exactly in time for the next group. Later I noticed a tall bouquet of peacock feathers waving from the doorway of the palace each time a new troupe had assembled on the steps, ready for their entrance. One gentle wave cued the dancers on the square it was time to switch.

The afternoon ended with the *tsowo*, the lead dancer, piercing the demon effigy with a religious dagger. When the last group of dancers had exited, tourists began to move toward the gates. The Lhobas remained still, showing deference to their king. Soldiers stepped solemnly forward and snapped to attention. Movement halted instantly. The king stood, leaning heavily on the arm of his bodyguard. The royal entourage almost carried the once robust horseman as he slouched forward, hobbling his way wearily back across the congested square, swarmed by camera-toting tourists. Raju, with an expression linking seriousness and despair, strode warrior-like by the royal's side, glued to the gold-coated monarch's every step. Up the steep cement stairway and through the double doors they disappeared into the palace.

No sighting of the queen. Perhaps she preferred the more comfortable quarters of their home in Kathmandu to the drafty palace. Originally the couple would have spent all year in Lo-Manthang's harsh environment. As the years sped by the length of their stay dwindled to five months in summer. Now visits lasted only a few weeks, if that.

There was much speculation about the absence of the crown prince. No doubt he was busy with his Kathmandu-based Royal Mustang tours. Soon to inherit the king's wealth in land and horses, he had also inherited the responsibility to lead the people of Lo into a rapidly changing future. No longer officially a crown prince, he remained a respected member of the royal family.

As the royals disappeared behind the massive wooden doors,

the crowd let out a collective, faintly audible sigh, realizing they had witnessed what might likely be the final appearance at Tiji of the last king of Mustang.

Day three began again in the monastery. Later, in the square, the *tsowo* led the proceedings as he offered ritualistic nectar, an appeal for assistance from the gods. Christians use wine or grape juice to represent the blood of Christ. These Buddhist monks used Everest beer poured into silver chalices to substitute for the nectar. Shouting followed. Dancers picked up the pace. A second effigy, this one made of dough, was brought out amid chants, prayers and dances. The dance ended as the *tsowo* raised his arm and pierced the effigy with a symbolic dagger, once again symbolizing triumph over evil.

Next a raucous procession led by the masked dancers and members of the royal family, the king conspicuously absent, wound its way through narrow lanes to offer prayers at *Jhiwa Chorten*, a *stupa* outside the gates of the city. The final destination was *Solang*, a desolate and barren patch of land on the edge of town. There, under a rainbow, with the glow of waning light illuminating the fields and distant pewter hills, the *tsowo* led the prayer to the gods. Bows and arrows were shot, muskets were fired, and the demons banished for another year. The crowd dispersed.

By late afternoon the main square was almost deserted. A few benches remained. A row of maroon cushions at the base of the wall where the ancient and modern thangka had been unfurled still showed slight indentations made by the weight of the monks. Low tables along the row held sets of platter-sized brass cymbals and ornate dungchens the length of Swiss alphorns. Young monks collected the ancient instruments, toting them gently, almost reverently, back to the monastery. Bits of discarded tourist ID nametags swirled in the afternoon whirlwinds.

I pulled a white plastic chair away from the wall of the guard station and sat down to catch the last of the afternoon sun slivering through twiggy firewood along the flat palace roof. Hours before, the cacophony of crashing cymbals, blaring horns and scuffles of dancing feet had delighted thousands of exuberant tourists. Now there was silence.

That's when I heard a faint, sonorous hum. A throaty, persistent murmur, low slow, continuous. *Om mani padme hum, om mani padme hum.* From the bench on my left, I noticed the source of the mesmerizing sound. An elderly man sat with his back to me, rocking side to side slightly in time with his intonations. Possibly a contemporary of the king, his long snowy white hair hung halfway down his back spreading across the orange down jacket he wore over his brown *chuba*. As he chanted his tanned weathered fingers moved meditatively over his *malla*, a necklace of 108 wooden prayer beads. One of five luminaries, he had presided over the ceremonial unfurling of the fragile, ancient silk *thangka* that had marked the beginning of Tiji.

My eyes filled with tears. I felt an all-encompassing sense of peace paired with the realization of my good fortune to witness this event. Then sadness crept in. I would likely never be back. We lingered for twenty minutes of companionable stillness. His haunting chants swelled my heart. Was he as reticent as I to let go of the magic of Tiji?

Without warning, his chanting stopped. He stood, picked up the large brass cymbals he had so adeptly played in the closing ceremony, and walked away. After a few steps he turned, smiled and waved. We had never exchanged a word but understood each other completely.

The past three days had drawn me closer to the web of the people of Upper Mustang. Yet I still felt on the periphery, an interloper in a Buddhist culture it would take years to fully understand. As the festival had unfolded I'd sat alone on a rooftop above the square, separate from fellow foreigners. Raj, Resham and Tika spent their days attending parts of the festival, sleeping in the sun and playing cards in Pema's back garden. Down jacket zipped to my chin against the chilly wind, I had wished Barry was sitting beside me.

——— • ———

That evening the dining room at the Lotus Holiday Inn was chock-a-block with tourists tucking in enthusiastically for a last dinner before heading south. For several evenings we had shared Lhasa beers, omelets, curries and rice, as well as nightly rehash sessions about Tiji events of the day. Now they were leaving. Part of me was sad, but another part of me relished the time I would have in what I hoped would be closer to the normal atmosphere of the village.

As an elementary school teacher I had always tried to treat all of my students equally. For me, the same rule applied for fellow travelers. However, it is inevitable that some students instantly capture your heart. As well, some fellow travelers stand out as more endearing and memorable than others. For me, it was those who opened my eyes and unexpectedly altered my attitude. And so, as memories of Tiji faded into the pink alpenglow of evening, I met my favorite fellow festival-goer.

I had seen her first parading around the white four-wheel-drive near the rock cairn of Nya La, the high pass between Ghilling and Ghami. A self-professed trekking snob I had felt superior knowing I was walking while she was getting a lift. We met again on my first morning in Lo-Manthang in front of the Lotus Holiday Inn. I watched as this seemingly objectionable woman set off on a sturdy horse to visit the Chhoser cave monastery, several steep miles away. Substantial, even though she stood only about 5 feet 4 inches in her boots, she clung tightly to the rough-hewn horn of the saddle with both hands, thick fingers intertwined in the leather reins. The guide kicked his horse and set out. She followed, swaying precariously across the first stream, then turned the corner and rode out of sight.

By mid-afternoon she had ridden back onto the flagstone dismount area of the hotel.

"How was the morning?"

"Magnificent."

One guide stood beside her horse's head to offer dismounting assistance. "Look away," she said, laughing. She seemed amused, not at all uncomfortable at her lack of skill.

First she looped one arm around her guide's neck. The taller of the two guides present, he stood erect, bracing her weight on one of his broad shoulders. She rolled toward him while a second shorter guide quickly stepped forward to disengage her boot from the stirrup. Her hands grasped the wooden frame of the saddle, then abruptly let go. Her weight shifted, pushing the taller guide over. She landed on top of him. The second guide held onto her foot a second too long and was dragged into the fray. The Three-Stooges-style maneuver ended with all three jumbled on the ground in a joyous heap of laughter, turning a potentially embarrassing situation into unbridled hilarity. She got up, brushed herself off and sauntered nonchalantly into the hotel gift shop.

I would have felt foolish and been humiliated for falling in front of strangers. She had better things to do than beat herself up. Apparently I could learn a thing or two from this upbeat tourist. That's when my fondness for her began.

For the next three days I had observed as she had attended every event of the Tiji Festival. From my aerie on the roof of the king's palace on the opposite side of the square, I watched her standing shoulder to shoulder and laughing with the locals, her bright plaid shirt, light pants and short white hair a sharp contrast to the dark tresses and traditional dresses of the women beside her. A small video camera formed a permanent extension of her right arm. I watched her chuckle at the antics of the pre-teen monastic clowns whose mock fights and tumbles entertained the crowd between serious dramatic dances. She appeared to be having fun interacting with locals of all ages. Exactly the opposite of what I had originally expected.

On the last evening, when the festival was over, the gathered travelers sat facing each other on carpeted benches of the dining room. She was seated directly opposite me. After scattered multilingual introductions, it became obvious that French was the *langue du jour.*

"*D'ou venez vous?*" she asked, her accent *parfait.*

"*Du Canada,*" I answered, haltingly. "*De la Columbie Britannique.*"

"*Ah. Du Canada.*"

She immediately jumped up from the bench, walked over, clutched my forearm with her meaty hand, and leaned into my personal space.

"I am from Germany. Berlin." A warm smile lit her azure eyes, commanding my full attention.

"You know Safeway?" she asked, having smoothly switched to English. "They have best meats. Great t-bone steaks. Thick, juicy. I visit the Pan Pacific Hotel in Vancouver every couple of years. I always go to your Safeway for steak. It is the best."

We laughed together, hers originating deep in her chest, mine more a muffled guffaw. Then she turned abruptly and perched again at her place on the bench.

Later, when I glanced in her direction over my veggie curry, I noticed she was hunched over a bowl of something vaguely resembling mashed potatoes. I love mashed potatoes, the perfect comfort food, gourmet garlic mashed with tasty bits of skins, lots of melted butter and salt. These looked like pureed, slightly aged, bland field potatoes left too long in the bin. The perfect bland food to combat the nausea of altitude sickness. She caught my inquisitive look.

"Stomach problems. Jeep trekking. Too much altitude, too fast."

She put down her spoon and held her farmer-sized hands in the shape of a steak, then thumb and forefinger of one hand switched to a vertical measure indicating her preference for two-inch thick cuts of beef. She rolled her eyes and sighed in resignation.

The following morning we said good-bye. This unusual character had in only a few days won my heart and cemented herself in my memory. I vowed to ease up on myself when I made mistakes, or couldn't keep up with others; to remember her positive, fun-loving attitude. Despite obviously feeling ill, she didn't let digestive issues dampen her spirit.

I never got her name. In my journal I referred to her fondly as Frau T-bone. Before we parted company I asked if I could take her photo. As I peered through the viewfinder she and the Nepali guide scrunched close, shoulders touching, on one of the dining room benches. They leaned toward the middle of the photo like a unified team, staring directly into the lens. Frau T-bone extended her muscular arm. Her hand rested comfortably on the guide's shoulder. Her eyes sparkled like someone who had been eating juicy steak all week instead of insipid mashed potatoes. Her lips a flat line above her angular jaw, she appeared almost vulnerable.

Photo op complete, she stood, hefted her daypack, and rewarded me with a grin. "See you in Safeway," she said, then followed the guide down the steep wooden stairs to the courtyard and out to the waiting vehicle.

CHAPTER 17
RETAIL THERAPY
AT 3,480 METERS

After a good night's sleep on a comfy bunk in the premier en suite room of the Lotus Holiday Inn, my enthusiasm for meeting locals was renewed. This luxurious accommodation included twin beds, one for sleeping and one for airing out the contents of my pack, which had been jammed into the corner of my tent for the past week.

It was time to discover Lo-Manthang, *sans* outsiders. Early winds drifted more gently than usual, as if the entire setting, like me, had been waiting to exhale. By noon the city seemed ready for a nap. Wondering what this next transition might bring, I headed to the community center in the hope there would be enough solar power to fire up the aging computers. I was feeling a bit guilty about the privilege of staying longer than others. I was also eager to connect with Barry.

As I left the hotel Pema lounged in the doorway, munching on an apple. A local horse-trader strolled by leading a black horse, its muscled flanks gleaming. Behind him a younger man straddled a shiny green motorcycle. Two men on horseback cantered by, sitting erect atop wooden saddles softened by blankets fashioned from Tibetan carpets. Ten horses without saddles followed. A drover was herding them out to pasture, their work done until the next influx of tourists. An ancient gentleman wandered along, his grey toque, red down jacket, and tattered brown pants lightly coated in dust. Nine teenaged girls approached, arm in arm in trios. Some wore traditional Tibetan dresses; others, vests over woolen leggings, heads swathed in plaid scarves. Stylish purple surgical masks protected their faces from the dust. Long ebony braids glistened in the mid-day sun. This tumult of traffic squeezed slowly along a street barely wide enough for a four-wheel drive vehicle. Three taxis idled around the corner, belching exhaust, waiting for stragglers to depart. Three short blasts of the Jeep's horn heralded imminent departure.

At the other end of the main street I stepped into a dimly lit room off the main library. The attendant raised his head from the book he was reading, but only long enough to accept my handful of rupees. I had my choice of three computers. Two posted "Not Working" signs. I pulled up a chair in front of the third.

Among a plethora of junk mail, two messages stood out. The first was from Barry, subject line: Kamloops. He had just returned from a weekend of mountain biking with friends. He sounded good. My lingering guilt lessened. The other message was also from him, written a few days later, subject line: Roseanne. Curious as to what Roseanne, who had briefly considered coming with me, was up to, I clicked on the message. The content was terrifying. Barry had heard the day before how she had travelled to Portugal alone. During her visit to a small village she somehow had plummeted twenty meters down a cliff. She wasn't found until the following morning. Having sustained multiple injuries she now lay alone in a hospital in Portugal. That's all he knew.

My throat tightened. Roseanne, by herself, in a hospital in a country where she didn't know the language. Selfishly, the incident made me worry about my own immediate future. If that kind of accident could happen to Roseanne in a seemingly safe European country, what might become of me, several days walk from the airport, in this cloistered kingdom with limited contact with the outside world? Six trekking days, rife with possibilities of injury from altitude, river crossings, and steep trails edged by precarious cliff edges, still separated us from Jomsom.

Mind in a fog, I stepped out of the community center and started toward the hotel. The thunder of tiny hooves jolted me back to reality. I leapt up the cement steps of the Mud Kingdom Bakery Shop just in time to avoid a stampede of slate and silver goats. Stunned, I was hardly able to focus on the teenaged herder behind them, his shrill whistle slicing the thin mountain air. I turned into the coffee emporium.

The proprietor stood with his back to me dusting an array of the usual drink offerings on the shelf above him, from Royal Stag and Khukuri rum to Red Bull and Fanta. I chose the table closest to the door, where the bright rays of sun illuminated the turquoise roughly plastered walls. During Tiji the place had been packed with Italians in name-brand jackets, boisterously sipping espresso in tiny glass cups, overjoyed to find genuine coffee after days of Nescafé instant crystals. Their lively gestures, conversation and exuberant cries of "*Café, bono, si bono*," resounded. Now, the melancholy silence weighed heavily.

The owner turned and welcomed me. "Namaste. The usual?"

During my first visit to the shop, I'd learned that Karsang Gurung and his wife Chhyumi Bista had opened the shop only a month before, in what had previously been the local kerosene depot. She baked bread and donuts. He served customers. A couple in their early thirties, they had one daughter, Sonam. She studied English, Nepali and, thanks to the support of the American Himalayan Foundation, Tibetan language at the local government school—again proving outside influence and funds can make a difference.

"I'm just the waiter," Karsang had said, a self-deprecating smile showing his dazzling white teeth. I had inquired about his feelings on the completion of the road. Further conversation had revealed his involvement in the Upper Mustang Youth Society. He had worked alongside Raju, from Ghami, to stage the tourism boycott that had forced the government to distribute more of the permit money to Lo-Manthang.

Now Karsang took one look at me and brought over a cup of sweet Nepali milk tea. "You look like you need this," he said. His down vest matched the cheerful hue of the walls, offering a rich contrast to his short-cropped black hair and dark eyes. He placed steaming tea before me. "Are you all right? Tired from Tiji?"

"*Dhanyabad.* I'm OK."

The news about Roseanne was too new and too disturbing to talk about. My pangs of loneliness, fear for my own safety, and feeling of distance from others tourists— definitely first world problems—should not be discussed here. When I searched in my waist wallet to pay, I realized I had spent all the rupees in my tiny travel wallet on computer time. The rest were at the hotel. I told Karsang my dilemma.

"No problem. You pay tomorrow. I know you."

That simple statement of trust and acceptance elevated my mood. Karsang must have sensed my respect for him, his friends and his home. Somehow he realized my interests fell deeper than the surface entertainment of Tiji. Maybe the next few days would take me closer to this culture I longed to understand and connect with more deeply.

———•———

My plan for the next few days was to make amends with someone I had neglected on my last visit, to reconnect with a fondly remembered acquaintance and to venture north of Lo-Manthang to the unspoiled Buddhist culture close to the Tibetan border.

The first person I looked for was Funsang Gurung. When Barry and I had passed him on the street in 2011, he had called out to me, "Please come to my shop, madam. Good things to show you."

My first impression of Funsang, who appeared soft around the edges, arguably from a high starch diet consisting of *dal bhat* (rice and lentils), had been one of persistent depression. But on his round face, under the rim of his faded gray ball cap, I also discerned an inquisitive look, a desperation tinged with sadness, a look silently screaming, "Please don't ignore me."

All that day, all the time we were in Pema Bista's shop talking about Buddhism and the brass *stupa* lamp, Funsang had been standing in front of his shop next door. He held the hand of a pre-school-aged child dressed in a grubby turquoise and white tracksuit, dark tangled hair sticking out in all directions.

While I longed to support all of the shopkeepers we were soon out of time and money, and so we had never entered his wretched-looking establishment. His face haunted me; the solemn shopkeeper we hadn't taken the time to visit. I wondered how he and his family survived the harsh winter months.

I needn't have worried. Funsang's fate had changed dramatically in the few years between my visits. Refreshed by coffee and biscuits, I made my way back to the Lotus Holiday Inn. Along the way a large gray sign with professionally painted yellow letters caught my eye: The Hidden Kingdom Souvenir Shop. Plate glass windows displayed postcards and exquisitely carved statues of Buddha and Ganesh, as well as expensive-looking silver, turquoise and coral necklaces. Architectural accents painted in the five prayer flag colors fronted the newly constructed white stucco shop.

Curious, I walked in. A young woman in Tibetan dress looked up from her jewelry making. I told her this was my second time in Lo-Manthang. "Yes," she said, "when my husband was out walking this morning he said he saw a tourist lady he was sure he had seen here before."

Was it possible he was the neglected shopkeeper I remembered?

Seconds later, her husband Funsang Gurung marched proprietarily into his shop, walked right over and extended his hand.
"*Tashi delek*. Welcome back." Decked out in a gray sweatshirt
and jeans, navy down vest and ball cap, decidedly Western and
prosperous, Funsang's conversion was dramatic. No longer
desperate and dejected looking, he smiled while he outlined the
recent changes in his life and home.

"I was born inside wall," he said. Everyone I met was quick to
claim this status if they could; it seemed to give them a feeling of
belonging, a pride of heritage of being a true Lhoba. "I went to
government school until class four. I had to stop. I was oldest. I
helped care for family. My first shop was in small chapel in my
house, then first real shop 2003, small one you saw last visit. But
rent to king fifteen thousand rupees a year." With a quick mental
calculation I realized he was talking about $190, a huge amount
in this country.

"In summer 2013 I built new shop on this land owned by
family. My wife, Karsang, makes jewelry. Our son now six. Goes
to government school. When he reach nine we send him boarding
school Kathmandu. We have relatives."

Again, I realized those whose income had been increased by
tourism now had the privilege of addressing the challenges of
education differently. What about those left behind, off the tourist
tracks, with fewer choices? Faces of the children of Aprik Village
appeared before me.

Perusing the shelves I spied many unusual items.

"Where do you get all this stuff?"

"For past eight years I spend five months in winter on horse,
trailing pack horse behind, sometimes alone, sometimes with
friend."

He told me Karsang would mind the shop for two more months,
then head to Kathmandu for the winter. Sounded like an arduous
existence to me, but Funsang was determined to do well by his

Patti showing off the Mongolian war bonnet.

family. He had already made great gains. Bundled against the blast of the harsh winter blizzards of the roof of the world, he annually braved remote desolate hamlets in search of treasures; far-flung, often isolated areas like Dolpo, Bhutan, Ladakh, Manang and Tibet.

"Villagers bring items, we bargain and I bring home to clean. Sometimes sleep in barns. Sometimes village homes."

Funsang and a friend travelled ancient trade routes, scavenging in hovels and crumbling fortresses in search of items to sell in his sparkling new establishment. From a high shelf he retrieved a massive silver filigreed Mongolian war bonnet.

"You want try?"

Without waiting for an answer, he plunked it on my head.

I staggered under its massive heft. His asking price was $1,800. His clientele now comprised mainly of wealthy Russians who arrived on horseback in search of unique treasures and left by helicopter.

My purchase, a lightweight turquoise and coral bracelet, custom made by Karsang, fit perfectly. Pleased to have been remembered, it felt good to finally patronize his shop.

Next I ventured inside the wall to search for a tiny establishment Barry and I had patronized on our previous visit. My quest to find a shop selling locally made items, representing authentic *Lhoba* culture, had led me to Karma, a soft-spoken young man. He was just beginning his business at that time. His greasy black waves had brushed the collar of his cracked faux-leather jacket. Sunken acne-scarred cheeks and sallow complexion hinted at a substandard diet. But his white teeth, fortified by ample childhood servings of fresh buffalo milk, shone as he blasted out a slow grin. His card read K K Karma, Souvenirs.

"My father and grandfather. We are all Karma," he had said, standing a bit taller.

Triple Karma, I thought. A good omen.

"My shop inside the wall," he had said. "Come. I serve tea. See things from land of Lo." Across the jagged flagstones of the main square, near the opening of a narrow street shaded by towering walls, Karma had a miniscule establishment. Barely out of his teens, a faint moustache shading his upper lip, third-generation shopkeeper Karma Wangyal already had a wife, two children and aging parents to support. Thin, fragile shoulders hunched, he beckoned us to follow him into the shop, a room below his family residence. Pale light filtered through the curtained window. Flames from two sooty brass lamps scarcely illuminated two narrow shelves. The cloying scent of burning rancid yak butter shrouded the air.

Karma's meager collection of statues, goat bells and bowls

had made other shops appear even more prosperous.

When I had requested to be shown only items made by fellow *Lhobas*, he had responded, not making eye contact, "My English not good. I show." He plucked a small black object from the shelf and handed me a rudely carved statue of Buddha. Another backpack-sized prize. "Made from Lo-Manthang mud. Do not put water. Carvers still learning," he added, his tone apologetic. I promised to treasure it. Mine for twenty dollars. I didn't bargain. The price of a Subway lunch for two would feed his family for a month.

I took a few sips of the salty butter tea he had poured. "So, what do you think about so many Westerners coming to your homeland?"

Karma's response hadn't been as positive as the others. He said he respected the American Himalayan Foundation who had worked with locals to restore monastery structures and artwork.

"They help Buddhist culture." But he also saw the downside to tourism.

"People come, learn about ancient treasures. In winter artifacts stolen from stupa outside city, nearby Tsarang." We had passed the *stupa* on our trek from Tsarang. Sadly, it was now surrounded by barbed wire.

Karma seemed to welcome trekkers who supported souvenir shops, food stores and camping areas. He appreciated those who encouraged local artisans.

"Most souvenirs from Tibet. Not show *Lhoba* culture. I am sad. My children losing language and culture. They like wear Western dress and speak English."

As if on cue one of his daughters, a four-year-old, peeked past a frayed curtain. Her bright orange sweater, cheery hello and plastic headband had proved his point.

Now, three years later I found Karma again. Like Funsang, his life had changed for the better. When I entered his shop a look of surprise, then recognition, flashed in his eyes, followed by a warm handshake.

"You come again. I remember."

In the same location, just off the main square, his shop had doubled in size. Larger windows let in more light. Robust in a gleaming white *I Heart Mustang* t-shirt, he flaunted muscular arms and clean navy blue jeans. His once straggly hair, transformed into a gelled Mohawk, set off his glowing countenance.

"Business better nowadays," he said. Now thirty-three, Karma and his wife had two sons and two daughters. The children all attended the local Nepali government school where they learned Nepali and English. The Jigme Foundation, the king's trust, paid for an extra teacher so they could learn Tibetan.

"I went government school to class eight, then started shop when I nineteen. No road then. Not many foreign trekkers came. Road done last year. Many foreigners and Nepali people come in Jeeps."

He took a sip of the butter tea his wife had poured. "Tourists coming helping with education, health and economics. Still, we losing our culture."

An added bonus, Karma's father, Karma senior, joined us, eager for an audience to listen to his story of the family's history.

"My family has lived here for six generations, inside the wall. There were no schools then. My parents were farmers, also raising cattle, sheep and goats. My mother died when I was six years old. At that time my grandfather traded *tsampa*, barley flour, for salt, wool and meat at the Tibetan border. Then my grandfather took the salt to Lower Mustang to trade for rice. He carried things on a donkey. Only rich people had horses. When I was a child, my father took me salt trading. He had six donkeys by then."

Realizing he had my attention, he continued. "When I was nine years old my father took me to India, to Dharamsala, the home of the Dalai Lama and the Tibetan government in

Karma returning from doing laundry in a nearby stream.

exile. While he worked in construction, I attended the Tibetan Children's Village School. Soon after I finished school I returned to Lo-Manthang."

His son smiled. "Now you know why father speaks English best."

As I wandered back to the hotel I realized how fortunate I was to have been welcomed by them, members of a family that represented many generations in Lo-Manthang, spanning from the ancient past to nomadic salt trader to successful shopkeeper, now comfortable meeting customers from all over the globe.

A few days later, Raj and I came upon Karma in a yak-dung-spattered alleyway outside the Thubchen monastery.

"Please come to our home. You are welcome. We serve fresh buffalo milk."

Worn out, I was wary of getting sick so far from home. I was tired of explaining why buffalo milk had to be boiled for me and worried I would insult him by insisting a cup had to be cleaned with boiling water to be safe. Exhausted from meeting new people, conducting interviews with tedious translations, straining to understand kind, well-meaning people speaking limited English, I am ashamed to say I declined his invitation.

"Maybe next time," said Karma. He turned away toward his front door. His gentle smile did little to mask his disappointment. I had hurt his feelings. My refusal had created an impassable chasm between us. How could I decline his kind offer of hospitality, an opportunity to be drawn into the culture I longed to know better?

The imposter syndrome reared its ugly head. For years I had suffered from this psychological pattern of doubting myself, an internal fear that any minute I would be exposed as a fraud. And the issue was compounded by my serious perfectionist tendencies. Over the years I had many periods when I felt smart and successful, but often there were dark times when whatever I did or said just didn't seem good enough. There were days when I was the principal of a large inner city school in Vancouver when I thought at any moment the superintendent of the school district would pay a surprise visit to my office. "We're very sorry," he would say, "There's been a terrible mistake. You never should have been promoted to principal. We think it's time for you to go back to the classroom." No surprise, then, that more recently while teaching at Ratmate village I had doubted my expertise as a teacher.

Afraid of being discovered as anything less than the perfect professional journalist, I foolishly passed on Karma's offer of buffalo milk and friendship. My reasoning seemed legitimate at the time. I'd read lots about what in me hovered as an ingrained personality trait that convinced me I had been fooling everyone for years into thinking I was intelligent and capable. It made me believe all my past successes were a fluke. There were times when I felt my good marks in school, fitness level, career accomplishments and hundreds of published articles had all happened by some odd mishap, that one day I would be found to be a colossal fake.

Was I being delusional supposing myself to be a travel writer, someone who insisted on understanding the culture of the area?

"I don't understand why you didn't go into Karma's house for buffalo milk," said Raj, as we walked away.

"Neither do I," I said, head hanging low.

The disappointment on Karma's face plagued me.

I dwelled on that missed opportunity for days, and weeks. I still do. Declining Karma's invitation erected a barrier between us, a wall we had come close to breaking down. I vowed in the time I had left in Nepal to suppress my fears, to be more of a risk taker. The fact that I insulted Karma and his family became the biggest regret of the entire trip. But, maybe, just maybe, my failure to honor his request was a sign. A sign I might have to return one day to Lo-Manthang. A sign I wasn't finished with Nepal, even if Barry was.

Perhaps it was good Karma, after all.

CHAPTER 18
KINDRED SPIRITS

It looked like a short hike, with generous servings of *ukalo, oralo*, to reach the thirteenth-century Namgyal monastery north of Lo-Manthang. With Raj as interpreter and accompanied by Resham, a curious soul interested in everything about Upper Mustang, I headed for the summer location of Namgyal Monastery School for my 10:00 a.m. appointment. With no way to check beforehand, we hoped the date and time, arranged earlier by the principal of the winter school near Pokhara, still worked for Khenpo Tsewang.

After a fairly sedentary week as a Tiji spectator it felt good to be trekking again. My elation soon gave way to trepidation. Outside the city we followed a roughly cut road strewn with fist-sized pieces of gravel. We lost altitude as it narrowed to a pebbly trail. Our boots scrambled and slipped across a rocky riverbed. When we started up the steep hill on the other side of the river, my shortness of breath hobbled my uphill progress. Walking at an altitude close to 4,000 meters seemed more challenging than ever after a week off. Concern about the long hike back to Jomson briefly clouded my excitement about meeting the great leader I had heard so much about.

Once on the plateau we passed hundreds of horses, goats,

and yaks, grazing on green pastureland bordered by rivulets descending from hidden sources in the desolation of the surrounding mountains. This isolated setting, adjacent to the crumbling red mud and stone walls of another ancient monastery set high on a windswept plateau, was the total opposite to the densely populated lands of the winter school near Pokhara.

An hour later we were settled in the simply furnished home of the venerable Khenpo Tsewang Rigzin, the abbot of the Namgyal monastery. A gentle creaking noise sounded from the worn Tibetan-style carpeted bench as the abbot leaned forward. Soft creases in the corners of his mouth created a look of contentment, yet I detected a brief flicker of worry in his eyes.

"I am happy here, but there are days when I am not sure how long I will be able continue. I am very tired." He hesitated, then settled back against the snow leopard motif of the cushion behind him.

"This is my home. I was born in the village of Phuwa, a few kilometers above us." Memories flooded his eyes. "I arrived here as a very young child and was ordained as a monk in the Namgyal monastery at the age of eight."

We sat spellbound as he recounted the story of his background. A child of poverty, Khenpo Tsewang started out the scruffy younger brother laboring in sandy barley fields, his small but sturdy hands working to support his family's subsistence farm. Buddhist tradition dictates sending the second son to the local monastery for both religious and secular education. Grateful for one less mouth to feed, his parents encouraged him to take advantage of the life-changing opportunity close at hand at Namgyal. Vibrant images formed in my head as he told his story. I could see him clearly, heading to an unknown future on that fateful day.

With a mixture of curiosity and trepidation the diminutive eight-year-old, then known only as Tsewang, brushed the dust from his ragged *chuba*—the only outfit he owned—and stepped outside the courtyard of his family home. Small even for his age, he wore his *chuba* in the traditional style, hoping to look like his father, one sleeve hanging off his right shoulder, his left arm warm in the second sleeve. His hand, calloused from farm work, reached into the pocket formed by the overlap of the sheepskin-lined knee-length coat. His fingers curved around a ball of *tsampa*, a baseball-sized morsel his mother had fashioned for him from barley flour and butter tea in the smoky kitchen of their tiny flat-roofed home.

Hungry for this first and perhaps only meal of the day, he stood alone in the pale morning light, munching his morning treat, gathering courage.

When the ball was half eaten he stuffed it back in his pouch. His plastic sandals scuffed through the barren cracked earth as he took his final steps toward the imposing red slope-walled monastery. Tentatively he ascended the wide cement steps, then slowly approached the massive wooden door. He hesitated again, not sure what to expect. Sent by his parents from the nearby village of Phuwa, all he knew of monks was from the distant glimpses he had caught of their sunset yellow and burgundy robes as he led the family goats to pasture. Now he was to become one of them. Summoning courage he raised his small trembling fingers to the massive wooden door. Shyly he grasped the ring hanging from the face of the angry lion depicted in the ancient hammered Tibetan silver knocker.

He drew it back as far as he could three times, letting it fall against the ancient wood, and waited. The monk who opened the door seemed to Tsewang as old as the monastery itself. The monk turned and removed his sandals. Tsewang noticed and did the same, then followed the kindly-looking man into the dim interior.

"I continued my studies there for the next thirteen years,"

Tsewang continued. "My father died when I was twenty-one. I was invited to study at the Ngor monastery in Manduwala, Uttarakhand, India by His Holiness Sakya Trizin, the head of the Sakya sect of Tibetan Buddhism." Khenpo Tsewang studied at the monastery for twenty-five years, including nine years at the Sakya College in Uttarakhand.

"I completed my studies with a traditional three-year retreat at Tsechen Samten Shedrup Phuntsok Ling Retreat Centre in Uttarakhand." The latter was no doubt partially the source of his serene countenance.

Although he seemed unhurried, I knew he had many commitments. The Namgyal monastery area was currently off limits to tourists, roped off because of ongoing construction. I was determined to optimize my allotted time with this respected leader. I shifted my notebook on my knees, in part to disguise my grimy trekking pants. Body temperature rising with imposter syndrome anxiety, I lowered the zipper of my down vest and continued. "And how did you end up back here after all that time away?"

"My guru, Sakya Trizin, on instructions of His Holiness the 14th Dalai Lama, instructed me to return to Upper Mustang to assume responsibility of Namgyal Monastery."

When Khenpo Tsewang returned, he viewed his homeland with fresh eyes. Struck by the difficulty of the lives of locals struggling to survive in the harsh one-crop-per-year high-altitude climate, he pledged to build a school for local children to impart traditional Buddhist monastic studies along with modern education. It soon became evident we shared a belief in the potential of every child.

"Students study the Buddha Dharma, Buddhist ritual practices, Buddhist scripture-making, reading and writing, Tibetan and English, Nepalese, math, science and social science. Every Friday we have spelling bees, debates, quizzes and elocution."

No wonder a place at the school is in high demand and expansion of facilities crucial.

"Our aim is to offer Buddhist studies, free formal education and complete care for children of the most destitute families from the mountainous regions of Nepal."

As an inner-city principal, my first school catchment area—a few destitute square blocks of inner city Vancouver—yielded 250 students; tiny in comparison to Khenpo Tsewang's vast Himalayan territory. Our school provided hot breakfast, lunch, basic education and counseling. While our concerns often extended twenty-four-seven, our legal responsibility didn't.

"When the students go to the school locations near Pokhara for the winter months, I go to Singapore and other parts of Asia for four to five months of travel for fund-raising every year. Some of the senior monks travel with me. I must make enough for the teachers' salaries, as well. I give dharma talks and meet with business people and NGOs. It is very tiring."

I was no stranger to fundraising. My travels as a principal had taken me throughout the industrial neighborhood of Vancouver's Downtown Eastside. Blasted by the winter rains of the Pacific coast I wandered the streets, copying addresses of companies who would later receive my letter of request for donations. It took fifteen months of work to raise enough money for a computer lab.

Khenpo Tsewang shifted on his bench. Perhaps in search of more warmth, he arranged his washed-out robes around his ankles. A deep, exhausted sounding exhalation whispered through his sun-cracked lips. The back of his closely shaven head rested on the wavy surface of the whitewashed wall behind him. Fragrant fumes from a yak dung fire smoldered above a narrow tin stove, stinging my nostrils with their pungent, earthy aroma. Swirls of blue incense-scented smog hung in the crisp late May morning air.

Streams of yellow light from several high windows, fashioned small enough to buffet the room from harsh winds, slashed the sepia tones of the mud walls and stamped earth floor. The low-ceilinged room served as his kitchen, living room and sleeping quarters. One room appeared all he needed. My middle class home in Canada suddenly seemed palatial. As orange as a Monarch butterfly's neon wings, his impeccably clean fleece sweater was zipped close to his throat, a shield against the chill roof-of-the-world winds sneaking into the room through gaps around the ill-fitted door. Wrinkles lined his forehead, perhaps the result of long days squinting at high altitude. Or, more likely the result of the constant concern inherent in his responsibility for more than a hundred young monks and nuns. His faded monastic robes, which had been repeatedly washed by slapping them over and over on the rocks of the nearby stream, looked almost as used up as he did.

His was the exact expression my face would have reflected when I opened the decrepit, paint-chipped doors of Admiral Seymour Elementary School in Vancouver's Downtown Eastside to welcome potential donors. A look of fatigue tinged with hope. A never-ending fatigue resulting from long days of collaboration with staff to develop and implement an academic, social and culturally appropriate program. We continually hoped for a more promising future for a multicultural crowd of immigrant and refugee children and families living in poverty.

Khenpo Tsewang had greeted me warmly. His radiant expression, the result of thousands of hours of meditation and months of solitary retreat, projected a sense of calm and I had felt instantly comfortable in his unassuming presence. He seemed a man who smiled easily, genuinely and often. I thanked him again for allowing me to come.

"Would you like to see the new classrooms and our monastery?" He led the way outside into searing sunlight in his regulation issue café au lait plimsolls. We continued past several mounds of hand-hewn slate gray bricks. Well-worn rock hammers lay discarded beside the heap.

"Work has ceased during Tiji. Our students went down to Lo-Manthang to help where needed. Some are cleaning the streets after the festival."

We picked our way through masses of rebar, rock and rough lumber. A motel-like row of rooms, each a quarter the size of the traditional North American public school classroom, was joined by a common cement foundation.

"The Indian Embassy in Kathmandu is funding most of the new school building. It is my job to find the rest of the money. There is still a lot to do before all ages of male students can study here during the summer." His statement rang with relaxed but firm determination.

I recognized the highs and lows, similarities and differences of our common world of education. All children started out eager to learn. But extreme discrepancies existed, even in the Western world. In wealthy Vancouver neighborhoods freshly scrubbed children, clutching Starbucks hot chocolates, sporting North Face backpacks and newly minted designer outfits from The Gap or LuluLemon Kids, stepped out of shiny BMWs in front of the school, chatting about their new iPads.

On the other side of the city, in the Downtown Eastside, Admiral Seymour students made their way to school from the cement block, graffiti emblazed apartments of the Raymur Housing Project across railway tracks, the route for transporting hazardous wastes to Vancouver's harbor. Garbed in donated clothing, savvy kids stuck together, picking a safe route along pavement littered with used condoms and needles, then hurried through the chain-link-fenced tunnel over the tracks, an enclosure designed to protect them from oncoming trains. They knew not to dally through the tube-like structure, especially if alone, for fear of entrapment.

On the other side of the world, in many areas of rural Nepal the ragged, dusty children, dressed in traditional clothing mixed often with T-shirts and jeans which would be deemed not worthy of Canadian children in poverty, rose early to fetch water from the village tap, gather feed for the goats, and then make their way past fields of grazing goats and horses to the village school. They skipped along, nibbling from time to time on a ball of *tsampa* or a handful of popcorn.

Pal Ewam Namgyal Monastic School held summer classes from May to October at more than 4,000 meters of elevation, looking down on Lo-Manthang, once listed as the highest capital city in the world. The neighborhood surrounding Admiral Seymour Elementary School, edging on Vancouver's Downtown Eastside, was until recently listed as the lowest socio economic neighborhood in Canada.

Fresh, thin air, characteristic of the cold, harsh climate of Upper Mustang, surrounded Namgyal. Above, desolate distant views punctuated only by the crumbling hilltop *dzong*, or fortress, which once housed the original capital of Upper Mustang. Below, narrow pastures, dust and rutted pathways.

Industrial smog typified the moderate Pacific coast temperate climate around Admiral Seymour School. From the playground students witnessed the distant majesty of the North Shore Mountains. So near, yet so far, ski and hiking terrain inaccessible to families without cars or even the price of a bus ticket. The gravel schoolyard offered the only play area close to the densely populated housing project the students called home.

Two institutions, one common mission: to educate and care for children living in poverty.

"There are twenty-five monks here this summer. They are sixteen, seventeen and eighteen years old. The younger students are staying at the other school in Sarangot, near Pokhara," said Khenpo Tsewang. "They all will be able to come for the summer every year when the new classrooms are ready."

"Yes. I enjoyed my visit to your school in Pokhara.

"When I started the school in 2005, we had only sixteen male students. We held classes here at the Namgyal monastery site. We soon realized the school was too small for the number of children we wanted to help and the winter too harsh for study, especially for the younger students, so we built the school near Pokhara. Now there are seventy boys, ranging in age from five to eighteen years, studying to be monks."

He hesitated a moment. "Students come from Lo-Manthang, from Chhoser and Thinngar to the north and also from remote areas to the west, like Dolpo, Manang, Jumla. Students stay with us all year. Not many parents can afford to visit. It is too far and too expensive to travel. Some children have no parents." The silence that followed acknowledged the loneliness and fear of many of his students.

Poverty crippled so many people the world over. A look of despair, an expression of exhaustion, the manner of walking slowly, wearily, leaning slightly forward, shoulders hunched, eyes glazed over, often characterized adults in poverty. Children, many still blissfully unaware of their plight, shared meager toys with friends, skipped on the way to school and invented playground games out of nothing. But they went to bed hungry.

My first day at Admiral Seymour School in 1989, the tired old brick building was chock-a-block with refugees. In Nepal and Canada alike, the price of hope, better health and education was separation, sometimes from siblings, sometimes from parents and often from extended family. At times, these separations became permanent. Death, unrelenting financial struggle, loss of original language or simply changes in lifestyle contributed to the ever-widening gap between the lives of family members and lost friends.

But poverty for the kids who made it to Canada and inner

city schools like Admiral Seymour paled in comparison to the day-to-day hardships and total lack of educational opportunities for some of the children of rural Nepal.

We ambled further along the row of hollow brick shells. "Many more students want to come. We will need even more classrooms and sleeping quarters. I need to raise more money." His back stiffened and he looked away, stress evident in his posture.

Admiral Seymour School, the grand old circa 1907 edifice, was built and maintained by the Vancouver School District. The building boasted the twelve-foot ceilings, tall windows and large, bright classrooms of the era. I hadn't had to worry about construction. Khenpo Tsewang's concerns began at a much more basic level than mine ever had.

He paused, then turned toward a small building, pale red paint barely covering its rough stucco exterior. The slanted walls of Namgyal Choede Thupten Dhargyeling Monastery, the heart and inspiration of his school, were raised in the 13th century. I followed Khenpo Tsewang up the crumbling cement stairs to the door he had knocked on so long ago. The damaged walls and deteriorating roof stood sentinel against the constant attack of the gritty winds and harsh winters. "No American Himalayan Foundation money up here," said Khenpo Tsewang, a trace of bitterness coloring his tone. He was referring to the monastery restoration project in nearby Lo-Manthang. One thousand feet lower, three major monasteries had been rebuilt and ancient paintings restored by locally trained artists under investment banker Richard Blum's supervision. Culture and the local economy had been revitalized. Tiji had become more popular than ever.

"Please, leave your shoes on. There is only a dirt floor," he said, producing a flashlight from his pocket and leading the way into the abyss of the assembly hall.

Ancient eyes stared back at us from centuries-old holy statues. Khenpo Tsewang shone a light on individual age-old ceremonial masks hanging atop red pillars. Dust motes, stirred by our footsteps, danced in the stagnant air. An angry red face topped with skulls scowled down on us. Another, shaped like the head of a mongrel dog, its jaw stretched to reveal yellow fangs below a scarlet snout, stared blankly, red eyes rimmed with golden flames. A second, slightly more benign-looking animal extended a curved cinnamon tongue, lolling over its swollen auburn lower lip. "Those are to scare away evil spirits. When the monastery renovations are complete, we will hold our own Tiji Festival up here. Our students are learning how to restore the ancient masks and create their own. It is a long process." His voice rose in pitch, excited and hopeful, sharing his vision of a brighter future.

Two rows of dust-coated wooden box-like benches, where monks once solemnly chanted puja ceremonies, were piled haphazardly on the side of the room, under several zigzag cracks in the wall. Beside them, a bookcase sectioned into small square glass-fronted compartments held ragged piles of priceless narrow Sanskrit scriptures. The sacred texts, bound between carved wooden covers, were barely visible through the soot-smudged glass.

Would renovations ever happen? Khenpo Tsewang would have to raise many thousands of American dollars to complete the project.

His eyes met mine, his gaze direct. "I'm not sure how long I can continue. In 2008 the work was very hard because of the recession. You can never count on donations."

Khenpo Tsewang went on to explain that while the Nepal government supported village schools, there were no funds for monastery schools. He had worked for ten years without salary. A pang of guilt mingled with personal relief rose in my stomach at the thought of my Western principal's salary and comfortable pension.

"There is also still so much to do for our young nuns." He went on to explain how in 2010, Francesca Stengel and Mariagrazia Ferro raised funds to build a summer school for the girls.

"It is in the nearby village of Trenkar, about a half hour walk further toward the Tibet border. But during the winter, the thirty-five nuns must live in a small, crowded rented apartment. Most classes must be held outdoors."

Despite the crushing weight of responsibility a sensation of warmth radiated from him as he spoke. He raised his hand to cover his heart. "But I love my job, helping children and the community."

We wandered in silence back to his living quarters. Khenpo Tsewang gestured for a young monk to join us. The boy handed him an ornately decorated royal blue *khata* scarf and a red fist-sized angry faced mask topped with tiny skulls, a replica of one hanging in the monastery. Khenpo bowed his head. I mirrored his action. He touched the scarf to his forehead then gently draped it around my neck. "Thank you for coming. Please take this Tiji mask made by the students. It will keep you and your home free from demons."

Then, as we parted, he added, "If you only earn money for yourself, only yourself and family can be happy. It is a great thing to work for the community and support others."

Lost in thought I hung back as Raj and Resham and I back up the steep bank to Lo-Manthang. My thigh muscles screamed with the effort. All my conditioning seemed to have disappeared. The trek back to Jomson could be a disaster. Did I have the stamina needed? Was altitude sapping my strength after all? My heart felt as heavy as Khenpo Tsewang's. The reality of the amount of fundraising needed to build a school in Aprik Village seemed insurmountable.

I'd once read about the theory of generativity. It said sometime between the ages of forty and sixty-five most people begin to

Patti with Khenpo Tsewang.

think about leaving a legacy. Clearly Khenpo Tsewang, at 56, was right on target. I, on the other hand, had always been a late bloomer. However, it was gradually becoming clear to me that the children and families of Aprik Village had somehow chosen me to be the one to help them. At sixty-seven, it was time to get moving.

But, first there was a long, long walk back to Jomson, and several flights, before I would reach home safely.

CHAPTER 19
RESTORING THE HEART
OF A CULTURE

One last day in Lo-Manthang stretched before me like a blank canvas: a day to absorb as much culture as I could cram into my head and heart, say some good-byes, and search out one last piece of backpack-friendly local art.

The Tibetan curtain hanging in a doorway across the street from the hotel intrigued me. The hand painted sign read Lo-Manthang Art Gallery. I'd never taken the time to investigate. Today was the day. From outside the dusty doorstep I spotted a stocky, tousled-hair artist. His bear-sized hands seemed incongruous with the slender paintbrush he held poised over an intricate *thangka* painting. His attention was focused on the canvas resting on a spattered easel. The meager solar illumination radiating from a single bulb barely brightened the fifteenth century deity. Manjushree, god of wisdom, was depicted in the painstakingly meticulous style of the nearby Thubchen monastery paintings. Haunted-looking ebony eyes stared. Pencil-thin black eyebrows slashed across the forehead of the bodhisattva's pale aristocratic face.

My fingers brushed the endless knot design of the door curtain. I pulled it aside and stepped over the wooden threshold. Out of the warmth of the sunlight I tugged my fleece jacket

Pasang working in the doorway of his art gallery in Lo-Manthang.

closer as my boots scuffed the stamped earth floor. The artist looked up from his position on a sack of rice cushioning the flat stool he had fashioned from a wooden packing pallet. His hopeful expression mirrored that of a young boy displaying his first artistic endeavor to his primary teacher. Colorful particles from the imported minerals he had been grinding to create paints worthy of centuries old images danced in the soft light, threatening my asthmatic lungs. Despite the claustrophobic surroundings I was drawn in, compelled to stay.

I had seen this artist the day before, when visiting the Thubchen Gompa monastery for a final morning puja ceremony. Raj, Resham and I had sat, steeped in serenity, as monks draped in burgundy and saffron leaned forward over their long narrow books of scriptures. Sonorous chants echoed through the assembly hall as they flipped the fragile pages, each well-thumbed sheet an almost transparent masterpiece of Tibetan Sanskrit. Barely visible in shadows the length of the tall red pillars, images of fifteenth century deities peeked through centuries of butter lamp soot and grimy bird droppings.

Pools of warm yellow lit the workspace of several artists, whose shadows hovered above them like ghostly spirits. Enveloped in North Face knock-off down filled jackets, each restoration artist sat on rustic bamboo scaffolding platforms. Pots of glue, richly hued mineral spirits, a rainbow of paints, and coarse brushes surrounded them. Upper bodies tilted toward the wall, hands never directly touching the surface, they stared into the faces of the Gods. Their meticulous cleaning would allow those 500-year-old eyes, blinded for centuries, to finally return their gaze.

When the crashing of cymbals and wail of *dungchen*, Tibetan horns, had signaled the end of the puja, Raj, Resham and I had silently filed out of the monastery, walking shoulder to shoulder along a maze of shaded, perpetually damp streets. Across the open square, past the royal palace, we exited through ancient gates. We strolled out into the wide sunlit avenues. Outside the wall, the straight-edged shadows of cement-rendered buildings of the newer part of town proved a stark contrast to the medieval mud and stone world we had left.

Now, in the dim gallery, not much larger than many Western walk-in closets, one of the restoration artists continued in fierce concentration. He seemed oblivious to the bleating and tramping of hundreds of goats stampeding out to pasture less than a meter from where he sat. The interior of his gallery provided scant haven from the motorcycles and Jeeps revving their engines and spewing exhaust into the formerly pristine mountain air.

Buddhas demonstrating myriad hand positions (mudras), sleek eyed Gods and goddesses, and gold-accented mandalas glared down. Almost every centimeter of the roughly plastered mud walls, ceiling to dirt floor, contributed in the creation of a tiny chapel of timeless countenances.

Amidst a display of photographs and credentials, I noticed the signature of Luigi Fieni, the monastery art restoration expert I had seen months before in a DVD about Upper Mustang.

"You trained with Luigi Fieni?" I asked. "Didn't I see you earlier working on restoring paintings on the monastery walls?"

Beaming a smile as expansive as the Tibetan plateau, he set down his brush and stood, wiping his brown pants with painted streaked hands.

"Yes. I am Pasang Gurung. Luigi is my friend and teacher."

Full-moon faced, he wore a ragged black and green striped sweater stretched over his broad barrel chest. Pasang looked more like the farmer he used to be than the artist he had become. I followed him around as he gestured to the artwork on the walls. First he told me the meaning of several of his paintings. Then he shared his own story.

He was born in Lo-Manthang, meters from where we stood, inside the time-worn city in a dark, dirt-floored house on the other side of the shop wall. "That wall, built by first king Ame Pal," he said, pointing to the back wall of his tiny gallery.

His words reminded me there was a certain cachet to being born inside the wall. That wall created a barrier between the past and present, the dividing line between ancient and rapidly encroaching Western ways. This right of birth attached those born inside the wall to the proud heritage of a people who had endured the cold, dust and hardship of more than twenty-five generations in an unforgiving climate.

He lived with his family in one of the two-story homes standing shoulder to shoulder along a warren of alleyways. Animals sheltered in beds of straw on the ground floor provided heat for the family above, who lived in quarters accessed by wooden ladders, notches smoothed by generations of footsteps.

Pasang, now a thirty-three-year-old master *thangka* painter, grew up tending goats in the nearby hills and plowing and cultivating barley fields.

"My family was too poor to send me to school. When I was eighteen, foreigners came to our village. They saw monasteries falling down. They said they would fix them if we would work with them. I was just a farmer. No education. But it was a chance to make money."

Once an independent kingdom closely tied to Tibet, Upper Mustang was annexed by Nepal at the end of the eighteenth century, then closed off. For five centuries the walls of Lo-Manthang had kept out most unwanted visitors. But when Richard Blum, founder of the American Himalayan Foundation, visited in 1991, he arrived with John Sanday—an architectural restoration specialist. They found ancient monasteries on the verge of collapse, Buddhist wall paintings disintegrating, and an impoverished community in need of health care, education and employment.

"Thubchen monastery temple is a classic example of Tibetan architecture," said Sanday in the 2003 documentary *Lost Treasures of Tibet*, "a single great hall with thirty-five columns supporting a flat roof. Rainwater leaking in where the roof meets the walls had destroyed several wall paintings. No one had used it for worship for over one hundred years."

Blum had assumed education would be the priority. King Jigme Palbar Bista saw things differently. He requested work on the crumbling monasteries take precedence in order to reignite the cultural identity of his people. He presided over several town meetings to weigh the merits of accepting foreign funds.

Once trust was gained, Sanday—who restored Cambodia's Angkor Wat—and Blum hired locals to rip out the centuries-old roof rafters and replace them with new round timbers, some carried from as far away as Tibet. Flat stones were then placed on top of the new rafters, followed by two layers of clay, mixed to an age-old consistency by village masters in mud laying.

The roof secure, the king granted permission in 1999 to complete the restoration work inside the temple. Sanday realized experts would be needed to train the locals. Newars, known throughout the Himalaya for their artistic skill as carpenters, sculptors in metal and stone, and painting, were hired from the Kathmandu Valley. The king and Richard Blum requested each family in the village send one member to be trained in carpentry, construction or art restoration.

Pasang had answered the call.

Italian art conservator Rodolfo Lujan Lunsford headed up the crew of volunteers trained in the same techniques used for the restoration of the Sistine Chapel. Hired by John Sanday through the King Mahendra Trust, he was accompanied by his former student Luigi Fieni, a recent graduate of Rome's Ars Labor Conservation Institute.

"Luigi came by horseback, 1999. No road to Lo-Manthang back then." Older than Pasang by eight years, Luigi had also followed the original path prescribed by his family. But, growing up in a more privileged environment, he'd had the benefit of a formal education. The route his parents advised was the study of aeronautical engineering at the University of Rome, *La Sapienza*. "He quit after two years," said Pasang.

Unlike Pasang, Luigi had been drawing since he could hold a pencil. Two years at the Ars Labor Conservation Institute cemented his future career. After graduation he jumped at the invitation to accompany his professor to Upper Mustang. When Luigi first saw the monasteries their beauty compelled him, but unlike Pasang he was not accustomed to working in the remote, rustic, high-altitude location. He rented a house, hired a cook and gradually acclimatized to the 3,840 meter elevation. Various materials, like special brushes and chemicals, were brought from Italy then transported to Lo-Manthang on horseback. The work began.

At the time, Pasang spoke only the local *Lhoba* language, a dialect of Tibetan. Luigi spoke only Italian. He used lots of miming to be certain Pasang and the other volunteers understood his instructions. To clean off the grease and surface dirt without removing the paint itself he used a carefully balanced blend of solvents, ethyl alcohol and powdered ammonium carbonate. The wrong combination could strip the 500-year-old pigments. Pure gold was the final paint applied, often to embellish the jewelry of Buddha's attendants.

Pasang, the one-time barley farmer, rapidly took to the meticulous work of restoration. "Those who did the best job got chosen," said Pasang, a shy smile spreading across his broad face. For the first time in his life he had paid employment. From May to September, 2000 to 2005, the cleaning project continued during the summer months, under Rodolfo and Luigi's supervision. Pasang and Luigi worked together, their ability in English growing along with their friendship.

The cleaning process finished, the images inside Thubchen documenting the historical life of Buddha remained incomplete. Sections of the walls were damaged beyond repair or had crumbled totally. "Missing pieces needed to be redrawn and painted," said Pasang. The American Himalayan Foundation asked Mukta Singh Thapa, the Nepali artist credited with reviving the classical Newar style of *thangka* painting, to find artists. "Thapa had to leave Lo-Manthang because of altitude sickness. Five of us were chosen to go to Kathmandu with him during the winter of 2006 to study *thangka* painting." Pasang had never held a paintbrush before that time.

"Luigi came to Lo-Manthang for five months every year for sixteen years. He doesn't come as long now. Now he comes in May for one month, gives us our work, then comes again to check in October."

"Is life better now?"

"If not for the art, I would still be a farmer," he said, settling down again on his rice bag cushion and picking up his brush. His life had been transformed in one generation. Pasang married fellow art restorer Yanjin, who had also worked on the Thubchen monastery project. The couple's daughter Kunsang attended school in Lo-Manthang. Pasang opened his own gallery and was selling fifteen to twenty *thangkas* per year. Prices ranged from $50 to $500. He wrapped my chosen treasure, an intricately painted image of Manjushree, the bodhisattva of wisdom and insight. In the painting he holds a sword in his right hand, symbolizing his ability to cut through delusion. In his left, near his heart, he clutches a lotus flower and a book of wisdom. Pasang slid the rolled *thangka* into a length of PVC plastic pipe. Virtually weightless, it fit in my daypack perfectly.

After a last Lavazza latte and good-bye to Karsang, we lounged on the raised cement wall beside the communal water tap outside the city gates. Local women garbed in traditional *chuba* dresses were clearing debris left after the festival. They bent over short-handled homemade straw brooms, sweeping the dung of yaks, horses, and goats from the uneven flagstones.

Children in tattered Western clothing gravitated to the huge copper prayer wheel to the right of the gate. They rotated the wheel, grimy hands grasping lengths of tattered fabric attached at various points around the base, feet dangling. Giggles rang out as they swung in circles, causing the clang of a bell with each rotation. I would need some of their enthusiasm for the days ahead.

Across the square several elderly gentleman, looking as if they had been there as long as the medieval wall, sat gossiping in the sun. One glanced over at me through gold-rimmed glasses, his brown face weathered by unforgiving winds and sands. I smiled and called out a "*shopa delek*," good morning. A study in effortless waking meditation, he rotated his prayer wheel clockwise with his right hand, while the fingers of his left constantly thumbed a circle of wooden prayer beads. His lips barely moved with the centuries-old *om mani padme hum* each time there was a break in the conversation. I took a mental picture of the scene, to revisit in times of stress.

Later we stopped in to say good-bye to Funsang and his wife. The crammed windows of his Hidden Kingdom Souvenir Shop proclaimed his status as a modern Marco Polo, collector of treasures as old as the Silk Road. Backs warmed by the sun, we made our way toward to the end of the street and back to the hotel.

Influence from the outside world had opened up an impressive range of possibilities for the people of Lo-Manthang. Overseen by a wise king, world-renowned British architect, an American Buddhist investment banker, and an Italian art restoration student had come together to improve the lives of one barley farmer, as well as hoteliers, restaurant owners and art dealers. All shared a common purpose—restoring the heart of Tibetan culture and showcasing it to the world.

I hoped I would be able to offer similar life-changing opportunities for the children and families of Aprik. Did I have what it would take to persuade others to join my team? The forces of generativity and the imposter syndrome clashed to the core of my being. Which would win out?

CHAPTER 20
WILL THIS TREK EVER END?

There comes a time in every journey when I decide I've had enough. On a Yukon River paddling trip it was when thunder and hailstorm left me soaked and chilled on the sixteenth day of paddling. In Tibet it was the dung-smoke scented greasy omelet and burnt chapatti served in the yak-hair tent hotel at the Tibet-side Everest Base Camp. On my first trip to Nepal it was the *eau de* kerosene permeated shortbread cookies from Mama's Bakery in the village of Dingboche on the way back from Everest Base Camp.

This time, one too many tediously tiring trekking days through the ceaselessly blasting sands of Upper Mustang threatened to overwhelm my usually resilient spirit. It was the end of May. The permit allowing me to stay in Upper Mustang had only a few days left on it. We had spent one week experiencing Tiji and a second exploring the area, visiting schools, and interviewing locals. It was time to head south. Snowflakes had swirled past the dining room windows the night before, demonstrating once again the harsh reality of the local climate.

The day began simply enough. Raj, Resham and I walked out of Lo-Manthang in the 6:00 a.m. chill into a shifting canvas of pale peach and tan, still dotted with patches of white from last night's storm. The tents were no longer needed, so Tika had left a few days before, striding out of town at a fast clip, eager to reach Jomsom, catch the bus for Kathmandu back to his family. We'd miss his smile and thumbs-up positive attitude.

Part of me envied him. Three grueling weeks of high altitude passes, countless conversations and interviews in a mélange of international languages and more fried eggs, veggies and white rice than my stomach ever wished to encounter again, had taken their toll. Spellbinding images of cavorting monks, blaring horns and cacophonous cymbals resonated in my consciousness. The Tiji Festival I had travelled thousands of kilometers to witness was over for another year.

We had at least five trekking days ahead. Daydreams of margherita pizza dripping with yak cheese and glasses of Australian wine were all I had to keep me motivated.

———— * ————

Raj caught up to me easily.

"You seem extra tired today, Patti Maam. Should I carry your pack for you?"

I knew Raj was trying to help, but his comment only served to make me feel more discouraged. For the first time in my life I considered swallowing my pride, giving in and surrendering my pack. Too many inactive days searching out optimum photos angles, conducting interviews and the occasional beer had left me soft.

I watched as Raj forged ahead. His professional presence had been honed by seven years of porter and guide experience. Tall and broad-shouldered, he carried himself with the confidence of a Brahmin, the highest rank of the now-unofficial traditional Nepali caste system. Despite his standing, Raj had been quite shy as a child. He once told me he was frightened of the white-skinned Westerners he had encountered for the first time at the age of four, but at our first meeting he had soon won me over with his conscientious manner and brilliant smile.

Now we both looked as worn and tattered as sun-bleached prayer flags. Well past the five o'clock shadow stage, Raj needed a shave and a trim to tame his tight black curls. A thin film of desert residue coated his red trekking shirt, quick-dry pants and hiking boots. But, as per Nepali guide tradition, his socks were clean. At the end of each trekking day, by the time I had unrolled my sleeping bag and set up my room, Raj and Resham had already found the closest creek or village tap, washed their socks and feet and meandered off to the household clothesline in foot-airing flip-flops. Thickly coated with grit, my own rarely-laundered socks were in danger of standing up by themselves.

I lagged behind. My knees warned of imminent strike action. My unwilling thighs screamed to be stretched, then left to wallow in self-pity. My lungs begged for at least one deep inhalation of oxygen-saturated air. I muddled along through the constantly altering sea of burnt brown sands, pebbles, stones and boulders punctuated by red earth monuments and monasteries. My spirits climbed, *ukalo*, and descended, *oralo*, as rapidly as the terrain.

For the first few hours of the morning my spongy legs fought the exertion bravely. *Bistari, bistari*. Slowly, slowly. My weary shoulder muscles reawakened to the weight of my backpack. Step by measured step, over rubbly trails edged by patchy meadow grass, the 4,920 meter crest of Marang La pass drew nearer.

A sense of foreboding clouded the joy of those initial southward steps, heading toward the comforts of Kathmandu. The email message Barry had sent about Roseanne still unnerved and saddened me deeply.

Sometimes I walked alone, happy to leave Raj and Resham barely in earshot, ahead or behind. They nattered away in non-stop Nepali like a couple of sari-wrapped ladies exchanging village gossip. Raj often absentmindedly sang as he walked, chorus after chorus of *Resham Piriri*. From time to time he bent and picked up a stone, tossed it in the air, then batted it with his right hand to keep his shoulder lubricated for the impromptu evening volleyball games with fellow guides and clients.

Sometimes he sensed I wanted company.

"Why are you looking so sad this morning?"

"It's the email I got a few days ago."

As our boots stamped side-by-side prints in the trail, I told him about Roseanne's horrific accident. "She was one of the women who considered coming with me. But she went to Portugal by herself." The details I knew of the tragedy, although still sketchy, frightened me. I hesitated. I wanted to erase the next image from my brain. "She fell down a cliff."

"What happened? Was she all right?"

"She lay there all night. A homeless person found her in the morning. She broke her hip and both her legs. It was three weeks ago. I just found out. I can't get her out of my head."

The image of my strong, independent friend, slipping in and out of consciousness, lying crumpled, injured and alone shook me to the core. Selfishly my thoughts bolted to my own safety. Would I make it home in good shape? The terror of Roseanne's story dwarfed the magnificence of the expansive surrounding scene. All I could think of was getting home in one piece.

I was satisfied with all I had accomplished so far: miles of challenging trekking, learning how to take what I hoped would be quality photos, interviewing complete strangers, completing my journal each day and eating and sleeping in all manner of accommodation. Despite my current state of fatigue I was delighted to be on my own with just Raj and Resham. I had seized the chance to prove my independence.

Sitting in the gravel at the top of Marang La, I pulled out a pristine package of prayer flags I had been saving and turned to Raj. "This is the perfect place." He knew what I was talking about. He had a sister, too. He understood my plan to place a fresh line of bright flags here at the top of this windy pass for my sister, Donna. I wanted the wind to carry good wishes back to Canada. I knew she wouldn't recover from Alzheimer's but I hoped her remaining days would be as peaceful as possible, filled with the serenity she so often instilled in others.

My thoughts drifted to an email I had received shortly before leaving on this trip. The name in my inbox read Arthur, Donna's husband. He kept family updated on my sister's condition. Sadly, there was seldom anything positive to report. I'd clicked on the message.

"Our dear Donna has suffered a stroke. She keeps losing her balance so has to be in a wheelchair from now on." My sister's rich, brilliant, compassionate life reduced to two short sentences. A quilt of sorrow weighed heavily on my shoulders. A vision of our last visit flooded my mind. We sat holding hands in the sunny lounge of the care facility where she lived.

"Is that your sister?" one of the staff asked her.

"Yes. It's Patti," she had declared with certainty. Her blue eyes stared directly into mine. I squeezed her fingers. When did they become so bony? The skin, so paper-thin? She rewarded me with almost imperceptible pressure.

"I have a treat for you."

From my purse I pulled out a CD produced by the Kitchener-Waterloo Woman-to-Woman Choir, to which she once belonged. I popped the disc into a CD player and selected a song we both loved, as much for the message as for the harmony. Our humming started with the first line, "There was music in my mother's house." A memory of two sisters singing with our mom while doing dinner dishes popped up. Mom's freckled hands immersed in dishwater, Donna and I drying with blue and white linen tea towels. The sound of our voices, blended in harmony, drifted out the kitchen window toward the sunset.

I passed one end of the line of flags to Resham, unfurled

the length, and handed the other end to Raj. I took the middle. Raj stood on his toes and stretched up to tie one end high on the pole marking the height of the pass. The other end Resham and I secured into a tangle of pale, practically translucent flags. The colorful squares billowed with the increasing current of the morning breeze. "Good wishes, Donna," I murmured and turned southward.

Once over the pass, boots soaked by myriad missteps in sections still boggy from spring snowmelt, we squished downhill to bone-dry beige hills. Lines of rectangular, pyramid-like red earth *chortens* guided us along the route to the village of Lo Gekhar and the Ghar Gompa monastery.

Our first glimpse of the settlement promised relief after four and a half hours of trekking. At the top of a gentle, grassy slope we encountered a solitary monk, seated on a cement pad next to the village tap. Soap suds up to his elbows, he crouched in timeless, pastoral elegance, scrubbing his burgundy and saffron robes. Scraggly goats grazed on the lush meadow grass beside a milk white horse. Barking mongrels rushed to yap at our ankles.

"Namaste," we called. "*Tashi delek.*" He looked up, radiating a beatific smile. "May we visit the monastery?" The monk stood and led us to the flagstone steps of Ghar Gompa.

"How long have you been here?"

"I take care Ghar Gompa twenty-five years." He settled on the steps for me to take his photo. "I lived here most my life."

Monastic robes abandoned in his laundry bowl, he sported civilian attire: a white golf shirt, scruffy brown corduroy pants and the plastic sandals worn by most of his order. Dried calloused feet casually crossed, he stared, squinting from the sun, directly into the lens. His gentle gap-toothed smile broadcast a sense of patience in the presence of one more tourist looking for a photo op.

Behind him, at the top of the steps, threadbare faded persimmon curtains shadowed the monastery entrance. Local legend told of Padmasambhava, also known as Guru Rinpoche, stopping here prior to 775, on his way to Tibet to build Samye, Tibet's oldest Buddhist monastery. He had apparently overcome a demon at this spot and left instructions for a monastery to be built.

We removed our shoes and stepped over the massive timber doorstep into the interior lit only by butter lamps. The chill of the stone floor seeped through the soles of my sweaty socks. A large gold-embellished statue of Padmasambhava dominated the tiny outer room. It was flanked by ancient images that looked surprisingly free from soot and grime.

"Has Luigi Fieni been here?"

"Yes. He came with workers one year ago."

With a large key he reverently unlocked the door into an even darker cave-like inner room, the original enclave. The eyes of thousands of kata-scarved Buddhas stared down. Fumes of the butter lamps, the presence of the ancient statues, and the dusky illumination combined to create a lost-in-time sensation. Not many outsiders were granted a glimpse of the inner sanctum. Honored and grateful, I tried to capture all the images in my mind's memory bank. Photos were forbidden.

Outside again, exposed to the scorching sunlight of late morning, I wondered what the rest of the day would bring. We still had a long way to go, over a second mountain pass. I tried to focus on all we had completed so far and not dwell too heavily on the challenges ahead.

The prayer flags at the top of the steep 300-meter path up to Mui La, the pass we still had to cross before lunch, formed a mischievously disappearing oasis in the sky. My back muscles twisted. Finally over the pass my confidence lagged. I hated how slowly I was walking. The gravelly, knee-knackering descent led to what I considered to be an embarrassing moment.

"Okay. I give up." I surrendered my pack to Raj for the first time.

The next hour was painful. Once on flatter terrain we entered a pastoral scene of handsome horses and rag tag goats grazing on the green meadows of the village of Dhakmar.

At the miniscule New Tenzin Guest House and Restaurant, dwarfed by towering carmine cliffs, Raj placed my pack on the doorstep.

"If you feel this bad, maybe we should rent a Jeep."

"You know I don't have enough money. I still owe you for beer in Lo-Manthang."

Inside, prone and exhausted, I stretched out on a hard bench in the damp, almost windowless dining room. Knees throbbing, back muscles wound like tightropes, I mentally reviewed my litany of woes. The high altitude sun had become my worst enemy. The thin skin on the backs of my aging hands, constantly skyward on the tops of my trekking poles, shouted an angry, peeling red. No amount of lip balm had prevented my bottom lip from continual cracking and bleeding.

Smoke belched from the kerosene stove. Dampness of lingering perspiration from seven hours of hiking from Lo-Manthang caused shivers up my back. Several more hours still separated us from my longed-for collapse onto a bunk in the Hotel Royal Mustang in Ghami.

Humiliated by my weakness I drifted into a clammy nightmare haunted by the unshakable picture of Roseanne lying alone in a hospital. An infinity of *ukalo, oralo,* stretched into the distance, an endless trail of prayer-flag-adorned passes, steep gravel pathways, and river crossings with slippery wooden bridges above roaring torrents, where one misstep could be my last.

The clatter of cooking pots jolted me awake. Raj lay snoring on a rice sack pillow. An apparition appeared in the form of an unbearably attractive ruddy-cheeked girl, wearing a purple wrap skirt and black hoodie. A leopard-patterned headscarf confined her glossy raven hair. She moved purposefully between the kitchen and dining room, noisily removing dishes and cutlery from high shelves barely within her reach. The incessant snapping of her bubblegum added to the din.

Moist air oozed up through cracks between the rough-hewn floorboards. On the storage side of the dining room a photo of the Potala Palace in Lhasa, Tibet graced the wall. Depicting the former residence of the 14th Dalai Lama, the photo served as a constant reminder of the predominantly Tibetan Buddhist culture of Upper Mustang.

The dingy, cheerless room was a far cry from the dining hall of the Lotus Holiday Inn where an eternity earlier we had eaten breakfast. At length the server produced a thick mass of mashed potatoes heavily laced with garlic and dripping with gooey cheese. She placed a plate full of *dal bhat* in front of Raj and Resham. Raj rolled over, stood up, stretched his arms over his head, and immediately hunkered down over one of the plates.

We ate in concentrated silence.

With a tin spoon I shoveled in two thirds of mine. Raj and Resham reverted to their village habit of eating without utensils. They efficiently gathered balls of rice with practiced fingers, rolling them though the lentil stew and popping them into their mouths. The guys were tired, too. I was glad they felt comfortable enough with me to eat in their customary way.

I pushed my plate aside and leaned back.

"Aren't you going to finish that? Our country is poor. It's bad to waste food."

I shoved my plate in his direction. He and Resham, having both wolfed down several servings of dal bhat, polished off the rest.

"Dal bhat power, twenty-four hour," said Raj, quoting his favorite trekking rhyme and patting his belly.

"Sorry." I managed a half-hearted smile. "I don't have the strength to laugh."

However, that lunch break proved the resilience of the human body and its power to recuperate. It also illustrated that given a nap and food I could be as obstinate as ever.

Outside again I shouldered my pack. Raj hesitated with Resham, leaving me to go ahead. Endeavoring to regain my sense of pride, I plowed ahead at what for me was a brisk pace, eager to complete the downhill trail to Ghami.

Hours later when I stumbled into the dining room of the Hotel Royal Mustang, Raju Bista greeted me.

"Did you come by feet?"

I confirmed we had left Lo-Manthang that morning.

"You are very strong."

Feeling somewhat exonerated, I hauled my pack up the makeshift ladder to my rooftop room. Sleeping bag unfurled, I tumbled, fully clothed onto the bed and exhaled a huge sigh. I felt exhausted but pleased with my transformation from my pudgy teenager to wiry, spiky-haired Himalayan solo trekker status. It had taken me almost five decades, but I'd made it.

At happy hour, eager for Everest beer, popcorn and some conversation with Raj and Resham, in that order, I made my way down the ladder to the dining room.

"How are you feeling, GranPatti?" inquired the ever solicitous Raj.

"Okay. But, I certainly hope we have an easy day tomorrow."

"Chicken curry, no worry. It will be a short day. I promise. Only four hours. Very easy."

My eyelids drooped as I struggled to consume my dinner of spinach *momos*. Twenty minutes later, I popped an Advil, rubbed analgesic cream on my puffy knees and stretched out on my bunk to read Cheryl Strayed's *Wild*, the epic story of her solo hike of the Pacific Crest Trail. I had had enough of my own adventure and longed to get lost in hers. I managed only a few pages before closing my eyes. I drifted off with thoughts of magically waking up between clean sheets at home at SilverStar with Barry by my side. Had I reached the point of no return? How many more trekking hours could my body sustain? Despite the incredible warmth and charm of my many hosts, their smoke-filled rooms, damp dirt floors and endless cups of salty butter tea had tested my limits. I'd need a mammoth dose of my trademark determination to make it the rest of the way to Jomson.

CHAPTER 21
THE LONG STAIRWAY TO HEAVEN

The next morning I awoke surprisingly rejuvenated, cautiously optimistic. I shouldered my pack and managed a smile. Despite the challenge of crossing Nya La, the highest pass on our route, my back muscles remained relaxed. The chocolate biscuits Raj had produced from a mysterious stash in the bottom of his pack had helped. The majesty of the Annapurna range created optimism about the rest of the trekking day ahead.

After a total of five months trekking together within a span of three years, Raj had known exactly what he was doing when he had offered to arrange a Jeep ride the day before. He knew me. I was far too resolute to admit defeat. His suggestion of a Jeep ride had been all it took for me to get up and start walking.

Trekking guide's relationships with clients can range from cool professionalism to mutual trust and comfortable companionship. Raj and I had developed understanding and appreciation of each other, taking our relationship one step further, into long-term friendship.

We had fun together. Our roles had evolved. Sometimes we teased, addressing each other as *didi*, sister, and *dai*, brother. He corrected my mispronunciation when I called his village Ramtate instead of Ratmate.

He chuckled when I mimicked his phone manners. I imitated him raising his cell phone and shouting "*Kiri?*" over and over, the not-so- polite local slang version of "What?" he used when gossiping with fellow guides. We developed pet names. To me he became Raju, which progressed to Rajuji when I tacked on the suffix "ji" adding extra endearment. He, however, took the high road, respectfully dubbing me Patti-Maam, GranPatti or *azurama*, meaning grandma.

Occasionally we bickered like an elderly couple clinging to each other out of habit. And we gave each other space to prevent arguments.

Sometimes I felt liberated, sometimes lonely. When I lit my travel candle and opened my journal at happy hour, Raj knew I longed for home, the solace of the familiar. He left me alone.

"I'm having an imaginary dinner with Barry tonight."

"Okay, GranPatti. See you in the morning." Raj sometimes slipped in the GranPatti nickname when I looked especially tired.

He would slip off to the guides' quarters, no doubt glad of extra time to himself. When I ordered popcorn and a large Everest beer at 5 o'clock, he knew beer-bonding was on the agenda.

Later that morning when our boots brushed the branches of the sea buckthorn bushes lining the trail my spirits danced along with a riot of minute orange butterflies floating above the white blossoms. Our gentle four-hour route for the day, dotted with rolling hills and river crossings, led us to the tiny village of Syangboche. We reached the whitewashed Dhaulagiri Guest House in time for a late lunch.

"That's it for me. I'm going for a nap. Wake me up at happy hour."

Sun streamed through the bedroom curtains, dappling red geraniums in old tomato cans clustered in the windowsill. Tortured by images of never ending mounds of white rice, veggies and fried eggs, I conjured dreams of chilled Kim Crawford

Sauvignon Blanc and fresh arugula salad with raspberry vinai-grette. For the remainder of the afternoon and evening I cocooned in my sleeping bag, lost again in the pages of *Wild*, attempting to mine even a fraction of Cheryl Strayed's strength and resolve.

Was I wasting my time reading and resting for the entire afternoon? Did I really need more than a one-hour nap? Shouldn't I be out doing interviews instead of reclusively hiding in my closed cell of a room, battered door locked against the world?

My refusal of Karma's hospitality still bothered me. I tried to stop beating myself up. I rummaged deep in my daypack for Roger, my scruffy, well-traveled mini golden retriever, and tucked him beside me in my sleeping bag. My furry talisman provided comfort, giving me courage.

As I drifted off to sleep a plan formed in my head. I would send Karma a letter and some framed photos of his family. I hoped the small gesture would persuade him I had not forgotten him.

————— * —————

The following morning I resolved to reclaim my status as an adventurer and risk-taker. The only foreign guest in the house, I was welcomed into the family kitchen, along with Raj and Resham, to a seat of honor close to the stove. Strong, sugared Nepali milk coffee helped me wash down a plateful of runny fried eggs mopped up with warm chapatti. I watched the lady of the house, a round-faced, dark-eyed woman about forty. She repeatedly plunged a broom-handle sized pole up and down in a yellow churn to create *po cha*, butter tea, generated from tea, salt and yak butter. When I indicated, through sign language, my interest in having a go, she relinquished the plunger.

"You do." She placed my hands on the pole. My arms tired in no time. I laughed, bowed, and pressed my hands together, acknowledging her superior expertise. Over a second cup up of coffee I relaxed, contented by the slurping of the butter tea churn, the hissing of the charred pot on the stove, and the crackling of the dry wood fire. I was back in the game.

"So what's up for today?" I asked Raj. That's when he suggested the alternate route to the Chyungsi Rhangchung Cave Monastery.

Our heads almost touched as we leaned in over the map in the smoky kitchen. Raj traced the route. "The owner of the lodge gave me clear directions." After some discussion, I agreed to the plan.

We started south on the usual gravel road. After an hour the path veered off to the left on an unmarked, barely discernible route, downhill into a dark and rugged-looking canyon. From time to time Raj sent Resham, second in command as porter and apprentice guide, on a reconnaissance mission. Resham scooted off the path to check what looked like cave openings in the rock wall. Garbed in a faded pink shirt and tattered brown pants, he smiled, was always courteous, never complained. We walked down, deeper into the canyon, past the warming rays of the morning sun. No cave in sight. My risk taker resolve began to fade.

Raj strode confidently alongside the turquoise bubbles of the *khola*, the Syangboche River. I lagged behind. My spirits darkened with the diminishing light. The path narrowed. Gray canyon walls rose on both sides like Wall Street towers, forming a cathedral of silence.

The darkness drew me back to my conversation with my Resham at the Hotel Royal Mustang in Ghami.

Thinking back to his story, my pitiful feelings of self-doubt seemed incredibly insignificant. If he could be cheerful, hefting my overstuffed duffel and working away from his wife and new young son for long periods of time, the least I could do was match his upbeat attitude.

Engulfed in shadows, tall cliffs rising on three sides, we stopped to consult the map. I leaned in past Raj's elbow for a look.

"Can you point out where we are exactly?" The khola

Chungsi Rhangchung Cave Monastery.

continued ahead but a stream was joining it from the right.

"Let's go a bit further, follow the stream around the corner, then decide which way to go."

Five minutes later our eyes followed the stream into the sunlight at the base of a long, vertical, stairway clinging to the sandstone wall. Above, almost out of sight near what looked like the top of the stairs, we glimpsed a confusion of faded prayer flags.

"OMLB, that must be it," I said. "Finally."

Raj responded to our secret saying with his usual Hindu version, "OMLS," (Oh my Lord Shiva). "You must be right."

Chyungsi Rhangchung Cave Monastery, hidden for centuries by the overhang of sandstone, visible only from certain angles, had remained undisturbed until rediscovered by wandering monks from nearby Ghilling village thirty years earlier.

We made our way up hundreds of zigzagging stone steps led

to a narrow sandstone veranda. At the end of a flagstone walkway the shaded entryway into the meditation cave opened. We bowed to enter. Light streamed through the transparent prayer flags illuminating a large room with natural rock arched cathedral ceilings. Printed Tibetan Sanskrit messages of Buddhist scripture had almost disappeared, lightening the flags to silvery-gray. Deep in the cave an altar rose above three red mud steps holding rows of gleaming butter lamps. Behind the altar four two-storey high, whitewashed, mound-like *stupas* ascended toward the ceiling. Hidden in their bases were bits of bones and remnants of fabric from the robes of long-dead high lamas. Thousands of fraying white *khata* scarves draped the sapphire hair, golden countenance and saffron robes of the image of Shakyamuni Buddha painted on each *stupa*. A tangle of prayer flags rained from the heights. A crudely constructed brick wall boasted a Tibetan flag, the national flag forbidden only a few hundred kilometers north across the border in China.

From behind the wall an ethereal young woman in a flimsy blouse entered the space. Her long gray skirt grazed the red stone floor as she moved toward us. She presented steaming butter tea in glass mugs on a silver tray. Her husband, his slim frame bulked by a red down vest over a worn wool sweater, continued his daily duties, lighting butter lamps on the altar.

In isolation, a four-hour walk from neighbors, food, and medical assistance, hundreds of steps above the river that provided their only source of water, the couple dedicated their lives to the care of this sacred monastery. No one knew how long it had been there in this windy wasteland.

After tea, Raj explained the caretaker had described a mini *kora* or sacred circumambulation we could walk, starting in the main room and continuing deep into the cave behind the giant Buddhas.

"It's a traditional spiritual practice, a way of gaining merit. Do you want to do it?" Always ready to gain merit and determined to continue to step out of my comfort zone, I agreed. We set out clockwise into the dark.

I groped along behind Raj. A gloomy stillness descended on my shoulders, draping them in a cloak of melancholy. Gray silt, smooth and cool, stuck to my palms. My ragged nails raked through the deep sooty residue left from centuries of butter lamps. I tugged at my fingerless rag wool gloves. I smelled like I'd slept in a goat shed, pungent with the odor of wet wool and sour milk. The waistband of my trekking pants, tight when I left home, hung loose around my hips.

With my next shuffling move the worn tread of my boots glanced over the smooth rock. My left foot skidded. I struggled to maintain balance. I was sure Resham, close behind, could hear the pounding of my heart. In an effort to calm myself, I leaned against the sooty wall and inhaled a deep cleansing breath, the kind they teach in yoga class. Turned out it wasn't so cleansing. Particles of centuries old dust rushed into my bronchial tubes. A whistling wheeze rasped from somewhere deep in my chest.

My hand traced the side of my pack for my water bottle. There was nothing there. My pack was back in the outer room of the cave. My tongue meandered around the parched crevices of my mouth searching for saliva, savoring the residue of butter tea. I checked my altimeter watch. Six hours since breakfast. I was thirsty, hungry and a bit afraid. But, I was exactly where I wanted to be.

Crouched too long, electric tingles crept up my legs. I tried a few steps forward. Like ropes stretched taut on a medieval torture rack my hamstrings stiffened. One ankle slipped out. That's when I landed, hard, directly on my right hip.

For me, part of the intrigue of travel is the moment when I ask myself, "How did I get into this situation, and, more importantly, how am I going to get out of it?" Cowering injured and frightened in the dark of Chyungsi Rhangchung perched at an altitude of 3,842 meters, I found that moment. What was I doing crawling forward in a remote ancient cave with two twenty-something Nepali guys?

I can't say for sure how long I remained in that position, shocked, stiff, and afraid to move. Finally I manipulated my legs into a kind of comfortable crouch. Leaning left on the forty-five degree slope I struggled to maintain balance. All I needed now was to slip again.

At least I was out of the sun for a while.

An involuntary shiver rattled my bones. Wheezing lungs, a sweaty back and a damp cave made for a dangerous combination. Cool air drifted over the unhealed crack in my lower lip. It actually felt good. For six weeks the crack had refused to heal despite constant slatherings of sunscreen and Vaseline. Every time I ate, the split opened again, excavating an annoying crevasse. Each night at dinner the taste of blood mixed with the startlingly spicy sting of curried vegetables.

I massaged the knot in my cranky hip. Pain shot down my leg. I remained still, waiting for the pain to subside. Had I broken something? Older women often didn't recover from a hip injury. What was next? The whirring blades of a rescue helicopter?

Finally, after my half-day rest, I had been feeling stronger, nervier, more willing to take the road less travelled. I pictured the faces of the children I had vowed to help. What would happen now to their dream of a school?

My athletic background was sketchy. A lifeguard in my university years, a tri-athlete in my forties, I had run one marathon and been a cross-country ski racer in my early fifties. But ski racing was fifteen years ago. Then came the two significant car accidents, T-boned on the passenger side where I was sitting. I couldn't rely on past athletic exploits to defend my bones forever.

It was now seven weeks since I'd left home. The novelty of long days of trekking and nights in tents or on lumpy guesthouses mattresses was beginning to wear thin.

Afraid to move, I sat and wondered what I was doing there. Why, despite my affliction with claustrophobia and asthma, was I, a small white-haired woman, squished behind towering statues of Buddha in the dusty dim of an ancient cave, in a far off corner of Upper Mustang?

I inched myself ahead through the narrow corridor. Slivers of sunlight dappled the countenances of the Buddhas. Deep shadows threatened to entomb me like the layers of sadness I had come all this way to escape.

Ahead, almost obscured, Raj's muscular silhouette loomed large. Strong shoulders, developed from years of carrying heavy loads as a trekking porter, gave him a self-possessed presence. More confident than I of his footing he continued ahead in a bent crouch. I could smell a month of trekking on him, too. Me, aroma of goat shed. His, the essence of *dal bhat* mingled with a hint of kerosene from kitchen stoves.

He turned to check on me. "Are you okay, Patti Maam?" Shuffling ahead, he waved his arms overhead in a ghostly slow-motion fashion. Wisps of tangled gray cobwebs flowed from his fingertips. My matted hair caught one. I didn't brush it away. I didn't dare. I needed both hands for support.

"Wait, Rajuji. Just a minute." I hoped my pet name for him would garner some compassion.

"Please. Wait." My spirit clung desperately to the faint glow of butter lamps barely visible ahead, flickering on what looked like the knee of the last of the three Buddhas. I hoped that was the exit from our *kora*.

Raj turned. The white of his eyes were a ghostly glow. "What happened? Are you okay?"

What was I thinking, so far from internet, other travelers, or cell phone reception? Would there even be any way to call a helicopter?

"I think so." My feeble response was meant as much to assure myself as well as him. Could he make out the grimace of pain contorting my features? Five trekking days from the airport at Jomson, I had to be okay. I had to complete the adventure.

I thought of Donna. I could hear her harmonizing, humming her alto line. Now at sixty-seven, the age she was when first diagnosed with Alzheimer's, the future terrified me. The email about her stroke had turned out to be a strong impetus, among others, to convince me to travel on my own. Now it gave me the courage to get up and continue. Donna no longer had choices. Her world had shrunk to one room. Outside the walls of this cave, a vast, exciting world waited for me. I still had choices about my fate, and my contribution to others. I vowed not to waste them.

Aided by Raj I crawled and slid the rest of the way around the statues and settled on the stone floor in the atrium. Resham followed. For a while, no one spoke. We sat in silent meditation in this belly of the Buddha-shaped cave, content in the tranquility.

———— • ————

Since my twenties I had felt I was meant to do something important, something meaningful, something of value to others. My career in education had fulfilled some of my personal legend. Early in my retirement I was drawn to Tibet. I imagined the next steps would have to do with Nepal. Before that nasty fall in the inner recesses of the cave, I didn't fully realize what I was capable of, and how I could fulfill my dreams. I was beginning to realize if I could get up and keep going after that fall, I could do anything. Maybe I could raise enough money to build a school for the children of Aprik Village.

Two months before one of my biggest concerns had been how to access cash from a foreign ATM. I had cowered at the thought of arriving in Kathmandu after dark. My nightmares had been peppered with scenes of becoming lost and alone on the roof of the world. In Lo-Manthang my interviews had gone smoothly. I had squatted companionably beside local women at the village stream, washing clothes, laughing and chatting in a convoluted combination of English and Nepali. Karma had invited me into his family home. Funsang and Pasang had openly shared their life stories. Khenpo Tsewang had given me a mask to ward off evils and inspiration to raise funds. I had begun to feel as if maybe, just maybe, I had a future as a travel writer and humanitarian. I had slept in dodgy places, surrounded by warm, hospitable people. And today, I had been brave enough to take the road less travelled.

———— • ————

After more tea we set out. Gingerly I hobbled down countless steps to the valley floor, rubbing my hip and stretching my leg every few minutes. The pain had subsided some. With measured strides and extra rest stops we made our way. Despite the jarring steps down to the riverbed and sun-scorched trail to the far end of the canyon, I worked to maintain a meditative state. At the base of the steep climb to exit the canyon, I pulled down my hat, adjusted my pack and took a deep breath. There was nowhere to go but up.

Rhythmically counting steps and mindful of the 300-meter drop-off, I picked my way steadily up the narrow trail. My mind wandered to Roseanne. I concentrated on every boot placement. I allowed myself a glance at the scenery only when I stopped every thirty paces. Raj wisely sent me ahead to set the pace. At the exact time when I thought another step impossible, he called out, "Patti Maam is a very strong woman."

By the time we reached Samar that evening my confidence was renewed, my purpose defined. I knew my attitude to trekking, my life and its infinite joys and challenges would vary, up and down, *ukalo, oralo*, as often as the trail. And, that was hazure, okay. I felt prepared. Ready for anything life could throw at me. I was ready to go home.

CHAPTER 22
HOMEWARD

When travelling in Nepal it's wise to expect the unexpected. An enormous amount of patience, an attitude of curiosity and a strong sense of resignation can also be a bonus. A sacred cow munching garbage in the middle of a Kathmandu street, a brass band leading a lengthy wedding procession through the alleys of Thamel or a herd of ornery yaks balking before a suspension bridge above a tumultuous river can cause massive delays in travel. For us, it took six more days, double the originally scheduled three, before we were gobbling pizza and sipping red wine at Café Concerto in Pokhara. Walking south from Samar we had retraced our original route. No more detours for me. My hip still aching, it took three hobbling half-day hikes to reach Jomson.

Resham left us in Jomsom, hopping the late night bus for Kathmandu. Despite sharing his personal stories he remained shy, thanking me profusely when I handed him a new trekker's water bottle full of snacks for the road, tiny gifts for his son, a heartfelt note of thanks and good wishes for his future as a guide as well as a tip. One brief warm hug and he was gone. I knew I would see him again one day.

Hiking portion of our trip completed, we were ready for a

flight to Pokhara. We waited, waited, and then waited some more. Three mornings of 4:30 a.m. airport wake-up calls in an effort to score places on the first flight of the day proved fruitless. Due to heavy pre-monsoon rains compounded by the usual late-morning winds, flights out were cancelled for the day. By the second morning I had read everything on my eReader. I rolled out of my sleeping bag, packed it again and forced down a cold breakfast before the short 6:00 a.m. walk to the airport. But at 9:00 a.m. we were still in Jomson. Back at the lodge there was only one magazine on the coffee table in the lobby: Vanity Fair, March, 2010. I spent the entire day poring over every page, including the story of Tiger Woods' indiscretions, while scarfing down coffee, cinnamon buns and—unwisely, as it would later turn out—chicken curry.

By 8:15 a.m. on the third morning, grounded again, Raj succeeded in persuading me to take a public bus. Time to face a final fear. Barry and I had travelled on a public bus with Raj during our first trip to Nepal. The driver had looked about twelve years old. He had blasted bus inhabitants with high volume Nepali music, aggravating both locals and foreigners. Landslides and rivers had washed out entire sections of road leaving them rutted, slippery and potholed. There were no guardrails. Twice we had to carry our luggage from one bus to the next through ankle-deep water across slippery rocks under the spray of a waterfall.

Raj and I joined the crowd milling around the bus ticket office, waiting for it to open. Remembering my dislike for viewing the precipice of the cliff from a window seat in the bus, Raj kindly rushed ahead to get seats on the side of the bus opposite the drop-off.

During the first leg of the 157 kilometer route I distracted myself by chatting with a lone male hiker from Australia and a couple from New Zealand. A quarter of the way to Pokhara, at

Ghasa, the first rest stop, I noticed a variety of empty vehicles. Bored-looking drivers lounged beside them, smoking and gossiping. My new friends and I conspired to rent a Mahindra four-wheel drive for the four of us, our guides, and porters. Trekkers up front, staff in rear jump seats, we bumped out again through potholes and ruts in marginally increased comfort and imagined safety.

Halfway to Pokhara we stopped. We watched in poorly veiled disappointment, known only to those who had not enjoyed the pleasure of a warm shower in three or four weeks, as a rickety dump truck deposited five loads of gravel to completely block the road ahead. The turbulent Kali Gandaki River rushed along one side of the road. A vertical cliff rose on the other. There was nothing to do but wait. Patience be damned, the Aussie and Kiwi found a shovel. Not to be deterred from anticipated creature comforts they took turns smoothing the pile. Their efforts barely made a dent. More patient and resigned than the foreigners, the Nepali men in the crowd stepped out of their vehicles to watch, gossip, and—in an expression of global camaraderie—occasionally take a short turn. The lineup of cars, motorcycles and cattle lengthened on both sides of the huge mound. Three hours later a bulldozer arrived and completed the impromptu roadwork. First the cattle, then the motorcycles, and finally the cars were nonchalantly waved ahead by a lackadaisical road worker.

It was dark when the rattling Mahindra deposited us in the busy town center of Beni. Half of the journey complete, we still had eighty-two kilometers to go to get to Pokhara. Raj had called ahead. A car and driver were waiting. We finally checked into the Landmark Hotel in lakeside Pokhara at 9:00 p.m. We ran all the way to Café Concerto. The road trip that usually took eight hours had taken us twelve. Red wine and pizza never tasted so good.

The next morning, showered and refreshed, we flew out of Pokhara on the 9:00 a.m. flight to Kathmandu. Back at Thamel

Eco Resort Hotel Raj persuaded the desk clerk to allow me an early check in. After a quick hug he raced for a taxi, eager to get home to Rojina, knowing we would have time for a final dinner before I left Kathmandu.

By 11:00 a.m. I was led upstairs to room 304, at Thamel's Eco Resort Hotel. When I saw the room number an eerie feeling descended. It was the same room where I had lain fully clothed, shivering, swaddled in a fluffy duvet during the first night of Barry's hospital stay in 2011. Thoughts of him, healthy at home, waiting for my return, soon squashed those melancholy memories.

The next morning I treated myself to an amazingly inexpensive spa session, a quarter of the price it would have been at home. By noon I sat relaxed in the hotel garden catching up on journal writing. Out of nowhere a disturbing gurgling in my stomach alerted me to trouble. For the rest of the day, I was attacked by a venomous bout of diarrhea. The culprit was probably the chicken curry in Jomson. I should have stuck with veggie curry until reaching a restaurant with more reliable refrigeration. The good news: I had a stash of Imodium. The bad news: I had already lost about ten pounds from trekking and now I couldn't have any alcohol, milk products, fruit, or salad—in short, all the things I had been craving.

Two days of white bread with tasteless red jam and wandering the streets of Thamel later, I stood under an umbrella at the end of the hotel lane. I was waiting for Prem to take me to a meeting of the Rotary Club of Mount Everest. Before I had left Canada my friend Pippa Shaw had invited me to join the Kalamalka Rotary in Vernon. I knew Rotary was an international service organization that supported local and global causes. For years I had been interested in joining but lunchtime meetings were impossible when I was a principal. I was eager to find out more. Now, plans for starting a non-profit to raise funds for Devi Jal

Kumari School in Aprik had been percolating in my brain for weeks, and the local Rotary would be a good place to learn more about global service projects and make some like-minded and service-oriented friends.

Rotary Club members welcomed me warmly, told me about their latest project of teaching reading and writing to adults in remote villages, and listened to my stories of Ratmate and Aprik. One member, Suman, Kathmandu's airport services manager for Cathay Dragon, even got me upgraded to business class on my flight back to Hong Kong. I was hooked. I decided to call Pippa as soon as I got home.

I never got to give Raj a final hug. As soon as we returned to Kathmandu he was offered the opportunity to guide a group to Everest Base Camp. The chance to lead a large group meant more salary and big tips, an opportunity he couldn't pass up now that he was a husband and about to be a father. I was pleased for him and just as happy to pour my thanks and thoughts into a letter. Farewells can be hard. I also left him my extra tube of L'Occitane hand cream. It was his favorite. It was fun to tease him about his princess hands. Of course, I left as generous a tip as I could afford and a promise to return.

The next night I held my own private celebration at the Sky City Marriott Hotel in Hong Kong. My digestive system had rallied. I splurged on a room-service dinner and a half-bottle of Australian merlot. With only a thirteen-hour flight separating me from Barry, I reflected on how far I had come. I had travelled to Asia on my own, kayaked through Hoi Ha Wan Marine Reserve with strangers, and reached Kathmandu unscathed. I had gained new friends, young and old, as I braved sweaty classrooms and dusty courtyard visits in Ratmate. In Aprik, villagers had recognized in me, their first foreign visitor, even before I could see it in myself, the possibility of creating a better future for their children. I had trekked over high passes to

Lo-Manthang, encountered welcoming, worldly monks, entre-preneurial hoteliers and enterprising shopkeepers. I had dared to take an unscheduled and risky route. I had been frightened by my fall behind three towering Buddhas in a monastery cave, travelled well beyond my comfort zone, and then back over the same high passes. I was stronger for the struggle, both physically and emotionally. And finally, I was on my way home.

Barry's warm hug in the Vancouver airport arrivals area felt as it always had, comfortable and loving, with a hint of more conscious intention on both our parts. We held on for a long time. Everything seemed the same. But it wasn't. Our love was still strong, but I was physically stronger, more self-assured, finally more myself, and more an equal partner. I suspected Barry sensed it. Finally, we separated to retrieve my luggage from the carousel. My fingers naturally laced through his as we walked out of the airport.

CHAPTER 23
NEPAL ONE DAY AT A TIME

SilverStar Mountain Resort; June 2019

Ten months after returning home I was still struggling to formulate a plan to raise enough funds to build a school in Aprik. I imagined a new school, and considered various options. I knew 225 students, thousands of kilometers away on the other side of the world, were waiting.

Then my friend Patti called. "Have you seen the news? There's been a huge earthquake in Nepal. Have you heard from any of your friends?"

"No, I'll check. Thanks."

Seconds later I was online. It was April 25, 2015. A massive earthquake had rocked Nepal. Say what you will about Facebook, it took me only a moment to find a posting from Prem declaring himself and his family safe. Having escaped their damaged apartment they were now sleeping in a tent in a field near their home. My fingers shook as I tried to find any notice of Raj or Resham. Five nerve-wracking hours later I learned they were also unhurt.

———*———

Over the next few days we learned more than eight thousand people had been killed, thousands more injured. In Aprik Village, only a few kilometers from the epicenter, every one of their well-kept homes had been reduced to a pile of rubble. Four villagers had been killed. After being buried in the rubble for several days the school principal had narrowly survived. The old school building had crumbled.

Prem, along with a team of international and local volunteers working with Sambhav Nepal, was the first to reach Ratmate and Aprik with relief supplies of rice, lentils, oil and tin shelter materials.

Though distant from the epicenter, Upper Mustang was not spared. The main shrine hall and wall paintings of the Namgyal monastery suffered severe damage. Police and locals rallied to remove holy statues, religious scriptures, and artifacts so they could be safely stored. Funds are still needed to repair the monastery and complete the summer school buildings, presenting insurmountable odds, even for the indefatigable Khenpo Tsewang. I pictured him surveying the damage, orange and burgundy robes vibrant against the desolate ecru landscape. His ongoing determination inspired me to ramp up our fund-raising efforts for the people of Aprik.

Jigme Dorje Palbar Bista, King of Upper Mustang from 1964 to 2008, died on December 16, 2016 at the age of 86. He would never witness the restoration efforts.

One month after the earthquake I stood in front of an auditorium packed full of friends, neighbors and wannabe trekkers at SilverStar Mountain Resort. My notes rattled as I raised them to begin the program. Barry sat beside his computer ready to cue the projector to start our first fundraising event. "Trek the Himalaya," his well-crafted slideshow presentation of the four treks we had completed together around the Annapurna Circuit and to Annapurna Base Camp Sanctuary, Upper Mustang and the Everest Base Camp circuit, was a hit. We raised our first $1,000 that night, through donations and the sale of art cards I had made of our photos.

Fueled by our success Barry and I and three friends formed a British Columbia registered non-profit, Nepal One Day at a Time. We presented the slideshow to several Okanagan Valley outdoor clubs. At one meeting of the Kelowna Alpine Club of Canada we had the good fortune of meeting Donn Aven, treasurer of Canadian charity Afretech Aid Society. Afretech has kindly taken us under their umbrella to enable us to offer tax receipts through Canada Helps.

That spring coincided with the fiftieth reunion of my high school graduating class from Neuchatel Junior College in Switzerland. Over drinks at Vancouver's Sylvia Hotel, class members decided to celebrate the legacy of our international education by donating funds to construct one classroom in Aprik. We were on the way. My friend Pippa Shaw had invited me to join Vernon's Kalamalka Rotary Club, and Kalamalka Rotary has been a champion supporter ever since, donating the majority of the funds needed to build Devi Jal Kumari School.

Our fundraising continues with slideshows, a crowd-funding campaign, public speaking engagements, the sale of photo art cards at summer festivals and applications to various charitable foundations.

———— • ————

In April 2017, two years after the earthquake, Barry and I and Mary Jackson, past president of the Kalamalka Rotary Club, stepped down from the four-wheel drive Toyota Land Cruiser at the tiny crossroads village of Arubang. The faint murmur of brass horns only hinted at the welcome to come.

Prem led us around the first corner. We were greeted by the cheers of a hundred villagers and the raucous sounds of the village band. Tika Ram, headman of the village, smeared generous portions of *rato tika*, the celebratory powder, onto our foreheads. Women and children came forward and strung layers of fragrant fuchsia *mallas* around our necks.

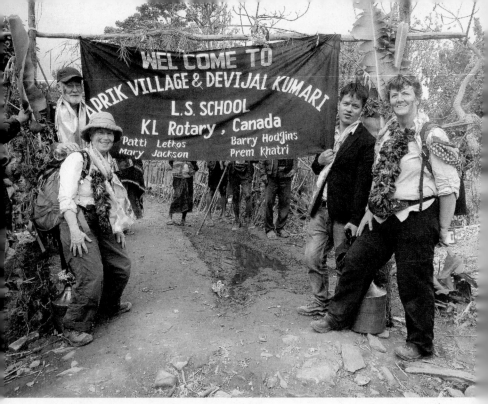

Welcome back to Aprik. Barry(l), Patti, Prem and Mary.

Warm fingers slipped around mine. I looked into the bright eyes of Kanchi, leader of the village women and wife of Tika Ram. "Come," she said, taking Mary's hand as well. The throng surged forward. I struggled to keep from bursting into tears. Each time we reached a new corner in the road I strained for a view of the village, afraid of what I might see. I knew the trimly built, slate roofed homes I remembered would no longer be standing.

On April 25, 2017, three years after my initial visit and two since the earthquake, we had arrived to celebrate the construction of the first four classrooms of Devi Jal Kumari School, coordinated on the ground by Prem and Sambhav Nepal. Sadness threatened as the village came into view. Aluminum shelters waterproofed with ragged plastic tarpaulins rose beside piles of stones that had once been attractive, well-maintained homes. But terraced fields of corn and wheat and a sturdy ten-room shelter school, fashioned from rusting sheets of corrugated tin, stood as a testament to the strength of the community.

We were seated in chairs of honor in front of four new earthquake-resistant classrooms. Exhausted but exhilarated, we joined the villagers dancing in celebration.

———•———

By February, 2018, thanks to family, friends, members of my Neuchatel Junior College 1965 grad class, SilverStar Mountain Resort, WL Seaton Interact Club and Kelowna Rotaract Club and especially the hard working Rotarians of Kalamalka Rotary Club with added assistance from Rotary International, funding was in place for eight furnished classrooms, a boys and girls toilet block, some school supplies and a beginning library collection.

In November, 2018, Kalamalka Rotarian Rob Bauml and his wife Corrie visited Aprik. With funds from Rotary members and their own donation they furnished the school staffroom.

By the end of 2018, NGO Japan International Cooperation Agency had signed on to complete twelve more rooms to house a kindergarten, library, staffroom, kitchen, hostel rooms for boys and girls who have a long way to travel, and storage. A fence to surround the playground is needed. Ball games don't last long when a ball goes over the edge of the field and down 300 meters to the valley below. As JICA does not provide furniture and supplies, the work of Nepal One Day at a Time and Kalamalka Rotary continues.

———•———

Time and travel change us all, not always in ways we expect.

Raj's parents lost their home in the earthquake. Raj tells me they have built a small cottage and still live in the village. Raj and Rojina have a son and a daughter. They live part-time in Kathmandu and in Lukla where Raj runs the Khumbu Lodge and Restaurant. He still guides when he can get away from the hotel.

Resham's parents also lost their home in the earthquake.

Resham is now a fully qualified guide. He and his wife and son are based in Kathmandu.

Prem's parents lost their home in the earthquake, too. His parents now live with him and his wife Geeta and two sons in their new earthquake-resilient home in Kathmandu. His father helps to oversee Sambhav Nepal's school and homebuilding projects in Ratmate. One of them is the rebuilding of Bhairabi School. Prem's trekking company Ace the Himalaya is listed as one of the top ten trekking companies in Nepal. He sends all of his Everest Base Camp trekking clients to Raj's hotel.

After several surgeries and determined rehabilitation, miraculously Roseanne is walking again, as well as hiking. Recently, while walking the Okanagan Rail Trail together, Roseanne shared her suspicion that she may have been drugged and robbed in Portugal causing her disastrous fall. But there is no stopping her. Currently she shares her passion for the outdoors by writing a nature column for a local newspaper encouraging people to experience, understand and enjoy nature. Roseanne also continues to inspire teachers by giving workshops in outdoor education and providing resources for BC teachers through her column Wild About Nature for HCTF, the Habitat Conservation Trust Foundation.

Barry and I, now over seventy, are healthy and fit, a formidable fundraising, skiing and trekking team. Following our 2017 visit to Aprik, our friend Mary set out on a solo cultural trip around Nepal. Barry and I completed the challenging twenty-five-day Manaslu Circuit trek, topping out at 5,100 meters at Larke La. The nine-hour hike over the pass was magnificent but our multi-day side trip into the recently opened treasure of Buddhist culture, the Tsum Valley, remains the highlight.

In November, 2018, I returned to Nepal alone for a brief visit to Aprik to celebrate the opening of eight classrooms and the second toilet block of Devi Jal Kumari School and catch

Teachers voluntarily provide extra early morning classes in the new eight-room school for grades 5 to 8.

up with friends. The new principal, Jivan, has ambitious plans for the school.

Barry and I still plan to put a few more kilometers on our trekking boots. Our sights are set on Upper Dolpo, another area near the Tibet border, even more remote than Upper Mustang. We know we have to get in the tough hikes while we're still young.

Our next project is Rotary 2020. We plan to lead a team of twenty-five members of Kalamalka Rotary along with family and friends to visit Aprik for two weeks in April, 2020, along with the funds and volunteer muscle to build two homes for villagers deemed most needy.

Back when I was a school administrator in Vancouver's inner city, it took me a long time before I finally realized that compared

Patti and students in front of the new school December 2018.

to those in my school catchment area, I came from a position of privilege. I came from a middle class background and had never seen poverty or met many immigrants or refuges. I learned a lot from the families of Admiral Seymour School. They taught me about resilience. Our daily interactions emphasized but also celebrated our similarities and minimized our differences. They made me realize I was in a position to make a difference. And I did. Now I have another cause, larger than myself, one that requires boundless perseverance but is equally rewarding.

Somewhere in that dark cave in Upper Mustang I discovered more courage than I ever knew had. I used it to get out of the cave and continue to the end of the trail. Now I'm using it to benefit a community of people thousands of kilometers away who want the best for their children.

To learn more:
- Visit us on Facebook at Nepal One Day at a Time.

In Canada to receive a tax receipt for a donation:
- At **Canadahelps.org** find charity **Afretech** (spelled with an e) Aid Society.
- Click on the link for the Donate Now page.
- In the FUND dropdown menu, choose NEPAL-ONE DAY AT A TIME.
- Make your donation and receive a tax receipt immediately.

For more information about Nepal One Day at a Time and Loon Island Press go to **pattishaleslekfos.com**

READING GUIDE

1. The author outlines countless fears around solo travel to a developing country. Were her fears were well founded? How did she overcome those fears?

2. Have you ever travelled alone to a developing country? What were the challenges and joys? If you have never travelled alone, why not? What are your biggest fears? What actions could you take to overcome them?

3. During her time in Nepal the author sometimes wishes she had a female interpreter. What questions would you ask local women if you could?

4. From the time of her first visit to Upper Mustang in 2011 and her solo visit in 2014, the road to Lo-Manthang was completed. Locals share their views as to the drawbacks and benefits of the road. What are your views about opening up this, or similar unspoiled cultural areas, to outsiders?

5. Compared to residents of rural Nepal, the author and the majority of tourists come from a position of privilege. What actions can a visitor take to be respectful of and contribute to local culture?

6. In rural Nepal people easily welcome strangers into their homes for tea. Have you ever invited a stranger into your home for tea or coffee? What was it like?

7. The author received varied reactions to her decision to go trekking in Nepal alone as a senior woman. What would

friends and family members say to you if you made a similar decision?

8. The author was worried about how leaving her husband behind would affect their relationship. How do you think your relationship with a loved one might change in similar circumstances?

9. At some point the author formulates her wish to become directly involved in the educational dreams of the people of Aprik. In what ways have you been involved in local or international humanitarian efforts? How would you like to be further involved?

10. Rotary has more than 1,000,000 members worldwide in 33,000 clubs. Have you ever considered joining a service club like Rotary? Why or why not?

ACKNOWLEDGEMENTS

When my maternal grandfather, the Reverend James Wesley Ross Gordon, died in 1956 he bequeathed $100 dollars to each of his grandchildren. My parents' only stipulation was to buy something lasting to remember Grandpa. I bought a typewriter and declared myself a writer. My parents, Doug and Anne Shales, encouraged me from day one.

Fifty years later I finally enrolled in the post-graduate journalism certificate program at Vancouver's Langara College. Thanks to my much younger pals Allison Kabernick, Geordie Clarke, Nathaniel Christopher, Wameesh George Hamilton and Adrian Nieoczym who helped me muddle through that challenging year.

Laurie Carter, TJ Wallis, Glenn Mitchell, Suzy van Bakel, Yvonne Turgeon, Bobbie Jo Reid, Spud Hilton and Marc Atchison accepted my first freelance queries. Thanks for publishing my articles.

Led by the inimitable Don George, the crew at the annual Travel Writers and Photographers Conference at Book Passage in Corte Madera, California has provided incredible inspiration and constructive advice on my early efforts at travel articles.

288   NEPAL ONE DAY AT A TIME

Thanks to family and special friends Sharonheart, Patti, Karen, Jan and the potluck posse for listening, reading, commenting and encouraging.

I wouldn't be skiing or trekking without the ongoing expertise of my physiotherapist Judy Fullerton at Easthill Physio in Vernon, British Columbia. I found her after the first car accident and continue to visit for seasonal tune-ups.

Thanks to the people of Upper Mustang, particularly those who shared their thoughts and endless cups of butter tea. I'll be back for the buffalo milk one day, Karma.

Will Johnson, thanks for your honest and constructive feedback on my first stories about my travels. I am grateful for the expertise and friendship of editor and writing coach Sylvia Taylor who, having read an early draft provided crucial feedback and encouragement.

When I asked for help raising money to take to Ratmate for the children at Bhairabi School, my friend Steffi van Dun jumped in immediately. Her Grade 5 students at Vernon's BX Elementary rose to the challenge. Her three children—our honorary grandchildren, Lars, Sophie and Kai—each donated half of their birthday money. After the earthquake, another teacher friend, Leah Scharf, encouraged her entire school to raise funds.

Friends Clayton Bussey, Dean Saddler and Joan Campbell willingly joined Barry and me to form the Board of Directors of Nepal One Day at a Time. Members of the graduating class of Neuchatel Junior College gave our fundraising campaign a kick-start.

Personal thanks to my friend Pippa Shaw, for her invitation to join Kalamalka Rotary Club. The continual involvement and support of Kalamalka Rotary has been truly incredible. Thanks to the Rotary Interact of WL Seaton Secondary in Vernon, Rotary District 5060 and the dedicated, hardworking members of

Vernon's Kalamalka Rotary Club. Several individual Rotarians have made the exciting and often arduous trip to visit Aprik: past president Mary Jackson, Rob Bauml and his wife Corrie and Interact past-president Bailey Morin. Many more have signed on to visit and build houses in 2020.

And, of course none of this would have happened without the expert planning of Prem K Khatry and his crew at Ace the Himalaya. His leadership, dedication and commitment to NGO Sambhav Nepal gathers volunteers and funds to provide assistance to the people of his home province, Gorkha, the epicenter of the 2015 earthquake.

Thanks to the teachers and villagers in Ratmate, who put up with my often misguided efforts at teaching their children, for their warmth and friendship and to the people of Aprik who saw possibilities in me I had yet to imagine.

Thanks to Resham Rana for his gentle smile, positive attitude, sharing of personal stories and lugging my enormous duffel all over Upper Mustang.

To Rajendra Neupane, my Rajuji, I am forever grateful for your patience, punctuality, friendship, classroom assistance, encouragement, shared beers, and popcorn. You stuck with me every step of the way.

A heartfelt *Namaste* to Gillian Gerylo who helped me clarify my intentions and started me on road to Kathmandu.

And, of course, thanks to Barry who taught me to love the mountains, who by example and love, encourages me to keep fit and follow my dreams.

RESOURCES

Books

Craig, Sienna. *Horses Like Lightning.* Boston: Wisdom Publications, 2008.

Gibbons, Bob and Pritchard-Jones, Sian. *Mustang, a Trekking Guide.* 2nd edition. New Delhi: Tiwari's Pilgrims Book House, 1997.

Dhakal, Prateek. *Beyond the Himalayas.* 2nd edition. Kathmandu: Himalayan Guides Nepal, 2008.

Dhungel, Ramesh K. *The Kingdom of Lo (Mustang) A Historical Study.* Kathmandu: Lusha Press, 2002.

Gelman, Rita Golden. *Tales of a Female Nomad, Living at Large in the World.* Reprint Edition. New York: Broadway Books, 2002.

Gelman, Rita Golden. *Female Nomad and Friends.* New York: Three Rivers Press, 2010.

Gregson, Jonathan. *Kingdoms Beyond the Clouds.* London: Pan Books, 2001.

Grennan, Conor. *Little Princes.* New York: William Morrow, 2010.

Guillebeau, Chris. *The Happiness of Pursuit.* New York: Harmony Books, 2014.

Gurung, Harka. *Vignettes of Nepal.* Kathmandu: Sahayogi Press, 1980.

Morris, Holly. *Adventure Divas, Searching the Globe for Women Who Are Changing the World.* New York: Villard Books, 2006.

Peissel, Michel. *Mustang, A Lost Tibetan Kingdom.* London: Futura Publications, 1967.

Shakya, Sujeev. *Unleashing Nepal, Past, Present and Future of the Economy.* Sonipat, India: Penguin Books, 2009.

Snellgrove, David. *Himalayan Pilgrimage, A Study of Tibetan Religion by a Traveller Through Western Nepal.* 3rd edition. Bangkok: Orchid Press, 2011.

Strayed, Cheryl. *Wild.* New York: Alfred A Knopf, 2012.

Spalding, Lavinia. *Writing Away, A Creative Guide to Awakening the Journal Writing Traveler.* Palo Alto: Travelers' Tales, 2009.

Sturgeon, Phillip with Judith Forrestal. *Himalayan Echoes, A*

Septuagenarian's Traverse of Mustang and Inner Dolpo. Delhi: Book
Faith India, 1998.

Thapa, Manjushree. *Mustang Bhot in Fragments.* 3rd edition. Lalitpur,
Nepal: Himal Books, 2008.

Tucci, Giuseppe. *Journey to Mustang.* 2nd edition. Kathmandu: Ratna
Pustak Bhandar, 2003.

Websites

Ace the Himalaya: trekking and adventure agency.
acethehimalaya.com.

Sambhav Nepal Foundation: Kathmandu based registered
non-profit founded by Prem Kumar Khatry in 2006.
sambhavnepal.org.

American Himalayan Foundation: San Francisco based
non-profit helping Nepalis throughout the Himalaya.
himalayan-foundation.org.

Fieni, Luigi. Conservationist, fine art photographer, photojournalist.
luigifieni.com.

On Facebook

Nepal One Day at a Time, British Columbia registered non-profit
supporting education in Aprik Village, Gorkha, Nepal.

DVDs

Mustang, Journey of Transformation, Restoring the Sacred Sites of Tibet's
Forbidden Kingdom. Parrinello, Will. Mill Valley Film Group, 2009.

Secrets of Shangri-La, Quest for the Sacred Caves. National Geographic.
Vivendi Entertainment, 2009.

Visions of Mustang, Bringing sight to the forbidden kingdom. Byers,
Daniel. Skyship Films, 2012.

ABOUT THE AUTHOR

P atti trained as a journalist after a career in education as a teacher, consultant and Vancouver inner city principal. Whether canoeing the Yukon River, backcountry skiing in British Columbia's Monashee Mountains, or trekking in Britain, Europe, Tibet or Nepal, Patti embraces the culture and environment of wilderness areas. Her stories have appeared in the *Globe and Mail, Macleans, the San Francisco Chronicle, Travelife.ca, Elevation Outdoors, Canadian Living, Okanagan Life, Profile Kingston,* and *Okanagan Woman* magazines. *Nepal One Day at a Time* is her first book. She and her husband spend winters at SilverStar Mountain Resort and summers at their Ontario island cottage. **pattishaleslefkos.com**